*Patchwork
Protectionism*

A book in the series

*Cornell Studies in Political Economy*

EDITED BY PETER J. KATZENSTEIN

A complete list of series titles appears at the end of the book

# *Patchwork Protectionism*

## Textile Trade Policy in the United States, Japan, and West Germany

H. Richard Friman

Cornell University Press

*Ithaca and London*

First published 1990 by Cornell University Press.

International Standard Book Number 0-8014-2423-2
Library of Congress Catalog Card Number 89-27400

Printed in the United States of America

*Librarians: Library of Congress cataloging information*
*appears on the last page of the book.*

⊗ The paper used in this publication meets the minimum
requirements of the American National Standard for Permanence
of Paper for Printed Library Materials Z39.48—1984.

# Contents

# List of Tables and Figures

# *Preface*

Protectionism since World War II has become a patchwork of selectively applied tariffs, unilateral and nonunilateral quotas, administrative restrictions, state subsidies, and production cartels. Each of these types of protectionist policy has differed in its ability to disrupt import flows and to incite retaliation in international economic relations. Why have advanced industrial countries responded with different types of protectionist policy to postwar trade competition and the resulting societal pressures for state action? The argument I develop and test in this book builds on the scholarly trend toward integrative, comparative analysis by offering a nuanced focus on the international and domestic sources of trade policy choices. Theoretically, the argument challenges and complements predominant approaches in the literature on international political economy. The book presents a systematic, comparative analysis of textile trade policy choices in the United States, Japan, and West Germany.

This project has benefited from the assistance of advisers, colleagues, and friends. I am deeply indebted to Peter J. Katzenstein, Richard N. Rosecrance, and T. J. Pempel for their invaluable insights, critiques, direction, and support. Each merits an additional word. I thank Peter Katzenstein for his multiple role as teacher, adviser, editor, and guide to the practice of systematic comparative analysis. I thank Richard Rosecrance for his support and emphasis on the international forces that shape the international political economy. I also thank T. J. Pempel for introducing me to Japan, a meeting I had never envisioned a decade ago and one for which I will always be grateful.

I am also deeply indebted to others who have helped shape this project. In Japan and West Germany, people devoted more time and effort to aiding me in my research than I could possibly have asked for. Their number is too great to allow a complete listing here; however, I especially thank Walter Engelmann, Wolfgang Fritzemeyer, Tsukasa Furukawa, P. C. Hauswedell, Mariko Higashi, Hirofume Katase, Wolf Morrison, Michio Muramatsu, Shoko Tanaka, Keiichi Tsunekawa, Georg von Netzer, Ippei Yamazawa, and Masayuki Yoshioka. As this project progressed, colleagues and friends also provided helpful insight, critiques, and support. I am especially grateful to I. M. Destler, Vinson Grace, Virginia Haufler, Stephen Krasner, John Kroll, Barrett McCormick, Ben Miller, Duane Swank, Susan Weatherwax, and several anonymous reviewers.

Earlier versions of some of the material in this book were published as "Rocks, Hard Places, and the New Protectionism: Textile Trade Policy Choices in the United States and Japan," *International Organization* 42:4 (Autumn 1988), © 1988 by the World Peace Foundation and the Massachusetts Institute of Technology, adapted with permission of the MIT Press; and "US Trade Policy: Hard Choices or Piecemeal Solutions," *Christian Science Monitor,* February 5, 1987.

A number of sources of financial support also made this project possible. Research in Japan and West Germany was funded by the Western Societies Program and Center for International Studies, at Cornell University, and the National Science Foundation (no. SES-8413332). Research in Washington, D.C., was funded, in part, by the Bradley Institute for the Study of Democracy and Public Values at Marquette University. Opinions, findings, conclusions, and errors are those of the author alone.

Over the past three years, the project has traveled through more word-processing and computer systems than the number of countries it discusses. I am grateful to Elaina Jeddry, Josephine Morstatter, Melinda Murakami, Angela Rodell, and Daniel Woodbeck for their assistance and patience through the transitions. I owe a greater debt to Roger Haydon's insights, patience, and humor, and Trudie Calvert's editing skills, which facilitated the project's final steps from manuscript to book.

Finally, I thank my parents. For my father, who always wondered what I would do with my undergraduate major, I am sorry you could not be here to read my answer. For my mother, who always taught me that being open to the world means learning from trial and tribulation as well as joy, I see once again that it pays to listen. I dedicate this book to you both.

H. Richard Friman

*Milwaukee, Wisconsin*

*Patchwork
Protectionism*

CHAPTER ONE

# Bridging the Gap: Broad Patterns, Specific Choices, and Theories of Postwar Protectionism

The postwar system of open international trade is slowly deteriorating. More important, advanced industrial countries have been either unable or unwilling to halt the system's decline.[1] By the early 1980s, roughly 40 percent of total world trade was being conducted under restrictive arrangements. Fifty years earlier, the trade wars of the 1930s had contributed to international economic collapse with cartel-like arrangements covering roughly 42 percent of world trade.[2] Yet the recurrent warnings of a world once again sliding down the "slippery slope" to economic Armageddon often overlook a key difference between the past and the present. In contrast to the across-the-board tariff wars of the 1930s, the postwar incarnation of protectionism is not only selective in its coverage but also a patchwork of different *types* of protectionist policy, each type distinguished by its ability to disrupt imports and incite retaliation in the international economy.[3] The 1947

1. Bahram Nowzad, "The Resurgence of Protectionism," reprint of *The Rise in Protectionism*, International Monetary Fund, Pamphlet Series no. 24, 1978; and Shailendra J. Anjaria et al., *Trade Policy Issues and Developments*, International Monetary Fund, Occasional Paper 38, July 1985.

2. Sylvia Ostry, "The World Economy in 1983: Marking Time," in *Foreign Affairs: America and the World 1983*, pp. 533–60. In 1982, *Newsweek* cited the estimate of Jan Tumlir, chief economist for GATT, at 40 to 48 percent in "On the Brink of a Trade War," *Newsweek*, 29 November 1982, pp. 77–81. See also the estimates in S. A. B. Page, "The Revival of Protectionism and Its Consequences for Europe," *Journal of Common Market Studies* 20 (September 1981), pp. 17–40; and estimates cited by Robert Gilpin, *The Political Economy of International Relations* (Princeton: Princeton University Press, 1987), pp. 192–95. On the 1930s, see Bela Balassa, "World Trade in the International Economy: Trends, Prospects and Policies, " in Balassa et al., *World Trade: Constraints and Opportunities in the 1980s* (Paris: Atlantic Institute for International Affairs, 1979), pp. 43–80.

3. Scholars of international trade have identified six broad types of protectionist policy: price-based restrictions (tariffs), unilateral quantitative restrictions, nonunilateral

General Agreement on Tariffs and Trade (GATT) clearly did not envision a future characterized by various arrays of price-based (tariff) restrictions, unilateral and nonunilateral quotas, administrative restrictions, state subsidies, and production cartels.

The predominant theoretical approaches to postwar protectionism offer only a partial understanding of the variation in trade policy choices. Approaches based on the structure of the international economic system fail to systematically link structure with actual policy decisions.[4] Similarly, the growing literature on international regimes has failed to account for countries that only selectively comply with regime constraints on trade policy choices. Domestic approaches argue that the structure of state and society matter, but static conceptions of structure often fail to capture the dynamic nature of trade policy choices.

A broad view of the specific strengths and weaknesses of these approaches reveals a basic theoretical premise that policy makers face international and domestic pressures on trade policy choices. Identifying these pressures and determining their relative importance in shaping policy decisions, however, remain the primary issues of contention among analysts of international trade and the stumbling blocks to understanding postwar protectionism. In this book, I contend that a more nuanced identification and integration of international and domestic factors than that offered by the predominant theoretical approaches in the political economy literature is necessary to understand the divergence in the types of protectionist policy adopted by advanced industrial countries.

To clarify the relative importance of international and domestic

---

quantitative restrictions, administrative restrictions, state subsidies, and production cartels. These can be ranked (see Appendix) according to their ability to disrupt imports and incite retaliation. See Balassa, "World Trade in the International Economy"; Herbert Giersch, "The New Protectionism: Hypocrisy and Bad Economics," *JAMA Forum* 2 (24 February 1984), pp. 3–8; Development Board, United Nations Conference on Trade and Development, *Growing Protectionism and the Standstill on Trade Barriers against Imports from Developing Countries: Report by the UNCTAD Secretariat*, 21 March 1978; Vinod Aggarwal, *Liberal Protectionism: The International Politics of Organized Textile Trade* (Berkeley and Los Angeles: University of California Press, 1985), p. 34; Charles Lipson, "The Transformation of Trade: The Sources and Effects of Regime Change," in Stephen D. Krasner, ed., *International Regimes* (Ithaca: Cornell University Press, 1983), pp. 233–72; and Lawrence G. Franco, "Current Trends in Protectionism in Industrialized Countries: Focus on Western Europe," in G. K. Helleiner et al., *Protectionism or Industrial Adjustment* (Paris: Atlantic Institute for International Affairs, 1980), pp. 29–46.

4. David A. Lake, "International Economic Structures and American Foreign Economic Policy, 1887–1934," *World Politics* 35 (July 1985), p. 540; and Vinod K. Aggarwal, "The Unraveling of the Multi-Fiber Arrangement, 1981: An Examination of International Regime Change," *International Organization* 37 (Autumn 1983), p. 619.

sources of trade policy choices, this book focuses on those cases in which state policy makers find themselves caught between international constraints against invoking certain types of protectionist policy and domestic pressures to invoke such measures. In such instances, I argue that domestic pressure—specifically the combined impact of industrial alliance strength and the degree of institutional access to the policy-making process—can override international constraints against the use of overt types of protectionist policy. The greater the domestic pressure, the more overt the policy response.

PATCHWORK PROTECTIONISM

Under the GATT, industrialized countries undertook extensive negotiations over tariffs on imported goods. As tariff barriers fell, however, policy makers took steps to ease the impact of rising competition from imports on domestic industries. A brief review of trade policies in three major industrial sectors illustrates the extent of the resulting protectionist patchwork among the United States, the larger members of the European Community (EC), and Japan.

*Textiles and Apparel*

✗ Despite seven rounds of multilateral tariff negotiations, tariffs in the textile and apparel sector remain relatively high.[5] Estimates of average, post–Tokyo Round, nominal tariff rates in textile products range from 3.3 percent for Japan to 9.2 percent for the United States. Tariff rates for West Germany, Great Britain, and France fluctuate between 6.7 percent and 7.4 percent. In wearing apparel, by contrast, the U.S. average rate of 22.7 percent clearly exceeds the 13.2 percent to 13.8 percent retained by the other four countries.

Quantitative restrictions in the textile and apparel sector have grown extensively since Japan's first voluntary export restraint in 1957 and the Short and Long Term Textile Arrangements of the 1960s. Since 1974, trade in this industrial sector has been conducted under the auspices of

5. Average tariffs for all industries by country: France, 6.0 percent; West Germany, 6.3 percent; Japan, 2.9 percent; Great Britain, 5.2 percent; and the United States, 4.3 percent. "The tariffs are weighted averages based on own-country imports, excluding petroleum, for 1976, which was the reference year used for the MTN." These rates reflect the planned (1987) completion of the phased-in reductions. See Alan V. Deardorff and Robert M. Stern, "The Economic Effects of Complete Elimination of Post–Tokyo Round Tariffs," in William R. Cline, ed., *Trade Policy in the 1980s* (Washington, D.C.: Institute for International Economics, 1983), pp. 674–76.

the Multi-Fiber Arrangement (MFA). By 1984, bilaterally negotiated agreements between exporting and importing nations under the MFA had produced quantitative restrictions on over 85 percent of world textile trade.[6] MFA coverage is extensive, but considerable variation exists in its use. Japan, for example, is heavily restricted as a textile exporter but has not invoked the MFA against textile imports. Instead, since the early 1980s Japan has turned to the tacit approval of "industry-negotiated" export-restraint agreements with countries such as South Korea. In contrast, the United States as of 1985 had invoked the MFA for thirty-one bilateral agreements covering 650 separate quotas.[7]

The European Community has also relied extensively on the MFA (twenty-three bilaterals in force in 1984); yet the Community has been by no means a totally cohesive body in textile trade. Of the 286 quotas negotiated under MFA III (1983–86), 84 quotas were "regional."[8] Through regional quotas, imports can be restricted by specific member states of the Community instead of by the Community as a whole. In addition, Community regulations under the Treaty of Rome have contributed to patchwork protectionism. Until a European Common Market is fully established, Article 115 protects individual countries from the trade policies of more liberal Community members. In textile trade during 1980 and 1981, for example, France successfully invoked this measure 118 times to prevent goods imported by other member countries (primarily West Germany) from injuring French industry.[9]

Other forms of protection in the textile and apparel sector have also been prevalent. In 1984, the United States introduced stringent "rules of origin" requirements aimed at limiting the ability of exporters to sidestep quantitative restrictions by shipping their goods through or processing them in third countries. Japan has relied instead on surveillance of imports and administrative guidance to monitor the flow of textile imports and, when necessary, to urge importers to slow the pace of import contracts.

6. Giersch, "The New Protectionism," pp. 4–5. This percentage is likely to increase with the 1986 extension of MFA coverage to ramie and silk products.

7. On U.S. use of the MFA see Gary Clyde Hufbauer et al., *Trade Protection in the United States: 31 Case Studies* (Washington, D.C.: Institute for International Economics, 1986), p. 146. I discuss Japanese textile trade policy with South Korea in Chapter 5.

8. Anjaria et al., *Trade Policy Issues*, p. 122; and Hans Teunissen and Niels Blokker, "Textile Protectionism in the 1980s: The MFA and the EEC's Bilateral Textile Agreements with Developing Countries," *Center for European Policy Studies: Working Documents*, no. 15 (Economic), July 1985.

9. R. J. P. M. van Dartel, "The Conduct of the EEC'S Textile Trade Policy and the Application of Article 115 EEC," in J. H. J. Bourgeois et al., *Protectionism and the European Community: Import Relief Measures Taken by the European Community and the Member States, and the Legal Remedies Available to Private Parties* (Antwerp: Kluwer Law and Taxation Publishers, 1983), pp. 119, 123.

As forms of indirect protection, state subsidies and production cartels have also varied by country. In the United States, assistance programs in force since 1962 have not been specifically targeted at the textile and apparel sector. Moreover, the requirements for assistance under the Trade Expansion Act of 1962 were excessively restrictive and relief under the Trade Act of 1974 failed to meet industry needs. From 1975 to 1980, and before eligibility and funding cutbacks began under the Reagan administration, approximately 30 percent of the firms qualifying for financial assistance went out of business while waiting to actually receive assistance.[10]

Western Europe and Japan have not shared American reluctance to provide assistance to the textile and apparel sector. Policy makers in West Germany have tended to avoid direct federal subsidies to the industry.[11] Yet indirect assistance through the Economic Recovery Program and regional assistance programs has been extensive. The Institute of Weltwirtschaft at the University of Kiel has estimated that the level of effective protection through subsidization for the textile and apparel sector in West Germany stands at 21 percent. Great Britain and France have more actively combined indirect and direct assistance measures.[12] Both countries experimented with wage subsidies, assistance to small firms, and assistance to regions with declining industries. Specific programs for the textile industry have included the United Kingdom's Clothing Industry Development Scheme and France's Codis Plan. European Community policy in this sector, by contrast, has been relatively limited. Guidelines for assistance to the textile and apparel sector have attempted to constrain rather than promote the use of such measures. Moreover, the European Commission's efforts to expand monetary assistance have been kept in check by the Council of Ministers, and divisions within the commission have inhibited the formation of production and scrapping cartels on the Community level.[13]

Finally, in Japan, direct intervention by providing assistance to the

10. Other general sources of limited assistance include the Economic Development Administration and the Small Business Administration. See Jose de la Torre, *Clothing Industry Adjustment in Developing Countries*, Thames Policy Papers no. 38 (London: Trade Policy Research Center, 1984), pp. 192–96. For an excellent overview of measures to assist industry in the United States, see Gary Clyde Hufbauer and Howard Rosen, *Trade Policy for Troubled Industries* (Washington, D.C.: Institute for International Economics, 1986).

11. For detail on indirect and regional assistance, see de la Torre, *Clothing Industry*, pp. 157–59; and Chapter 5.

12. De la Torre, *Clothing Industry*, pp. 151–57, 177–89.

13. For detail on the role of the European Economic Community in textile industry adjustment, see Chapter 2.

textile and apparel sector appears to be the rule rather than the exception.[14] Laws regulating the textile industry passed in 1956, 1967, 1974, 1979, and 1984 incorporated financial assistance as a tool to alter the structure of the industry. Before the 1970s, the major focus of such legislation was on promoting export competitiveness through structural adjustment. Since 1974, assistance measures have been targeted at reducing surplus capacity and at promoting the integration of computers and other high-technology components (knowledge intensification) in the industry. Although often not explicitly viewed as import relief measures, the textile industry laws contain the implicit message from Japanese policy makers that a more competitive industry will be less vulnerable to import pressures. In addition to textile legislation, general programs for small and medium-sized industries and aid for "structurally depressed industries" have acted as sources of financial relief. Finally, portions of the industry have been granted temporary exceptions to Japan's antimonopoly regulations to cut excess capacity through recession cartels.

*Steel*

Cross-national differences in tariff protection for the steel industry are not as extensive as those in the textile and apparel sector. Estimated averages for nominal tariff levels in iron and steel following completion of the Tokyo Round reductions range from Japan's 2.8 percent to France's 4.9 percent.[15] Beyond this point, however, the patchwork becomes more complex.

The steel industry in the United States has been heavily protected since the late 1960s.[16] Negotiated restraint agreements with Japan and the European Community set quantitative limits on steel exports to the United States from 1968 through 1974. In 1978, Japan reached an informal understanding with the United States that set a ceiling of 6 million tons on Japanese steel exports. From 1978 to 1981, the United States sought to dissuade dumping by foreign steel producers by introducing a "trigger price mechanism" (TPM). Imports priced below the trigger price were automatically subject to an accelerated antidumping investigation. In 1982, the TPM was replaced by an extensive voluntary

---

14. This issue is discussed in greater detail in Chapter 5.
15. Deardorff and Stern, "Economic Effects," pp. 674–75.
16. This section is based on Ingo Walter, "Structural Adjustment and Trade Policy in the International Steel Industry," in Cline, ed., *Trade Policy in the 1980s*, pp. 491–97; Anjaria et al., *Trade Policy Issues*, pp. 36–38; and Hufbauer et al., *Trade Protection*, pp. 170–73.

restraint agreement with the European Community on carbon steel products and alloys. The agreement was similar to the MFA for textiles in setting overall ceilings on a range of products and including subceilings on specific goods. An agreement in principle was also reached on tube and pipe steel. By November 1985, a new set of fifteen restraint agreements had been negotiated by the United States covering 80 percent of American steel imports.[17]

Reliance on export restraints and pricing schemes only partially characterizes steel policy in the European Community. During the 1970s, the EC combined restraints on Japanese exports with a "basis price system" to dissuade dumping. The system differed from the American TPM by automatically waiving dumping proceedings if the exporter in question would agree "voluntarily" to restrain its exports.[18] Yet the greatest difference between the United States and the EC lies in the latter's reliance on direct involvement in the industry. In 1976, the Community introduced a crisis cartel to stabilize pricing in the industry. Following the onset of crisis conditions in 1980, the EC introduced mandatory production quotas, select minimum prices, and a code regulating the extent of financial assistance that member countries could provide to their respective steel producers.[19] According to figures released by the European Commission in 1981, financial support to the steel industry by member countries totaled 32.97 billion ECU (European Currency Units).[20] These internal measures were supplemented by additional means of external protection. By 1984, the EC had instituted fifteen bilateral restraint agreements covering 75 to 80 percent of total steel imports.[21] Those countries not covered by restraint agreements faced an import price system that set minimum price levels and monitored import trends.

17. Hufbauer et al., *Trade Protection*, pp. 170–73; and I. M. Destler, *American Trade Politics: System under Stress* (Washington, D.C.: Institute for International Economics, 1986), Appendix. Acting on a campaign pledge, President George Bush extended steel quotas (set to expire in 1989) for an additional 30 months in July 1989. See "Big Steel Gets a Breather," *Business Week*, 7 August 1989, p. 34.

18. This clause resulted in the adoption of restraints by Eastern European countries, Western European countries not belonging to the EEC, South Korea, and Japan (Walter, "Structural Adjustment," pp. 497–500).

19. Anjaria et al., *Trade Policy Issues*, pp. 39–40; and Walter, "Structural Adjustment," pp. 497–500.

20. Great Britain accounted for 5.76 billion ECU, West Germany for 4.2 billion, and France for 7.61 billion (Patrick Messerlin, "Comment," in Loukas Tsoukalis, ed., *Europe, America, and the World Economy* [New York: Basil Blackwell, 1985], p. 39).

21. These imports were also regulated by a "triple clause" by which imports would be staggered by year, by product, and by Community member (Anjaria et al., *Trade Policy Issues*, pp. 39–40).

Japanese steel policy, characterized by an apparent absence of quantitative restrictions, reflects a third pattern of protectionism. Japan lacks the extensive bilateral restriction of the United States and the EC. The absence of any noticeable increase in the import penetration of the Japanese market by South Korean steel exports during the 1980s, however, prompted charges by the Korean Traders Association that nontariff trade barriers in the area of government procurement were at fault. The Japanese government countered with attacks on the quality of South Korean steel, and Japanese steel producers cited the "self-restraint" efforts of South Korea's Pohang steelworks.[22] The record of Japanese adjustment assistance to the steel industry is much clearer. The Japanese government has alternated since the 1970s between approval of recession cartels to stabilize steel production and the provision of indicative production guidelines.[23] In 1986, the industry also began to take advantage of government programs to subsidize wages at times of temporary layoffs.[24]

*Automobiles*

Cross-national differences in tariff protection in automobiles are roughly comparable to those found in the textile and apparel sector. Tariffs on passenger cars for Japan, the United States, and the EC are 0 percent, 3.0 percent, and 10.9 percent respectively. U.S. tariffs on imported light trucks, which are seen primarily as passenger vehicles, are set at 25 percent.[25] The range in tariff protection is overshadowed by differences in quantitative restrictions. Japan has avoided such restraints, but the United States and individual members of the EC maintain quantitative restrictions, which apply primarily to Japan. In 1981, Japan agreed to limit exports to the United States to 1.68 million units per year. The quota was increased to 1.85 million units in 1984 and phased out by the Reagan administration the following year. Since 1985, Japan has "voluntarily" maintained a quota of 2.3 million units.[26]

22. Imports were stable at roughly 2.5 percent of domestic production (Kubota Akira, "Transferring Technology to Asia," *Japan Quarterly* 33 [January–March 1986], p. 40). Recent reports attribute Japan's limited imports from South Korea and Taiwan to "strong steel demand" in the latter two countries (*Far Eastern Economic Review*, 13 November 1986).

23. Stephen Woolcock, "Iron and Steel," in Susan Strange and Roger Tooze, eds., *The International Politics of Surplus Capacity: Competition for Market Shares in the World Recession* (London: George Allen & Unwin, 1981), p. 72.

24. *Far Eastern Economic Review*, 13 November 1986.

25. Robert B. Cohen, "The Prospects for Trade and Protectionism in the Auto Industry," in Cline, ed., *Trade Policy in the 1980s*, pp. 533–34.

26. Anjaria et al., *Trade Policy Issues*, p. 46; and James A. Dunn, Jr., "Automobiles in

Members of the EC have adopted more extensive quantitative restrictions. France, Great Britain, and West Germany limit Japanese automobiles to 3.0 percent, 11.0 percent, and 10 percent of their respective markets.[27] Since 1981, the Community itself has taken steps to limit imports of Japanese automobiles. In 1983 calls for "moderation" in the growth of automobile exports were included in the three-year export-restraint agreement with Japan.[28]

Protectionism in the automobile trade is also characterized by a range of additional nontariff barriers. All five industrialized countries maintain regulations on safety and emission standards. With the exception of the United States, all of the countries impose some tax on imports. Japan places a 15 to 20 percent commodity tax on all automobiles; Great Britain, France, and West Germany rely on value-added taxes ranging from 13.0 to 33.3 percent. Beyond this point, Japan emerges as the predominant user of nontariff trade barriers. Exporters to Japan complain about the difficulty complying with Japanese standards, the complexities of the Japanese distribution system, and the dealer margins added to imported vehicles.[29]

## RAMIFICATIONS OF PATCHWORK PROTECTIONISM

This brief overview of the range of protectionist measures in only three industrial sectors provides some sense of the nature of postwar protectionism. Readers familiar with the complexity of the international economy are unlikely to be surprised at the manifestation of this complexity in international trade. Thus, why focus on protectionism? The answer to this question lies in the economic and political ramifications of the patchwork.

The economic impact of postwar protectionism affects both developed and developing countries. In developed countries, selective quantitative restrictions have inconsistently alleviated pressures for addressing changes in technology and comparative advantage. Specifically, selective protection has accelerated the shift of foreign competitors into new product areas while retarding similar shifts in domestic production.[30] Restric-

International Trade: Regime Change or Persistence," *International Organization* 41 (Spring 1987), p. 225.

27. Anjaria et al, *Trade Policy Issues*, pp. 46–47; Cohen, "Prospects for Trade," pp. 533–34; and EIU (Economist Intelligence Unit), "The Japanese in Western Europe," *Japan Motor Business*, June 1986, pp. 47–49.

28. Anjaria et al., *Trade Policy Issues*, p. 47.

29. Cohen, "Prospects for Trade," pp. 533–34.

30. Nowzad, "Resurgence of Protectionism," p. 14; Giersch, "New Protectionism," p. 6; and Balassa, "World Trade," p. 64.

tions on cotton textile trade in the 1950s and 1960s accelerated the shift of foreign producers into man-made fiber goods just as the restrictions on man-made fiber goods in the 1970s accelerated the shift into ramie and silk blends. In both instances, U.S. producers shifting to higher value-added products found themselves facing foreign competition much sooner than anticipated. More recently, the restrictions on exports of automobiles negotiated between the United States and Japan have led to unintended results. Quantitative restrictions pushed the Japanese toward the higher value-added end of the automobile market and opened the lower end of the market to new competitors such as South Korea. The American automobile industry's obsession with Japan resulted in increasing competition across a wider range of the market.

Postwar protectionism has also taken its toll on developing countries that have been unable to adjust to selective restrictions.[31] Many Latin American and Southeast Asian countries attempting to replicate Japan's rapid industrialization face a wide array of trade barriers, including those imposed by Japan itself. The difficulties these countries face are often compounded by the need to export to meet international debt obligations. Facing restricted foreign markets and low prices for commodity and raw material exports, these countries often turn to the International Monetary Fund (IMF) for debt relief. As a condition of this relief, the IMF requires the devaluation of the debtor country's currency, ideally to slow the country's imports and to boost its exports. Yet as long as foreign markets remain closed to the debtor country, devaluation can lead to less export revenue from the same quantity of exports and can increase the financial pressures on the debtor country. The reluctance of developed countries to make the connection between reductions in protectionism at home and debt relief abroad threatens debtors and creditors alike.[32]

Postwar protectionism has also involved broader political issues. Trade disputes between the United States and Japan have often threatened the political relationship between the two countries. From 1969 to 1971, U.S. negotiators attempted to force Japan into a voluntary restraint agreement on noncotton textiles.[33] During one meeting, Japanese

31. For an analysis of the factors that facilitate adjustment by developing countries, see David B. Yoffie, *Power and Protectionism: Strategies of the Newly Industrializing Countries* (New York: Columbia University Press, 1983).

32. For detail on the issue of international debt, see Miles Kahler, ed., *The Politics of International Debt* (Ithaca: Cornell University Press, 1986); and Gilpin, *Political Economy of International Relations*, pp. 317–28.

33. I. M. Destler et al., *The Textile Wrangle: Conflict in Japanese-American Relations* (Ithaca: Cornell University Press, 1979).

officials responded to American demands by reminding the American negotiators that Japan was not "Vietnam the enemy" and should not be treated as such. To break the stalemate caused by intense Japanese resistance, President Richard Nixon finally threatened to invoke the 1917 Trading with the Enemy Act unless Japan complied with American demands. More recently, American criticism of Japanese trade policies has again raised the specter of political ramifications. During 1985, protests by the United States and Western Europe evoked renewed fears of massive retaliation against Japanese exports. In an unprecedented appeal to the Japanese people, Prime Minister Yasuhiro Nakasone called for increased consumption of imports to prevent a repeat of the "tragedy of World War II."[34]

CONTENDING APPROACHES

Concern over postwar protectionism has produced a prolific quantity of scholarship, most of which has sought to account for policy makers' choices among the broad options of protection and liberalization or protection and adjustment. Four such theories of policy choices are international economic structure, international regime, statist, and domestic structure. Other approaches exist, and many will be noted in this analysis. Yet the four approaches discussed here represent the predominant arguments currently informing the debate over trade policy choices in the literature on international political economy.

*International Economic Structure and International Regimes*

International theories of postwar protectionism stress the influence of the international system on policy makers' choices. Although these approaches contend that systemic factors matter, the nature of the international system remains open to debate.[35] Perhaps the best example of systemic-level approaches argues that the rising hegemon works to create and maintain an open system in international trade and capital flows. As the hegemonic nation's capabilities decline relative to

34. *Wall Street Journal*, 10 April 1985.

35. For a discussion of systemic approaches, see Robert Keohane, ed., *Neorealism and Its Critics* (New York: Columbia University Press, 1986); Kenneth Waltz, *Theory of International Relations* (Reading, Mass.: Addison-Wesley, 1979); and Richard Rosecrance, "International Theory Revisited," *International Organization* 35 (Autumn 1981), pp. 691–713.

other nations, however, the open system created and maintained by the hegemon collapses in a wave of protectionism.[36]

The strength of this approach lies more in its parsimony than in its historical accuracy. The movement toward openness during the mid-1800s does correspond with the rise of British hegemony, and the closure of the 1930s saw the absence of a clear hegemonic power. From 1900 to 1913, however, Great Britain's decline was accompanied by increasing openness. The rise and fall of Pax Americana also failed to match the predictions of the hegemonic model.[37] This study and others reveal that the onset of international closure occurred at least ten years before the peak of American hegemony in the mid-1960s. Moreover, the fall of Pax Americana has not been characterized by the abandonment of international openness. Both nontariff trade barriers and international trade have increased during the period of hegemonic decline. Despite a rise in the percentage of "managed trade," postwar protection remained highly selective and international trade continued to expand until the 1982 world recession. That recession had a minimal impact compared to the 28 percent drop in world trade between 1926 and 1935. From 1980 to 1985, roughly twenty years after the onset of America's hegemonic decline, world trade declined only 1.9 percent.[38]

The apparent paradox of hegemonic decline without full-scale closure has sparked two lines of research. Some scholars have argued that the presence or absence of a hegemon does not automatically lead to openness or closure.[39] One must consider a wider array of actors. All

36. Robert O. Keohane, "The Theory of Hegemonic Stability and Changes in International Economic Regimes, 1967–1977," in Ole Holsti et al., eds., *Changes in the International System* (Boulder: Westview Press, 1980), pp. 131–62; Stephen D. Krasner, "State Power and the Structure of International Trade," *World Politics* 28 (April 1976), pp. 317–47; and Robert Gilpin, *U.S. Power and the Multinational Corporation: The Political Economy of Foreign Direct Investment* (New York: Basic Books, 1975).

37. Lake, "International Economic Structures," pp. 527–38; and Krasner, "State Power," pp. 335–41.

38. For an overview of the rise of international closure before the onset of America's hegemonic decline, see Aggarwal, *Liberal Protectionism*, pp. 43–94; and Yoffie, *Power and Protectionism*, pp. 43–80. For detail on the limits of international closure since the hegemonic decline of the United States, see Susan Strange, "Protectionism and World Politics," *International Organization* 39 (Spring 1985), p. 242; Gilpin, *Political Economy of International Relations*, pp. 192–95; and U.S. Bureau of the Census, *Statistical Abstract of the United States: 1987* (Washington, D.C., 1986), p. 813.

39. Lake, "International Economic Structures"; David A. Lake, "Beneath the Commerce of Nations: A Theory of International Economic Structures," *International Studies Quarterly* 28 (1984), pp. 143–70; John Conybeare, "Public Goods, Prisoners' Dilemmas and the International Political Economy," *International Studies Quarterly* 28 (1984), pp. 5–22; and Duncan Snidal, "The Limits of Hegemonic Stability Theory," *International Organization* 39 (Autumn 1985), pp. 579–614.

countries seek to maximize their interests as determined by their position and those of other countries in the international economic structure. The configuration of major, intermediate, and minor countries in the international economic system gives policy makers three options: avoid protection, turn to protection, and/or cooperate when necessary to minimize the protectionist actions of others. David Lake has argued that the absence of full-scale closure since the late 1960s is attributable to the continued presence of a "multilateral supportership." Instead of a hegemonic power shouldering the burdens of openness, fears of retaliation have prompted a modicum of cooperation among key intermediate-level countries with a stake in avoiding closure. As evidence of cooperation based on fear, Lake cites the "only marginal substantive increases" in the level of protection provided by the use of direct nontariff barriers (bilateral quotas) in the United States.[40]

Although this interpretation offers a tighter correlation between structure and the outcomes of openness and closure than its predecessors, it is incomplete. Specifically, why do fears of retaliation lead to the use of quotas as opposed to other, less direct types of protection? Lake acknowledges that there are strong domestic pressures for protection but fails to systematically link the actual strength of protectionist forces, the nature of policy-making institutions in the United States, international economic structure, and choices available to policy makers.

A more basic critique of these hegemony scholars is that they, like their predecessors, discuss hegemonic decline without adequately showing what distinguishes a hegemon from an intermediate country in the international economic structure. By broadening the attributes of hegemons to include knowledge, security, and cultural dominance, for example, Bruce Russett and Susan Strange have rejected the argument that the United States has fallen to the rank of an intermediate power. Yet such critiques risk shifting focus away from a narrow conceptualization of international economic structure that may provide insights into trade policy choices. Lake's efforts to add greater precision to the analysis of the international economic structure are cautious as seen in his own caveats and skepticism concerning the demarcations among categories of countries; the demarcations are explicitly based on Lake's judgment, intuition, and historical interpretations of hegemony arguments. The tentative conceptualization of the international economic structure thus calls for further refinement.[41]

40. Lake, "Beneath the Commerce of Nations," p. 165.
41. Bruce Russett, "The Mysterious Case of Vanishing Hegemony; or, Is Mark Twain Really Dead?" *International Organization* 39 (Spring 1985), pp. 207–32; Susan Strange, "Cave! Hic Dragones: A Critique of Regime Analysis," in Krasner, ed., *International*

The second approach to the paradox of hegemonic decline and the absence of full-scale closure contends that international regimes act as intervening variables between the structure of the international system and outcomes of openness and closure. As defined by Stephen Krasner, regimes consist of "sets of implicit or explicit principles, norms, rules, and decision-making procedures around which actors' expectations converge in a given area of international relations." Krasner has argued that a time lag occurs between changes in the structure of the system and changes in the regime created by a given structure. Once formed, the regime perseveres until incongruities between international structure and international regime force a realignment.[42] Thus, although U.S. hegemonic status has declined, the remaining regime would prevent a reincarnation of the trade wars of the 1930s.

According to the second approach's adherents, regimes constrain the choices of policy makers. Robert Keohane has argued that in the short run, policymakers constrain themselves by following the regime's dictates out of a belief in the long-run benefits of such action.[43] Keohane rejects the idea that policy makers engage in clear calculations comparing their own restraint with future similar action by others. Vinod Aggarwal, by contrast, has argued that a major reason why policy makers enter into regimes is to control the actions of others.[44] The extent of this control hinges on the regime's strength, nature, and scope. Despite these contending interpretations of how regime constraints operate, international regime theorists argue that variations in postwar trade policy reflect the uneven impact of the international trade regime on policy makers.

---

*Regimes*, pp. 337–54; Susan Strange, "The Persistent Myth of Lost Hegemony," *International Organization* 41 (Autumn 1987), pp. 551–75; and David Lake, *Power, Protection, and Free Trade: International Sources of U.S. Commercial Strategy, 1887–1939* (Ithaca: Cornell University Press, 1988), pp. 31–33.

42. Stephen D. Krasner, "Structural Causes and Regime Consequences: Regimes as Intervening Variables," and "Regimes and the Limits of Realism: Regimes as Autonomous Variables," in Krasner, ed., *International Regimes*, pp. 1–22, 355–68. Although Krasner's definition holds a predominant position in the regime literature, alternative formulations exist. In an effort to simplify Krasner's formulation, for example, Vinod Aggarwal classifies rules and procedures as the components of the regime and norms and principles as making up the "meta regime" (Aggarwal, *Liberal Protectionism*, pp. 17–18).

43. Robert O. Keohane, "The Demand for International Regimes," in Krasner, ed., *International Regimes*, p. 158; and Robert O. Keohane, *After Hegemony: Cooperation and Discord in the World Political Economy* (Princeton: Princeton University Press, 1984).

44. Aggarwal, *Liberal Protectionism*, pp. 29–33. Two other reasons Aggarwal posits for entering regimes are to bring a narrow issue in line with broader concerns and to reduce the costs of regulating interaction between states (pp. 17–18).

Although regime approaches illustrate a possible source of international constraint on policy makers, they provide at best only a partial understanding of how such constraints have shaped postwar protectionism. Krasner's argument would state that the regime of open international trade created under Pax Americana should have been at its strongest before the peak of American hegemony. Yet in the trade conflicts of the 1950s with Japan and Hong Kong U.S. policy makers bypassed GATT rules and procedures for the resolution of trade disputes and violated the GATT regime's norms against discriminatory trade policy.[45] Studies of international regimes have also failed to account for selective compliance with regime constraints. Despite discriminatory quantitative arrangements in textiles and other products, the United States has continued to adhere to GATT's efforts at nondiscriminatory tariff liberalization. Japan, as a signatory to the MFA, has allowed its exports to be restricted but has refused to exercise its right under the textile regime to impose similar quantitative restrictions on East and Southeast Asian countries.

In a theoretical discussion of regimes as social institutions, Oran Young has argued that deviant behavior by individuals does not call a regime into question.[46] Yet in applying this formulation to international politics, Young fails to recognize that the individual deviant does matter, especially when the deviant is a major or intermediate power. Moreover, as deviant behavior becomes more extensive, at what point does it still make sense to speak of a regime? In contrast, Keohane traces compliance in regimes to a country's concerns with retaliation, precedent and reputation. Deviant behavior occurs in the absence of such concerns.[47] This argument still fails to account for selective compliance within a single regime. In addition, Keohane forgoes the possibility that domestic considerations could override policy makers' fears as to how the rest of the world will react to deviant behavior. A focus on regime constraints alone provides an incomplete explanation of trade policy choices.

## Statist and Domestic Structure Approaches

Forgoing the parsimony of international approaches, a number of international political economy scholars have sought to reintroduce

45. Jock A. Finlayson and Mark W. Zacher, "The GATT and the Regulation of Trade Barriers: Regime Dynamics and Functions," in Krasner, ed., *International Regimes*, pp. 273–314; and Aggarwal, *Liberal Protectionism*, pp. 43–76.

46. Oran Young, "Regime Dynamics: The Rise and Fall of International Regimes," in Krasner, ed., *International Regimes*, pp. 94–97.

47. Keohane, *After Hegemony*, pp. 98–106.

aspects of state and society into trade policy analysis. Statist approaches contend that the strength of the state determines the policy maker's ability to act autonomously from societal pressures for protection.[48] In weak states, power and authority are fragmented and dispersed across state institutions. The weaker the state, the more easily strong societal actors can gain access to the policy-making process. Stephen Krasner has argued that faced with strong societal pressure for import relief, the weak American state will adopt protectionist concessions whereas strong states such as Japan or France will promote changes in industrial structure.

Yet the contention that strong societal actors can penetrate weak states says little about the nature of the penetration. Broad typologies based on the structural characteristics of state institutions reveal only a variety of possible access channels to what Krasner has termed "central decision-makers." Each channel offers societal actors different degrees of input into the policy-making process, from mere advice to binding recommendations. In the United States, industry appeals to the International Trade Commission lead to nonbinding recommendations for presidential action, and appeals to Congress can lead to unilateral quotas on imported goods despite presidential opposition.[49] State fragmentation is not the entire issue. Insights into trade policy choices lie in the nature of access channels actually chosen by societal actors in trade policy disputes.

The issue of state strength also begs the question of strength relative to what. The typology of strong, moderate, and weak states assumes strength relative to strong societal actors. Yet societal actors are not static. Coalitions between and within industries rise and fall. Expanding the statist matrix to include weak and moderate societal actors leads to confusion. What policy response should be expected from the combination of a weak state and weak societal actors? Does the weak state behave as a strong or a moderate state? The statist approach challenged the basic pluralist model of interest group behavior by rejecting the

48. Stephen D. Krasner, "United States Commercial Policy: Unraveling the Paradox of External Strength and Internal Weakness," in Peter J. Katzenstein, ed., *Between Power and Plenty: Foreign Economic Policies of Advanced Industrial States* (Madison: University of Wisconsin Press, 1978), pp. 47–66. For the application of this argument to raw materials policy see Krasner, *Defending the National Interest: Raw Materials Investments and U.S. Foreign Policy* (Princeton: Princeton University Press, 1978), pp. 55–73, 10–20. For a detailed critique of Krasner's argument, see J. G. Ruggie, "Book Review: Defending the National Interest," *American Political Science Review* 74 (1980), pp. 297–99.

49. Krasner, "United States Commercial Policy," p. 65; Destler, *American Trade Politics* pp. 11, 111–15, 118.

notion that the state serves merely as an arena for competing societal coalitions.[50] Moreover, the statist approach appeared to relieve scholars from determining what constellation of societal groups results in what specific policy (a task made more difficult by the absence of agreement on the sources of interest group strength).[51] The statist approach, however, offers little systematic analysis of societal coalitions and their interactions with the state.

Peter Katzenstein has expanded the statist approach by systematically incorporating international as well as societal characteristics in the analysis of policy choices. Drawing on the literature on interdependence, Katzenstein argues that small states such as Switzerland and Austria will remain open because of their dependence on the world economy but that relatively larger states such as the United States and Japan have greater flexibility in dealing with economic change. Moreover, within the parameters set by relative size, a country's domestic structure shapes its proclivity toward protectionism or adjustment.[52] Domestic structure differs from state strength by combining governing coalitions of major public and private actors with what Katzenstein has termed the "policy network": patterns of public and private organizations linking state and society (centralization); patterns of shared ideology linking state and society; and patterns of private representation (concentration). Katzenstein has argued that weak centralization, business-labor-government hostility, and weak societal concentration in the United States result in "limited, ad hoc protectionist policies." In Japan, strong centralization, a greater sense of state-societal partnership, and

50. Krasner, *Defending the National Interest*, pp. 28–29. For a review of interest group analysis, see J. David Greenstone, "Group Theories," in Fred I. Greenstein and Nelson W. Polsby, eds., *Micropolitical Theory: Handbook of Political Science*, vol. 2 (Reading, Mass.: Addison-Wesley, 1975), pp. 243–318.

51. On the sources of interest group strength and influence, see Mancur Olson, *The Rise and Decline of Nations: Economic Growth, Stagflation, and Social Rigidities* (New Haven: Yale University Press, 1982); David B. Truman, *The Government Process: Public Interests and Public Opinion* (New York: Knopf, 1962); Raymond A. Bauer et al., *American Business and Public Policy: The Politics of Foreign Trade* (New York: Atherton Press, 1963); E. E. Schattschneider, *Politics, Pressures, and the Tariff* (New York: Prentice-Hall, 1935); and Peter Gourevitch, *Politics in Hard Times: Comparative Responses to International Economic Crises* (Ithaca: Cornell University Press, 1986).

52. Peter J. Katzenstein, *Small States in World Markets: Industrial Policy in Europe* (Ithaca: Cornell University Press, 1985), pp. 23–24, 33, 83–85; Katzenstein, *Corporatism and Change: Austria, Switzerland, and the Politics of Industry* (Ithaca: Cornell University Press, 1984); Katzenstein, "Introduction: Domestic and International Forces and Strategies of Foreign Economic Policy," and "Conclusion: Domestic Structures and Strategies of Foreign Economic Policy," in Katzenstein, ed., *Between Power and Plenty*, pp. 16, 19, 297, 306, 308, 333.

strong societal concentration produce short-to-medium-term protection and policies of structural adjustment.[53]

Katzenstein's framework of international size and domestic structure offers a clear step toward systematically integrating international and domestic sources of postwar protectionism. Yet this approach still raises several concerns. First, is the degree of openness based on international size an accurate indicator of international constraint on state action? Through the 1970s, Austria remained reluctant to liberalize textile trade despite its extreme vulnerability as well as pressure from GATT, the United Nations Conference on Trade and Development (UNCTAD), and Switzerland.[54] Factors such as reliance on foreign capital, imports of investment goods, and the nature of exports make small states such as Austria vulnerable to change in the world economy. Less clear is the extent to which small states actually face threats of retaliation by other countries should they choose to adopt selective closure. Lake's arguments, for example, suggest that small states may be able to free-ride under certain international economic structures. This example suggests that a more extensive integration of international factors may help to understand policy choices.

Second, the degree of state centralization, like state strength, offers a static conception of structure. The Japanese state's greater centralization than its American counterpart does not preclude direct societal access to central decision makers or other state actors taking steps on behalf of societal actors. Overlapping jurisdiction among Japanese ministries, prime ministerial directives, and an increasingly active Diet all offer potential sources of influence (both binding and nonbinding) on the Ministry of International Trade and Industry (MITI).[55] Nor has the absence of American-style business-government relations in Japan always led to smooth relations between state and society. MITI's failures at structural adjustment include resistance by the automobile industry over thirty years to consolidation proposals and by the textile industry over thirteen years to vertical integration plans.[56] Import competition

53. Katzenstein, *Between Power and Plenty*, pp. 297, 333; and Katzenstein, *Small States*, pp. 23–24.

54. Katzenstein, *Corporatism and Change*, pp. 182–85.

55. For the nature of changing relations between the legislative and executive branches in Japan, see Michio Muramatsu and Ellis Krauss, "Bureaucrats and Politicians in Policymaking: The Case of Japan," *American Political Science Review* 78 (March 1984), pp. 126–46. For overlapping ministry jurisdiction in Japanese trade policy, see Chalmers Johnson, "MITI and Japanese International Economic Policy," in Robert A. Scalapino, ed., *The Foreign Policy of Modern Japan* (Berkeley and Los Angeles: University of California Press, 1977), pp. 229–53. I discuss these issues in greater detail in Chapter 2.

56. For detail on Japanese automobile policy, see Ira C. Magaziner and Thomas M.

from East and Southeast Asia has caused increasing pressures for protection in Japan. The Japanese textile industry is at the forefront of these trade policy disputes, and the Japanese steel industry is waiting in the wings.

Finally, societal centralization and concentration, as operationalized by Katzenstein, capture only the static institutional aspects of societal actors. Centralization reflects the number of industry associations included in a country's peak business association. The greater the number of associations, the greater the peak association's hierarchical (organizational) control over other associations. Broader control over the business community also hinges on the concentration (inclusiveness) of the industry associations.[57] The missing dimension is the actual degree of interest convergence among and within the industry associations. High levels of formal organization and extensive membership rolls mean little if the members of the peak association are unable to agree on a common trade policy stance.[58]

## An Integrative Approach to Trade Policy Choices

The call in this book for a more nuanced, integrative focus on the domestic and international sources of trade policy choices both challenges and complements the predominant approaches in the literature on international political economy. This section grounds my integrative focus in the current theoretical debates concerning strategies of adjustment and protection, and conceptualizations of state, society, and international constraints.

### Disaggregating Protection and Adjustment

The previous discussion of the extent of the protectionist patchwork in the textile and apparel, steel, and automobile sectors reveals a mix of

---

Hout, *Japanese Industrial Policy*, Policy Papers in International Affairs no. 15 (Berkeley: University of California, Institute of International Studies, 1980), pp. 67–79. On textile adjustment policy, see Brian Ike, "The Japanese Textile Industry: Structural Adjustment and Government Policy," *Asian Survey* 20 (May 1980), pp. 532–51.

57. Katzenstein, *Small States*, pp. 32–33, 91, 106 note to Table 3.

58. In case studies of Switzerland and Austria, Katzenstein links interests and organization to his discussion of centralization (*Corporatism and Change*, pp. 162–238). Moreover, the importance of interest convergence as facilitating centralization is implicitly raised when Katzenstein discusses shared ideology and receptiveness to informal bargaining (*Small States*, pp. 32–33). To facilitate cross-national comparison among noncorporatist countries, however, a more precise and explicit operationalization of the societal component of domestic structure is needed.

different overt measures directly affecting imports—such as price-based, quantitative, and administrative restrictions—as well as different, less overt measures indirectly affecting imports—such as state subsidies and production cartels. Combining the industrial sectors at a broad national level of analysis and combining the trade policy choices into broad categories of protection (overt) and adjustment (less overt) measures reveal three rough patterns of trade policy choices. U.S. trade policy appears to be characterized by a reliance on protection and limited adjustment assistance, Japanese trade policy is characterized by the opposite pattern, and West German trade policy lies between these two poles. This pattern conforms to the analysis of Katzenstein and others as to how domestic structure has shaped the protection and adjustment (industrial) policies of advanced industrial states.

Yet the protectionist patchwork also reveals considerable variation within the broad categories of protection and adjustment both cross-nationally and intranationally. In explaining this more nuanced variation in patterns of protectionist policy, however, the predominant theoretical approaches in the political economy literature run into difficulty. Why do policy makers choose quotas instead of tariffs, or state subsidies instead of production cartels, or state subsidies and quotas instead of state subsidies and administrative restrictions? The literature on international political economy has offered only partial answers to this important question. Although broad patterns of protection and adjustment clearly have ramifications for the international political economy, it is often the specific choices among types of protectionist policy that provide the spark to ignite underlying tensions at the domestic and international levels.

This book's integrative approach accounts for these choices by disaggregating the state, giving primacy of place to alliances of producer associations as key societal actors, and nesting international economic constraints in political-military considerations. The price of such a focus is that the book is less able to explain or predict other aspects of trade policy such as cross-national differences in broader patterns of protection and adjustment. Nevertheless, it is more able to account for cross-national and intranational differences in the specific choices among types of protectionist policy made by state policy makers.

This trade-off is similar to that noted in J. David Singer's seminal work on the level-of-analysis problem. Disaggregating one's focus can lead to richer explanations of causation but at the price of a narrower breadth of focus. Yet where Singer compared the strengths and weaknesses of the international systemic-level approach versus an eclectic national-level approach, a number of scholars including Aggarwal and Katzenstein have integrated variables drawn from different levels of analysis. This book is distinguished by a similar integration as well as a systematic disaggregation of the national level of analysis and a narrower focus on types of protectionist policy. Heeding Singer, I take these steps in a consistent manner and with "full awareness" of their implications.[59]

### State, Society, and International Constraints

I define the state as an organization distinguished by the following characteristics: a set of differentiated institutions and personnel, primacy of place as the center or focal point of political relations in a given territory, monopoly power over "binding rulemaking" within this territory, and capability of acting autonomously from societal actors (groups based outside of the state).[60] This definition offers a starting point for a cross-national and intranational analysis of trade policy choices.

By definition, states are conceptualized as being similar in their primacy of place as a focal point of political relations and as a source of binding rulemaking within their given territories. States need not be similar, however, in their patterns of institutional differentiation or in their capability for autonomous action relative to society. This dichotomy begins to separate the integrative approach from contending arguments. First, by raising the potential for differentiation among states, the definition challenges the logic of international system-level conceptualizations of states as unitary, rational actors responding to the external environment. Second, the definition suggests that by focusing on the relationship between overall patterns of institutional differentiation and state autonomy—such as in the distinction between strong and weak states—statist and domestic structure arguments have tended to overshadow alternative conceptualizations of patterns of differentiation and autonomy.

One such alternative is the integrative approach offered in this book. The state's attributes of political centrality and rulemaking monopoly over a given territory and its capability for autonomous action from society, for example, suggest that the state lies at the nexus of international and societal pressures. Yet the state also contains differentiated

59. J. David Singer, "The Level-of-Analysis Problem in International Relations," in Klaus Knorr and Sidney Verba, eds., *The International System* (Princeton: Princeton University Press, 1961), pp. 77–92.

60. See the discussion of Weber's conceptualization of the state (as drawn from Weber's *Economy and Society*) in Michael Mann, "The Autonomous Power of the State: Its Origins, Mechanisms and Results," in John A. Hall, ed., *States in History* (London: Basil Blackwell, 1987), p. 112. Eric Nordlinger et al., "The Return to the State: Critiques," *American Political Science Review* 82 (September 1988), pp. 881–84.

institutions and personnel, suggesting interaction between state personnel closer to and further removed from the core of the policy-making
process. Although this distinction has been widely recognized by political scientists, attempts to conceptualize distinct state actors as well as the
state have contributed to the absence of agreement on what "the state"
actually is.[61]

This book seeks to avoid this pitfall by explicitly disaggregating the
institutional and personnel component of the state into three groups of
actors: state policy makers, state officials, and peripheral state actors.
State policy makers are the narrow core of public officials who serve as
the primary sources of state policy in a given issue area. State officials
consist of those state personnel who by virtue of their position within
the state's legislative, executive, bureaucratic, and judicial institutions
are able to become involved in the given issue area. Peripheral state
actors are those state personnel who are not relevant to the given issue
area. The state is, therefore, conceptualized according to the four-part
definition discussed above, and state actors are conceptualized as falling
into three groups. Moreover, because there are cross-national differences in the structure of state institutions and the potential for intranational
changes in the distribution of power and authority across state institutions, Chapter 2 identifies state policy makers and state officials by
country, by issue area, and by time period under analysis.

My focal point for analysis is the state policy makers and the way they
balance domestic and international pressures. To gain insight into the
relative influence of these pressures on trade policy choices, I narrow
my theoretical focus to account for those instances when conflicts exist
between the dictates of international and domestic forces. The price of
such a focus is to discount those instances when such conflicts do not
occur. Yet, much as in the case of the scholarly practice of focusing on
periods of international crisis to throw variables into stark relief, I
believe that insights can be gained from focusing on cases of contending

61. Theda Skocpol, *States and Social Revolutions: A Comparative Analysis of France, Russia,
and China* (Cambridge: Cambridge University Press, 1979), pp. 30–32; and Otto Hintze,
"Military Organization and the Organization of the State," in Felix Gilbert, ed., *The
Historical Essays of Otto Hintze* (New York: Oxford University Press, 1975), pp. 178–215.
For discussion of competing views of the state, see Ruggie, "Book Review," pp. 297–99;
Stephen D. Krasner, "Approaches to the State: Alternative Conceptions and Historical
Dynamics," *Comparative Politics* 16 (January 1984), pp. 223–46; Peter Evans et al., eds.,
*Bringing the State Back In* (Cambridge: Cambridge University Press, 1985); Gabriel A.
Almond, "The Return to the State," and Nordlinger et al., "The Return to the State:
Critiques," *American Political Science Review* 82 (September 1988), pp. 853–901; and James
A. Caporaso, ed., "Special Issue on the State in Comparative and International Perspec-
tive," *Comparative Political Studies* 21 (April 1988).

international and domestic forces.[62] I also narrow my focus by choosing not to extend my analysis to the socioeconomic class, specific belief systems, knowledge, or experience of state policy makers. I base this decision on considerations of feasibility and parsimony as well as the relative importance of the following explanatory variables in accounting for state policy makers' choices among types of protectionist policy.[63]

These caveats aside, the domestic pressure faced by state policy makers consists of two components: industrial alliance strength and the degree of institutional access. Both components provide insights into the current theoretical discourse over the nature of domestic constraints on foreign economic policy. Although interest group theories have long stressed the importance of societal groups in shaping trade policy choices, the questions of which societal actors matter and to what extent they determine policy choices remain points of contention.

From the standpoint of trade policy analysis, I contend that industrial alliances rather than alliances between producer associations and organized labor are the primary source of societal pressure on state policy makers. Industrial alliances are coalitions of producer associations, each association representing a subsector within a single major manufacturing industry. The strength of industrial alliances reflects the combination of the coalition's organization, inclusiveness, and convergence of interests.

As advocates for the economic health of their subsector, producer associations directly represent business and indirectly represent labor on international trade issues. Although organized labor may support the demands of producer associations, unions have had limited influence on trade policy issues without the support of such associations. It is important to stress, however, that these arguments do not necessarily hold true for the relative importance of business and labor in other issue areas such as incomes policy or foreign investment policy.

In contrast to both interest group and statist theories, industrial alliances do not necessarily determine trade policy choices, nor can state policy makers, regardless of the strength (centralization) of their state, necessarily resist the demands of industrial alliances. The intervening factor here is the second component of domestic pressure,

62. Peter A. Gourevitch, "Breaking with Orthodoxy: The Politics of Economic Policy Responses to the Depression of the 1930s," *International Organization* 38 (Winter 1984), p. 99; and Katzenstein, *Small States*, pp. 35–37.

63. For a discussion of the costs and benefits of dropping the level of analysis down to cognitive levels, see Singer, "Level-of-Analysis Problem," pp. 84–89; and Stephan Haggard and Beth A. Simmons, "Theories of International Regimes," *International Organization* 41 (Summer 1987), pp. 509–13.

degree of institutional access. This concept draws a key distinction between access and access with influence. The greater the latter, the greater the degree of institutional access.

The fragmentation of state power and authority across state institutions determines the array of access channels into the policy-making process available to societal actors. In other words, state structure determines the number of access channels or points of access. To define states as strong or weak based on the extent of fragmentation, however, does not reveal the nature of the access provided by a given access channel selected by a societal actors at a specific time.[64] Although state strength may help to explain general patterns of access, a more dynamic focus is necessary to capture the actual influence gained by a societal actor in a given policy dispute.

Industrial alliances, for example, attempt to gain access to state policy makers either through direct appeals or through the efforts of state officials on the alliance's behalf. As illustrated for the United States, Japan, and West Germany in the following chapter, different access channels available to an industrial alliance within a given country offer different degrees of influence over that country's policy-making process, ranging from the limited influence of nonbinding recommendations on state policy makers' action that some channels offer to the power of binding recommendations offered by other channels.

By separating domestic pressure into two components, I seek to illustrate that the mere emergence of a strong industrial alliance matters little if the alliance is unable to gain the right kind of access to the policy-making process. To gain access with influence requires tapping an institutionalized channel that links the alliance, either directly or indirectly, to the state policy maker in such a way that the

---

64. Helen Milner has accurately noted that the distinction between weak states (the United States) and strong states (France) on the continuum of "points of access to trade policy structures" is not extensive. Milner's strong societal focus, however, fails to take the additional step of addressing the nature of the access that these points provide (Milner, "Resisting the Protectionist Temptation: Industry and the Making of Trade Policy in France and the United States during the 1970s," *International Organization* 41 [Autumn 1987], pp. 652–55). In contrast, Michael Atkinson and William Coleman have called for disaggregating the state to the meso or sectoral level—focusing on bureaucratic arrangements and relationships linking specific state bureaus and societal organizations—when seeking to explain sectoral industry policy choices in advanced capitalist economies. By conceptualizing policy makers' autonomy in a given sector as a function of the mandates of relevant state bureaus and in-house capacity to meet such mandates, however, the authors still are limited to predictions of general patterns of access based on static conceptions of state structure (Atkinson and Coleman, "Strong States and Weak States: Sectoral Policy Networks in Advanced Capitalist Economies," *British Journal of Political Science* 19 [January 1989], pp. 47–67).

24

policy maker is bound by the recommendations of other actors that become involved in the policy-making process.

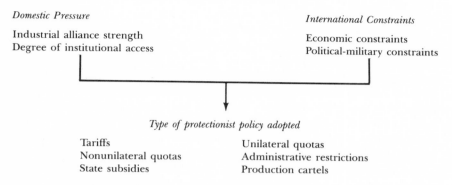

*Domestic Pressure*

Industrial alliance strength
Degree of institutional access

*International Constraints*

Economic constraints
Political-military constraints

*Type of protectionist policy adopted*

Tariffs
Nonunilateral quotas
State subsidies

Unilateral quotas
Administrative restrictions
Production cartels

*Figure 1.* An integrative framework

As illustrated in Figure 1, however, state policy makers do not have the luxury of merely looking inward. The different types of protectionist policy demanded by societal actors often entail international costs. In this book, I conceptualize international constraints as those international economic and political-military factors that impose costs on the country that adopts overt types of protectionist policy.

Retaliation is the bottom line of international economic constraints. Although considerable scholarship exists on international economic sources of constraint on trade policy, treatment of retaliation has tended to be overly compartmentalized. For example, interdependence approaches note the constraints inherent in a country's dependence on trade, whereas structural approaches stress the constraints stemming from a country's position in the international economic structure (Lake has termed the latter the country's "fear of retaliation"). Drawing on both theoretical traditions, I recast international economic constraints in terms of two dimensions of retaliation.

Specifically, if a country is highly dependent on trade, it may be vulnerable to retaliation from trading partners. Yet, in the absence of a focus on the structure of the international economic system and the position of the country in that system, it is not clear to what extent the country actually faces a threat of retaliation. For example, small countries, although vulnerable, may be able to free-ride in the presence of a hegemonic country. At the same time, however, limited vulnerability may lead state policy makers to discount the implications of a given international economic structure. Theorists of international strategy recognize that the threat of retaliation becomes pressing only if one is vulnerable to retaliation. Thus, combining the two dimensions of retaliation offers a more accurate conceptualization of international economic constraints.

Economic considerations, however, do not exist in an international vacuum. Therefore, I include political-military constraints as a second source of international constraint; the potential for adverse political-military consequences (such as the loss of support from or injury to strategic allies) in the event of overt, protectionist policy choices. This decision is grounded in the arguments raised by Susan Strange and other scholars that international political economy analysis should not lose sight of "the realities of power." The debate between scholars arguing from the realist and economic liberal traditions, however, shows that one point of contention is how much "sight" one should devote to political-military considerations versus international economic considerations as factors shaping state action.[65]

My contribution to this debate is twofold. First, drawing on Aggarwal, I "nest" international economic constraints in broader political-military constraints. Specifically, in instances when low levels of international economic constraint suggest the opportunity for introducing overt types of protectionist policy at low international cost, this suggestion can be overridden by high levels of political-military constraint. Second, in contrast to this international focus, I argue that international constraints must contend with domestic pressure in shaping trade policy choices.

Combining international constraints and domestic pressure produces the following general hypothesis: rising domestic pressure in the form of strong industrial alliances gaining institutional access to state policy makers will lead to the adoption of increasingly overt types of protectionist policy despite the existence of international constraints against such choices. I expect this relationship to hold even though overt types of protectionist policy are more likely than less overt types to disrupt imports and incite trading partners and may entail international economic and political-military costs.

Why will domestic pressure win out? First, by the very nature of their position, state policy makers attempt to mitigate between international considerations and domestic concerns. The emergence of an industrial

65. Susan Strange, "What about International Relations?" in Strange, *Paths to International Political Economy* (London: George Allen & Unwin, 1984), pp. 183–98; Strange, *States and Markets* (London: Pinter, 1988); and Robert O. Keohane and Joseph S. Nye, *Power and Interdependence* (Boston: Little, Brown, 1977).

alliance, however, increases the difficulty of this task. State policy makers are concerned with major manufacturing industries because of the employment and financial resources such industries represent.[66] By mobilizing the producer associations that represent the subsectors of a major manufacturing industry, industrial alliances begin to threaten the state policy makers' ability to acquire and maintain political support, to exercise influence over vital sectors of the economy, and to ensure economic stability.[67] Although other societal actors opposing the demands of the industrial alliance may vie for the state policy makers' attention, the absence or presence of opposing coalitions does not change the fact that the industrial alliance exists and must be dealt with. (As discussed in Chapter 7, however, such opposing coalitions may affect the receptiveness of certain access channels to the demands of the industrial alliance.)

Second, the extent to which state policy makers are forced to deal with the industrial alliance hinges on the degree of institutional access achieved by the industrial alliance or state officials acting on the alliance's behalf. As these actors turn to the access channels offering greater degrees of institutional access, state policy makers will have less flexibility to act according to the dictates of international constraints. Instead, rising domestic pressure will increasingly lead state policy makers to adopt the protectionist policies demanded by the industrial alliance.

Thus the book's integrative approach and the general hypothesis provide a starting point for assessing the variation in trade policy choices that characterizes postwar protectionism. Why has variation occurred? My contention is that for the trade policy choices of advanced industrial countries this variation is rooted in the cross-national and intranational differences in domestic pressure and international constraints faced by state policy makers.

66. Major manufacturing industries are distinguished by levels of employment and/or output greater than 10 percent of total manufacturing. The cutoff point of 10 percent is an intuitively applied demarcation, albeit somewhat arbitrary. I would expect such industries to be structurally important to the economy and the focus of state policy makers' interest. A cutoff point of 15 percent would unrealistically rule out all but one or two industries in a given country, but a cutoff point of 5 percent would offer little distinction between industries. Rather than an attempt at numerical precision, therefore, the purpose of such a demarcation is to add greater rigor to comparative analysis.

67. Gourevitch, "Breaking with Orthodoxy," pp. 95–129; and Kozo Yamamura, "Success That Soured: Administrative Guidance and Cartels in Japan," in Yamamura, ed., *Policy and Trade Issues of the Japanese Economy: American and Japanese Perspectives* (Seattle: University of Washington Press, 1982), pp. 77–112.

## METHODOLOGY AND CASES

I test this hypothesized relationship between international constraints, domestic pressure, and types of protectionist policy against nine cases of textile trade policy drawn from the United States, Japan, and West Germany.

### Methodology

Scholars have analyzed postwar protectionism using both quantitative and qualitative methods. Quantitative approaches tend to cluster around numerical data such as trade flows, tariff rates, regional concentration, employment levels, unionization rates, and gross national product.[68] Yet the cost of statistical precision is that available data in quantitative form are not always the best data for understanding trade policy choices. Qualitative approaches, in contrast, have relied more on the historical analysis and comparison of less precise constructs such as state strength and domestic structure. Moreover, the historical analysis of qualitative data makes establishing indicators that can be compared across historical contexts and national boundaries an extremely difficult task.

To gain precision as well as more informed analysis requires the integration of quantitative and qualitative data. I operationalize key variables and indicators with this goal in mind. My operational framework ranks each variable against a nine-point ordinal scale, from Low − to High +. The small number of cases addressed in this book precludes the use of these ordinal indexes to test for precise statistical correlations.[69] The indexes, however, do offer a rough framework from which to trace change in specific variables as well as relations between variables. To avoid spurious correlations at this level of analysis, I rely on the process-tracing techniques explained below. The analytical techniques employed to measure international constraints, domestic pressure, and type of protectionist policy as well as the resulting indexes are presented in detail in the Appendix. For those seeking a minimal exposure to operationalization, a brief overview of key variables and criteria for determining the ordinal indexes is offered in Table 1.

68. For examples of quantitative approaches, see J. J. Pincus, "Pressure Groups and the Pattern of Tariffs," *Journal of Political Economy* 83 (August 1975), pp. 757–78; Robert Baldwin, *The Political Economy of U.S. Import Policy* (Cambridge, Mass.: MIT Press, 1986).

69. A larger data set would allow testing through nonparametric measures of correlation such as Spearman's rho and Kendell's tau.

*Table 1.* Summary of operationalization

| Variables | Indicators | Index |
|---|---|---|
| *International constraints* | | |
| International economic constraint | | |
|   Vulnerability to retaliation | (Exports + imports)/GNP | Index derived from thirty-year unweighted average of trade dependence for fourteen industrialized countries |
|   Threat of retaliation | Country's position in the international economic structure (IES) | Index derived by combining David Lake's four possible IES (hegemonic leadership, multilateral supportership, bilateral supportership, and unilateral supportership) with three possible identities of the individual country in question (hegemonic leader, supporter, or spoiler) |
| Political-military constraint | Adverse political-military consequences (i.e., loss of support from or injury to strategic allies) | Index derived from typology of state policy makers' concerns with war, spheres of influence, and international alliance politics |
| *Domestic pressure* | | |
| Industrial alliance strength | Organization (merged, federated, separate) Inclusiveness (proportion of industry employment and production represented by alliance members). Interest convergence (demands of alliance members by type of protectionist policy) | Indexes for organization and interest convergence derived from possible combinations of types. Index for inclusiveness ranked from zero to 100 percent |
| Degree of institutional access | Degree of binding input on state policy makers' action | Index derived by ranking types of institutionalized input. These include nonbinding recommendations, setting parameters on state policy makers' initiatives, and binding recommendations |
| *Type of protectionist policy* | | |
| Type | Tariffs, unilateral quotas, nonunilateral quotas, administrative restrictions, state subsidies, production cartels | Index derived by ranking these types according to their ability to disrupt import flows and incite retaliation from trading partners |

Alexander George and Vinod Aggarwal have sought to increase the methodological rigor of case study analysis. George's "method of structured, focused comparison" introduces structure by requiring the analyst to ask "the same questions of the different cases."[70] I structure my nine cases by centering on the following question: how do state policy makers respond to contending international and domestic pressures on trade policy choices? In addition, I try to explain the policy choices in these cases from the standpoint of several alternative theoretical approaches. George's "focused" comparison requires the analyst to address those aspects of the case that are "interesting from a theoretical perspective." I focus my nine cases by specifically addressing textile trade policy disputes between textile alliances and state policy makers.

Aggarwal argues that process tracing uses interviews and archive work to "trace" the way in which a "postulated theoretical model affects policymakers."[71] This approach allows the analyst to test for a "spurious" relationship between independent and dependent variables. The case studies that follow rely on process tracing to assess the impact of international constraints and domestic pressure on state policy maker's choices. For the U.S. cases, I supplement the strong secondary literature on textile trade policy with a detailed examination of congressional hearings and industry petitions during the period of the industry's first postwar exposure to major competition from imports. Since the secondary literature is much weaker on Japanese and West German import policy in textiles, however, my analysis has relied heavily on field research conducted in both countries. The book is based on extensive interviews conducted with state policy makers, producer association representatives, labor union representatives, trade and import association representatives, and industry analysts from the media, banking, and academic communities. In addition, the analysis is informed by newspaper archival research and detailed review of industry trade journals.

## Cases

Why did I select the textile industry for an analysis of postwar protectionism? The answer to this question lies in the characteristics of

70. Alexander George, "Case Studies and Theory Development: The Method of Structured Focused Comparison," in Paul Gordon, ed., *Diplomacy: New Approaches in History, Theory, and Policy* (New York: Free Press, 1979), cited in Aggarwal, *Liberal Protectionism*, pp. 38–39.

71. Aggarwal, *Liberal Protectionism*, pp. 38–39.

the industry itself as well as the lessons the sector holds for trade policy choices in other industries. For example, the industry encompasses a range of activities, including man-made fiber production, natural and man-made fiber processing into yarns and cloth, and apparel production.[72] Over the past four decades, this industry has experienced extensive technological change and international competition.[73] Breakthroughs in synthetic fiber technology facilitated capital intensification and the growth of high value-added products. Innovations also emerged in the form of air-jet and water-jet looms, open-ended spinning, and, more recently, computer-aided design and manufacturing techniques. The gradual spread of technological innovations across developed and developing countries, as well as the relative labor intensity of segments of the industry, increased the sources and competitiveness of low- and high-wage imports in the markets of advanced countries.

Although technological change and import competition are not unique to textiles, it was the first major manufacturing industry where policy makers in the more industrialized countries responded to postwar international competition. As such, disputes between state and societal actors over international textile trade shaped patterns of interaction in subsequent import-competing industries.[74] Finally, textiles continues to be a major industry in the world economy and to be characterized by continuous trade disputes despite the pace of technological change. An analysis of the sources of variation in textile trade policies, therefore, offers a viable starting point for addressing the current pattern of postwar protectionism.

Why focus on the United States, Japan, and West Germany? First, these three countries represent the core economies of the industrialized "North," accounting for 45.9 percent of exports and 46.4 percent of

72. Industrial use and household furnishing textiles constitute only a small proportion of downstream textile products and thus will not be addressed here in any great detail.

73. Textile Institute, *Computers in the World of Textiles: Papers Presented at the Annual World Conference, September 26–29, 1984, Hong Kong* (Manchester: Textile Institute, 1984); Geoffrey Shepherd, *Textile Industry in Developed Countries*, Thames Policy Papers no. 30, Trade Policy Research Center, 1981; Geoffrey Shepherd, "Textiles: New Ways of Surviving in an Old Industry," in Shepherd et al., *Europe's Industries: Public and Private Strategies for Change* (Ithaca: Cornell University Press, 1983), pp. 26–51; Rianne Mahon and Lynn Krieger Mytelka, "Industry, the State, and the New Protectionism: Textiles in Canada and France," *International Organization* 37 (Autumn 1983), pp. 557–61; and Geoffrey Edwards, "Four Sectors: Textiles, Man-Made Fibers, Shipbuilding, Aircraft," in John Pinder, ed., *National Industrial Strategies and the World Economy* (Ottawa: Allenheld, Osmun, 1982), pp. 85–112.

74. I have benefited here from discussions with Peter J. Katzenstein.

imports by industrialized countries in 1986.[75] Full-scale protection by these three countries would sound the death knell of the open international economy. Second, although these three countries have attracted considerable attention from political scientists, systematic, sectoral analyses of all three countries in a single study are rare. As a result, assessing the lessons of the American, Japanese, or German "models" for other countries is often difficult. More important, the political economy literature has treated these countries as more different than similar in their international constraints and domestic structures. On the narrow continuum of large, advanced industrial countries, the United States and Japan are most often placed on opposite poles with West Germany somewhere in the middle.[76] This study seeks to introduce a cross-nationally applicable explanation of trade policy choices. The heterogeneity of the United States, Japan, and West Germany offers a strong challenge for such an attempt.

For each of the three countries, I focus on the respective textile industry's first major exposure to competition from imports. As state and societal interaction in textiles shapes interaction in other industries, so did state policy makers' responses to the first major period of exposure to imports in textiles shape subsequent textile trade policy. The cases are drawn from each country's first decade of major import competition. The onset of major competition is difficult to determine because what is major for one country may be of little consequence in another. During the 1950s, U.S. textile producers considered import penetration ratios of 2 percent as major. Yet Japanese textile producers did not become concerned until imports had surged to over 15 percent of domestic consumption. Thus, to facilitate cross-national analysis I define major import competition as occurring when dominant producer associations begin to call for state action to restrict imports. These actors are introduced in Chapter 3. For the United States, the first period of major import competition covers three case studies from 1954 to 1962. For the Japanese industry this period covers three case studies from 1974 to 1983. Finally, the three West German case studies span the period 1963 to 1969.[77]

75. Figures calculated from the International Monetary Fund, *International Financial Statistics, January 1988* (Washington, D.C., 1988), pp. 74–75.

76. Katzenstein, *Between Power and Plenty*, pp. 304–23; and Katzenstein, *Small States*, pp. 22–30. The accuracy of this continuum at the level of domestic politics is addressed in greater detail in Chapter 2.

77. During these periods, the textile industries also meet the criteria for major manufacturing industries set out above. From 1954 to 1962, the U.S. textile industry accounted for 13.7 percent of total manufacturing employment and 8.5 percent of

CONCLUSION

This study builds on international and domestic approaches to the international political economy to account for the sources of the post-war protectionist patchwork. Postwar protectionism differs from its counterpart in the 1930s in the selective use of different types of protectionist policy. Each of these policy types differs in its ability to hasten closure, either through disrupting the flow of imports or by inciting retaliation in the international economy. Assessing and responding to the future directions of international trade, therefore, requires insights into the sources of state policy makers' choices among these types of protectionist policy.

The predominant approaches in the literature on international political economy, however, have had greater success in accounting for broad patterns of protection and adjustment than in accounting for variation at the level of specific direct and indirect protectionist policies. This book, therefore, introduces a more nuanced identification and integration of the international and domestic sources of trade policy choices to fill this gap in the international political economy literature. The nine cases presented in Chapters 4, 5, and 6 address the origins of the postwar protectionist patchwork in the textile trade policy decisions of the United States, Japan, and West Germany.

Chapters 2 and 3 serve as an introduction to the three countries. More important, the purpose of these chapters is directly linked to the integrative approach introduced above. Chapter 2 disaggregates the state in each of the countries to identify state policy makers and state officials active in the issue area of textile trade policy and to identify access channels and potential degrees of institutional access faced by these state policy makers. Despite differences in state structure, the chapter reveals that state policy makers in all three countries face access channels that allow societal actors and state officials access with influence. Chapter 3 disaggregates society in each of the three countries to identify the potential members, supporters, and opponents of industrial alliances. By focusing on the centralization and inclusiveness of producer

---

manufacturing output (value added). From 1974 to 1983, the Japanese textile industry accounted for 13.3 percent of total manufacturing employment and 6.7 percent of manufacturing output (shipments). From 1963 to 1970, the West German textile industry accounted for 11.6 percent of total manufacturing employment and 8 percent of manufacturing output (shipments). These figures are calculated from the sources listed in the respective industry tables in Chapter 3 and from OECD, *Main Economic Indicators: Historical Statistics, 1964–83* (Paris: OECD, 1984), p. 342.

associations this chapter also begins to reveal how interest convergence among alliance members can offset their structural weaknesses. Chapters 4 through 6 integrate the state and societal actors introduced in the previous two chapters in a systematic analysis of textile trade policy choices in the United States, Japan, and West Germany. Finally, Chapter 7 summarizes and discusses the implications of the study's findings.

CHAPTER TWO

# Inside State Structure: Access Channels and the Authority of State Policy Makers

Statist and domestic structure approaches suggest that broad patterns of protection and adjustment strategies adopted by advanced industrial countries are shaped by state structure. Japan, characterized by a strong, centralized state, possesses the means and institutions to alter the economic structure of the country through adjustment strategies and limited protection. West Germany and, to a greater degree, the United States, by contrast, are characterized by weaker, decentralized states and therefore lack the means to follow Japan's statist strategy. Instead, these countries place a greater emphasis on protection to deal with economic change.

This chapter begins from the premise that though state structure is important and structural arguments are useful for capturing broad patterns of protection and adjustment, a focus on overall state structure is less suited for capturing state policy makers' choices among types of protectionist policy. This premise draws, in part, on the proliferation of scholarship citing paradoxical cases in which, in specific instances or in specific industrial sectors, strong states act like weak states and vice versa. In disaggregating the state, this chapter reveals that cross-national differences in the fragmentation of state power and authority in these countries are not as extensive as has been commonly portrayed in the political economy literature. Not only are the states in all three countries fragmented, but state policy makers in all three countries must deal with access channels that allow the binding influence of other actors in trade policy decisions.

A key step in the integrative approach proposed in this book is to identify state policy makers and state officials involved in textile trade policy. Peripheral state actors are not covered in this chapter. In disaggregating the state for the respective case study periods, this chapter also illustrates that state structure sets the array of potential access channels into the policy-making process from which the degree of institutional access emerges. Where applicable, trade regulations and policy-making procedures are updated in the chapter notes.

## UNITED STATES, 1954–1962

During the 1950s and early 1960s, the president, selected members of the White House staff, and selected bureaucratic appointees were the core public officials who set American textile trade policy. Because he is directly elected, the president is less bound by the faction and coalition politics that constrain chief executives in Japan and West Germany. American cabinet members, such as the secretaries of state and commerce, are politically subordinate to the president and play diverse roles ranging from advisers to international negotiators. Under the Eisenhower administration, such officials were active participants on issues of textile trade policy. The president also has access to a White House staff of key assistants, councils, and offices exclusive of the cabinet departments.[1]

American state policy makers have not held exclusive authority over textile trade policy. From 1954 to 1962, access channels into the policy-making process reflected extensive institutionalized checks on the exercise of power and authority between and within the branches of the government. Authority over international commerce constitutionally rests with the legislative branch. Yet as I. M. Destler argues, in 1934 "Congress legislated itself out of the business of making product-specific trade law" by conditionally delegating tariff-negotiating authority to the executive.[2] The 1934 Reciprocal Trade Act (RTA) amended the 1930 Smoot-Hawley tariff legislation to empower the president to negotiate reductions in tariff levels on a bilateral basis by 50 percent over a three-year period. Extensions of this amendment continued to set limits on maximum allowable reductions in tariff levels as well as time limits on the president's negotiating authority. In 1962, the RTA was incorporated into John F. Kennedy's Trade Expansion Act.[3]

1. I. M. Destler et al., *Managing an Alliance: The Politics of U.S.-Japanese Relations* (Washington, D.C.: Brookings Institution, 1976), pp. 61, 62, 66; and Lewis J. Edinger, *Politics in West Germany*, 2d ed. (Boston: Little, Brown, 1977), p. 20.

2. U.S. Constitution, Article 1, Section 8, Paragraphs 3 and 18. Destler, *American Trade Politics*, p. 11.

3. The RTA was extended in 1937, 1940, and 1943; expanded by a second 50

During years when the delegation of negotiating authority was up for renewal, trade acts could be held hostage in Congress in exchange for presidential concessions. As a result, extensions of the RTA during the 1950s included forced modifications—such as setting of peril points that placed maximum allowable ceilings on tariff reductions for specific products—aimed at mollifying protectionist opposition in Congress. Destler has argued that the strong congressional committee system limited the impact of protectionist forces in Congress through the late 1960s. Since tariffs were a source of state revenue, the tax committees— the Senate Finance Committee but particularly the House Ways and Means Committee—held jurisdiction over foreign trade legislation and could act as gatekeepers by limiting the trade proposals presented to the full Congress.[4]

Once the parameters of negotiating authority and tenure were in place and presidential efforts at negotiations begun, however, fewer access channels were available to industrial alliances through the RTA. Until 1962, interested parties to proposed trade concessions were allowed only nonbinding input through the Committee for Reciprocity Information. The committee's representatives drawn from the Tariff Commission and the Departments of State, Commerce, Agriculture,

percent cut in 1945; and extended in 1948, 1949, 1951, 1953, 1954, 1955, and 1958 with different negotiating ranges and inclusion of escape clause and peril point regulations. The RTA was incorporated into the Trade Expansion Act of 1962 along with a shift to a linear tariff reduction formula, abolition of the peril point, and the introduction of new presidential powers to enter into multilateral negotiations. Tariff-negotiating authority was implicitly rejected by a protectionist Congress from 1968 to 1975 only to be introduced with modified constraints on presidential action under the 1974 Trade Act. The 1974 act allowed presidential action to reduce tariff as well as nontariff barriers. The former could be reduced to zero when rates were under 6 percent or up to 60 percent on other rates. See Robert A. Pastor, *Congress and the Politics of U.S. Foreign Economic Policy, 1929–1976* (Berkeley and Los Angeles: University of California Press, 1980), p. 329; Jose de la Torre et al., *Corporate Responses to Import Competition in the U.S. Apparel Industry* (Atlanta: Georgia State University, 1978), pp. 5–6; Krasner, "United States Commercial Policy," pp. 75–78. For details on the 1979 and 1984 trade acts see Destler, *American Trade Politics*; and Stephen L. Lande and Craig VanGrasstek, *The Trade and Tariff Act of 1984: Trade Policy in the Reagan Administration* (Lexington, Mass.: Lexington Books, D. C. Heath, 1986).

4. Destler argues that congressional reforms and the rise of subcommittees during the 1970s have undercut this gatekeeper function (*American Trade Politics*, pp. 25–29, 59–60). Robert Pastor makes a similar argument on changes in Congress. Pastor's contention that Congress has played more of a role in sending signals—bills, resolutions, speeches, and hearings—to the executive than formulating policy on trade issues also lends support to my focus on the executive as state policy maker. See Pastor, "The Cry and Sigh Syndrome: Congress and Trade Policy," in Allen Schick, ed., *Making Economic Policy in Congress* (Washington, D.C.: American Enterprise Institute for Public Policy Research, 1983), pp. 158–95.

and the Treasury, would hold public hearings on pending negotiations. Although these hearings offered industry representatives little input on the scope of trade concessions, they fulfilled the obligation set by the 1934 RTA that the president engage in "prior consultation" with industries affected by planned tariff reductions.[5] In 1962, Kennedy's Trade Act and Executive Order 11075 established the office and staff of a new special trade representative (STR) to carry out trade negotiations on approved items and to coordinate the "trade policy activities" of other government agencies.[6] Yet advisory committees for industry, labor, and agricultural representatives were not attached to the STR until 1974.[7]

In addition to input from industry through the Committee for Reciprocity Information, a series of congressional acts granted state officials the right to recommend modifications in previously negotiated trade agreements. The director of the Office of Defense and Civilian Mobilization, the secretary of agriculture, and the Tariff Commission were allowed to act when the national security was impaired, agricultural programs were disrupted, or domestic producers were injured or threatened because of tariff reductions (thereby requiring use of the escape clause). In all three cases, however, the president was delegated the power of final approval over recommended modifications.[8] The

5. Grace Beckett, *The Reciprocal Trade Agreements Program* (New York: Columbia University Press, 1941), p. 18, n. 4; Krasner, "United States Commercial Policy," p. 65; and Pastor, *Congress and the Politics,* p. 330.

6. The creation of the STR reflected congressional dissatisfaction with the negotiating role played by the Department of State (Destler, *American Trade Politics,* p. 353). It is not clear to what extent the STR supplanted Kennedy's Cabinet Textile Committee established in 1961. According to R. Buford Brandis, this committee created an Interagency Textile Administration Committee (chaired by the Department of Commerce) to coordinate negotiations under the Short Term Arrangement in Textiles. In addition, the Cabinet Textile Committee established a Management-Labor Textile Advisory Committee in 1962 to "provide advice to textile negotiators" (Brandis, *The Making of Textile Trade Policy, 1935–1981* [Washington, D.C.: American Textile Manufacturers Institute, 1982], p. 22).

7. Under the 1974 Trade Act, representatives from the Departments of Commerce, Labor, and Agriculture were empowered to chair these committees. The STR's role as "executive broker" for the United States in international negotiations was increased by the 1974 Trade Act. The act boosted the STR, with cabinet ranking, to the Executive Office of the President. The Trade Agreements Act of 1979 expanded the STR at the expense of the Department of State (GATT, East-West trade responsibilities) and renamed it the Office of the United States Trade Representative (Destler, *American Trade Politics,* pp. 87–109; Krasner, "United States Commercial Policy," p. 64; de la Torre, *Corporate Responses,* pp. 5–6; and Pastor, *Congress and the Politics,* p. 330).

8. The director of the Office of Defense and Civilian Mobilization was granted authority by the 1955 extension of the RTA. The secretary of agriculture was granted authority under Section 22 of the Agricultural Act of 1933, as amended. Escape clause

one exception, although never invoked, empowered Congress under the 1958 RTA to override a presidential decision by a majority vote. The difficulty of mobilizing support for such an override suggests that the potential for industrial alliances to invoke high degrees of institutional access through such channels would remain limited.

Congress was less generous in its delegation of authority over quantitative restrictions on imports. Although Section 204 of the Agricultural Act of 1956 empowered the president to negotiate quantitative limits on foreign textile exports, Congress retained the right to legislate unilateral quotas and, if necessary, to override a presidential veto of such measures.[9] Thus key congressional committees and the congressional floor remained the battlegrounds for potentially strong degrees of institutional access.

In addition to action through Congress, industrial alliances could turn to the access channels embodied in existing dumping and countervailing duty procedures. Under the Tariff Act of 1897 and the

provisions originated in a 1947 Executive Order and the 1951 extension of the RTA. The role of the Tariff Commission (succeeded in 1974 by the U.S. International Trade Commission) and provisions for determining injury have changed during the course of the 1958 extension of the RTA, the 1962 Trade Expansion Act, the Trade Acts of 1974 and 1979, the Trade and Tariff Act of 1984, and the Omnibus Trade and Competitiveness Act of 1988.

See U.S. Congress, Senate, Committee on Interstate and Foreign Commerce, *Problems of the Domestic Textile Industry, Hearings before the Subcommittee of the Committee on Interstate and Foreign Commerce*, 85th Cong., 2d sess., 1958 (hereafter cited as *Pastore Hearings 1958*), pp. 1252–53; Krasner, "United States Commercial Policy," p. 65; de la Torre, *Corporate Responses*, pp. 5–6; Judith L. Goldstein, "The State, Industrial Interests, and Foreign Economic Policy: American Commercial Interests in the Postwar Period," paper delivered at the 1981 Annual Meeting of the American Political Science Association, New York, September 1981, pp. 4–6; Destler, *American Trade Politics*, pp. 114–15, 118; and Omnibus Trade and Competitiveness Act of 1988, Pub. L. No. 100–418, 102 Stat. 1107.

9. With authority provided by the Agricultural Act, American state policy makers acted as the driving force in the creation of the Short and Long Term Arrangements to regulate textile imports in 1961 and 1962. As a further extension of congressional authority, in 1962 under HR 10788, the president was authorized to restrict the products of nonsignatories to negotiated agreements when such agreements covered a significant portion of world trade in these products. Presidential authority to enter into multilateral arrangements was reinforced by the 1962 Trade Expansion Act. Since 1974, the president has also had broad authority to restrain imports through the use of tariff and nontariff policies in cases of unfair foreign trade practices (Section 301 of the 1974 Trade Act, as amended). See the Department of State, Department of Commerce, and the Department of Treasury, *Economic and Foreign Policy Effects of Voluntary Restraint Agreements on Textiles and Steel* (Washington, D.C.: General Accounting Office, 1974); Warren S. Hunsberger, *Japan and the United States in World Trade* (New York: Harper & Row, 1964), p. 318, n. 64; and Julia Christine Bliss, "The Amendments to Section 301: An Overview and Suggested Strategies for Foreign Response," *Law and Policy in International Business* 20 (1989), pp. 501–28.

1921 Antidumping Law, both modified by subsequent legislation, Congress delegated control over the levying of countervailing duty and antidumping judgments to the Department of the Treasury. The Department of the Treasury was bound only by prior Tariff Commission rulings on whether domestic producers had been "injured" by imports.[10] Thus positive findings regarding dumping or countervailing duties by the Department of Treasury would act as binding recommendations for state policy makers.

Finally, access channels to force the granting of adjustment assistance measures did not exist in any specific form before the introduction of President Kennedy's Seven Point Textile Plan in 1961. As part of his relief package for the textile industry, Kennedy directed the Department of the Treasury to review machinery depreciation allowances and to instruct the Small Business Administration to aid firms in obtaining financial assistance. In both cases, approval authority appeared to be left to the respective agencies. Under assistance measures included in the 1962 Trade Expansion Act, the Departments of Commerce and Labor were granted the authority to review industry applications for adjustment assistance following "authorization" of such applications by the president and rulings by the Tariff Commission that the industry had been injured by imports. In the absence of presidential authorization, the input of other state actors became nonbinding.[11]

10. See sections 731 (Dumping) and 701 (Countervailing duty) of the Tariff Act of 1930. In 1979, the Department of Commerce's International Trade Administration replaced the Department of Treasury in enforcing these actions. The Trade Act of 1974 allowed the secretary of the treasury to waive the imposition of countervailing duties for four years when steps were being taken to reduce subsidization and when the imposition of duties would disrupt ongoing negotiations under the Tokyo Round. In 1979 the criteria for injury were changed to cover subsidization leading to "material injury." The change brought U.S. legislation in line with the GATT subsidy agreements reached under the Tokyo Round. Under the Trade and Tariff Act of 1984, the USITC is allowed to combine the effects of imports from numerous suppliers when determining injury. The USITC is also allowed to consider subsidization at upstream stages of production. In addition, the Department of Commerce can initiate dumping proceedings itself (Destler, *American Trade Politics*, pp. 120–22; and Lande and VanGrasstek, *Trade and Tariff Act*, pp. 19–20).

11. For detail on the 1961 and 1962 measures, see Hunsberger, *Japan and the United States*, p. 327. Under the Trade Act of 1974, assistance requirements were relaxed. Imports had merely to "contribute importantly" to job losses instead of being the "major cause." The Tariff Commission was also bypassed to shift responsibility for determining adjustment assistance to the Departments of Commerce and Labor (Destler, *American Trade Politics*, p. 115; de la Torre, *Corporate Responses*, pp. 211, 214–17; Krasner, "United States Commercial Policy," p. 64; and Goldstein, "The State, Industrial Interests, and Foreign Economic Policy," p. 6).

Destler argues that the Trade Adjustment Assistance program was "gutted" in 1981. Although Congress managed to keep the statute, budget cuts under the Reagan adminis-

## JAPAN, 1974–1983

State policy makers in Japanese textile trade policy during this period were located in the Ministry of International Trade and Industry. Although the MITI minister and parliamentary vice-minister are politically appointed members of the prime minister's cabinet, the difficulty in creating a working cabinet from representatives of factions with the ruling Liberal Democratic party (LDP) has meant that the average tenure of these appointees has been approximately one year. Thus, in most cases, political appointees to MITI rely heavily on the ministry's senior and midlevel career bureaucrats at the vice-minister, bureau chief, section chief, and deputy section chief levels.[12]

The number of these bureaucrats devoted to textile issues decreased in 1973 as part of a change in MITI's focus and organization that shifted the jurisdiction of its bureaus from the traditional practice of vertical linkages between major industries and bureaus to new assignments making bureaus responsible for horizontal groupings of similar industries. In textiles, the nine sections of the pre-1973 Textile Bureau were reduced to three textile sections in the new Consumer Goods Industries Bureau (Sei Katsu Sangyō Kyoku).[13]

MITI advisory councils supplement this structure by creating a forum in which representatives from MITI, industry, labor, and other interested parties can air views and, upon reaching a consensus, draft recommendations on state policy. On textile issues, the Textile Committee of the Industrial Structure Council and the Textile Industry Council serve as the major advisory councils. The ministry also "exercises control" over seven public corporations through credit approval and/or expenditure authorization power. Of these, the Japan Development Bank, the Smaller Business Finance Corporation, and the Small and

---

tration have severely decreased the benefits and duration of available assistance (*American Trade Politics*, p. 160). For a more detailed analysis of adjustment assistance programs in the United States, see Hufbauer and Rosen, *Trade Policy for Troubled Industries*.

12. T. J. Pempel, "Japanese Foreign Economic Policy," in Katzenstein, ed., *Between Power and Plenty*, p. 147; Haruhiro Fukui, "The GATT Tokyo Round: The Bureaucratic Politics of Multilateral Diplomacy," in Michael Blaker, ed., *The Politics of Trade: U.S. and Japanese Policymaking for the GATT Negotiations* (New York: Columbia University East Asian Institute, 1978), pp. 83, 102; and Robert E. Ward, *Japan's Political System*, 2d ed. (Englewood Cliffs, N.J.: Prentice-Hall, 1978), pp. 157–59.

13. Johnson, "MITI and Japanese International Economic Policy," pp. 273–75; and Chikara Higashi, *Japanese Trade Policy Formulation* (New York: Praeger, 1983), p. 38. For a detailed breakdown of the reorganized MITI, see Chalmers Johnson, *MITI and the Japanese Miracle* (Stanford: Stanford University Press, 1982), pp. 336–38.

Medium Enterprise Agency play major roles in allocating financial assistance to the textile industry.[14]

The shift in bureau structure decreased the relative importance of textile issues within the ministry. Although the new Consumer Goods Industries Bureau ranks second to last in the hierarchy of bureaus and agencies, textile trade policy issues still work their way up to the vice-ministerial level through formal interbureau committees and ad hoc meetings. Formal committees exist at the General Affairs Section deputy chief, General Affairs Section chief, and bureau directors levels. These committees reflect an "internal democracy" of policy formation aimed at building consensus from the bottom up.[15] The process of working for consensus within and between bureaus allows the demands of a single industry to be considered in the context of broader issues such as overall trade policy. Similarly, in the United States, the president's large constituency facilitates his ability to view the demands of a single industry from the perspective of broader trade policy concerns.[16] Yet differences between U.S. and Japanese state policy makers must not be overlooked. The president is supported by a staff and cabinet. As a result, the direction of policy initiatives is predominantly from the top down. Top MITI officials, by contrast, rely more on the efforts of sections and bureaus within the ministry to build consensus from the bottom up.

What is the potential for high levels of institutional access as state policy makers seek to build consensus across state institutions on trade policy issues? In contrast to the United States, constitutional authority over international commerce in Japan is not explicitly delegated to either the executive or legislative branch. Constitutionally, the parliament (Diet) is the sole lawmaking organ of the Japanese state, and the executive branch is charged with administration of the law, managing foreign affairs, and, with Diet review, concluding treaties. In practice, legislation enacted by the Diet has placed considerable authority over international commerce in the hands of a number of executive minis-

14. The Textile Industry Rationalization Agency acts as an agent for the Small and Medium Enterprise Agency on textile issues. See Ronald P. Dore, *Flexible Rigidities: Industrial Policy and Structural Adjustment in the Japanese Economy, 1970–80* (London: Cambridge University Press, 1986), pp. 230–33; Johnson, *MITI*, p. 79; Johnson, "MITI and Japanese International Economic Policy," pp. 274–75; and Higashi, *Japanese Trade Policy*, pp. 38–39.

15. Textile policy issues may also work from the top down when key LDP Dietmen and/or the prime minister attempt to influence the MITI minister (Johnson, *MITI*, p. 79; Higashi, *Japanese Trade Policy*, p. 39; and Fukui, "GATT," pp. 101–2).

16. Krasner, *Defending the National Interest*, pp. 63–64, 73.

tries and agencies.[17] As a result, in textile trade policy institutional access to MITI officials can stem from the Ministry of Agriculture, Forestry, and Fisheries, the Ministry of Finance, the Fair Trade Commission, and the Ministry of Foreign Affairs.[18] This granting of statutory authority among executive ministries by no means allows the bureaucracy to disregard the LDP-dominated Diet in trade policy formation.[19] MITI legislative initiatives can be modified and delayed in Diet committees or in key LDP committees such as the Policy Affairs Research Council (PARC). Although less common, expressions of concern over MITI trade policy may also lead to the formation and promotion of policy initiatives by groups of Diet members such as those belonging to the LDP Textile Committee. As groups of long-standing LDP Diet members gain expertise, the potential for pressure from the Diet on state policymakers has increased. Finally, Diet officials can appeal to the politically vulnerable prime minister (usually the LDP party president) and MITI minister to gain their assistance in altering MITI policies.[20] In sum, the nature of Diet pressure on the

17. For a summary of Japan's constitution, see Ward, *Japan's Political System,* pp. 236, 233. For detail on the establishment laws for the respective ministries, see Johnson, "MITI and Japanese International Economic Policy," pp. 229–45.

18. Johnson, "MITI and Japanese International Economic Policy," pp. 248–53; Fukui, "GATT," pp. 103, 81–82, 114–36; and interview held in Tokyo, Japan, April 1984.

19. Johnson, "MITI and Japanese International Economic Policy," pp. 227–80; and Pempel, "Japanese Foreign Economic Policy," p. 147. The nature of this interaction is a subject of extensive debate among analysts of Japanese politics. Recent surveys of bureaucrats and politicians appear to lend credence to the increasing relevance of a "shared influence" model of Japanese politics, with both actors citing the importance of bureaucrats and politicians in the policy-making process. See the summary of major arguments in Muramatsu and Krauss, "Bureaucrats and Politicians in Policymaking," pp. 126–46. In a 1987 review of Japanese politics, the *Far Eastern Economic Review* also reported that the LDP was emerging as the primary source of decisions in Japanese policy making. See Charles Smith, "Who's in Charge Here? Increasingly It's 'the party,'" *Far Eastern Economic Review,* 11 June 1987, pp. 87–88. By late 1989, a debate over the relative influence of bureaucrats and politicians had become further clouded by the paralysis of the LDP over the Recruit scandal and the success of the opposition parties in the upper house of the Diet. See "Kaifu Snafu," and "All Kaifu Needs Is a Miracle," *Economist,* 12 August 1989, pp. 15, 25–26.

20. The influence of MITI political appointees on career bureaucrats is not entirely clear. For example, Shigeo Misawa argues that if a minister should veto a decision reached from below he will gain the distrust of the ministry. If the minister is not well prepared for his post he will have to take time to learn. In light of the average length of a minister's stay, this learning process would reduce the minister's effectiveness. Even if the minister is prepared, Misawa notes that he would still need to cooperate with the bulk of the ministry. In contrast, Kanji Haitani has argued that LDP officials in the Diet can work through the minister to influence personnel decisions within the ministry, thereby placing a premium on considering Diet interests for those officials interested in advancement within the ministry. In addition, the desire of individual bureaucrats to participate in

action of state policy makers encourages MITI officials to consider the interests of Diet members.

Although state policy makers in the United States and Japan face the prospect of legislative pressure, Japanese state policy makers have not been held hostage by temporary legislative delegations of authority over key aspects of trade policy making. The 1949 Foreign Exchange and Trade Control Law (FECL) gave MITI officials formal legal authority to regulate trade flows for an indefinite period.[21] During the 1960s, however, liberalization of the Japanese economy decreased the applicability of MITI's formal authority in areas such as import licensing. To retain the ministry's sphere of influence, MITI officials increasingly turned to "administrative guidance" (gyōsei shidō). Although administrative guidance is not legally binding, MITI officials can "'recommend' ... 'advise' ... 'or' ... 'mediate' on any matter within their jurisdiction as specified in the establishment law of their ministry." MITI's 1949 establishment law grants the ministry regulatory authority over the "production and circulation ... [of] ... manufacturing products." The

---

politics following their tenure in the ministry can be tapped. In the case of MITI, however, the bulk of MITI retirees go into industry rather than politics. See Haitani, *The Japanese Economic System: An Institutional Overview* (Lexington, Mass.: D.C. Heath, 1976), p. 40; Misawa, "An Outline of the Policy-Making Process in Japan," in Hiroshi Itoh, ed., *Japanese Politics—An Inside View: Readings from Japan* (Ithaca: Cornell University Press, 1973), p. 31; and Johnson, "MITI and Japanese International Economic Policy," pp. 257–58.

21. The FECL (revised in 1980) set out the "basic framework" for the regulation of international commerce. The law granted authority to the cabinet to elaborate on this framework through the use of cabinet ordinances. The cabinet, in turn, delegated powers to ministerial ordinances. Cabinet measures based on FECL included the Foreign Exchange Control Cabinet Order (1950), Export Trade Control Order (1949), and Import Trade Control Order (1949). MITI ministerial ordinances included Regulations for the Control of Export Trade (1949) and Regulations for the Control of Import Trade (1949). In general, MITI was granted primary responsibility over trade matters (including import licensing: FECL Article 52), and the Ministry of Finance's authority centered on setting exchange rates and the authorization and review of bank activity in foreign exchange transactions. The 1980 modifications in FECL lie primarily in the area of capital flows and general support for the concept of liberalization.

This note is based on Robert S. Ozaki, *The Control of Imports and Foreign Capital in Japan* (New York: Praeger, 1972), pp. 144–55; Hiroshi Kawakami, "Foreign Trade Regulations," in Zentaro Kitagawa, ed., *Doing Business in Japan*, vol. 6 (New York: Mathew Bender, 1984), pp. 5, 15–16; Michele Schmiegelow, "The Reform of Japan's Foreign Exchange and Foreign Trade Control Law: A Case of Qualitative Economic Policy," in Schmiegelow, ed., *Japan's Response to Crisis and Change in the World Economy* (Armonk, N.Y.: M. E. Sharpe, 1986), pp. 1–27; and Dan F. Henderson, "Access to the Japanese Market: Some Aspects of Foreign Exchange Controls and Banking Law," in Gary R. Saxonhouse and Kozo Yamamura, eds., *Law and Trade Issues of the Japanese Economy: American and Japanese Perspectives* (Seattle: University of Washington Press, 1986), pp. 131–51.

ministry is also authorized "to formulate plans concerning fundamental policies for the production, distribution, consumption and foreign trading of commodities under its jurisdiction."[22] The ministry's increased reliance on administrative guidance has also enhanced the importance of MITI advisory councils in state-societal consultation. Emphasis is placed on reaching a consensus among council members; yet the consensus is not required to be strong. Thus ministry representatives potentially face only a limited degree of institutional access through the advisory councils.[23]

The degree of access to MITI officials reflects jealously guarded overlapping jurisdictions among key ministries and may vary according to the type and scope of policy at issue.[24] When silk concerns overlap with mainstream textile issues, MITI officials face potential input from the Ministry of Agriculture, Forestry, and Fisheries.[25] On questions of the setting and administration of tariffs or tariff quotas MITI officials must address the potential input of the Ministry of Finance's Customs and Tariff Bureau and Tariff Council. In contrast to the overlapping

22. Administrative guidance is exercised through meetings with top officials or associations, sending representatives to association meetings, phone calls, and written requests. These activities take time and personnel and thus have finite limits in application. For detail on MITI's administrative guidance efforts, see Johnson, "MITI and Japanese International Economic Policy," pp. 253–56; Uchihasi Katsuto, "Behind the Scenes at MITI," *Japan Echo* 10 (1983), pp. 45–46; Ippei Yamazawa, "Japan's Adjustment to the Industrial Growth of Asian NICs and ASEAN Countries," forthcoming; and Yamamura, "Success That Soured," pp. 83–85. John Haley has argued that administrative guidance has offered MITI and other ministries only an extremely limited tool of influence ("Administrative Guidance versus Formal Regulation: Resolving the Paradox of Industrial Policy," in Saxonhouse and Yamamura, eds., *Law and Trade Issues of the Japanese Economy*, pp. 107–25).

23. It is not clear who benefits most from the councils. Industry representatives are guaranteed access to the ministry, and MITI representatives must consider the industry positions. Yet by routing industry demands and input through institutionalized channels, the councils give the industry representatives a stake in the successful operation of the councils. Pressures for successful consensus may slightly distance industry representatives from the industries they represent, decreasing the pressure on MITI officials. In addition, the advisory councils tend to "depend for information and advice on the very ministries which they are supposed to advise." See Haruhiro Fukui, "Studies in Policy Making: A Review of the Literature," in T. J. Pempel, ed., *Policymaking in Contemporary Japan* (Ithaca: Cornell University Press, 1977), p. 34; and Peter J. Katzenstein's argument concerning the role of "proporz" in the Swiss advisory council network in "Capitalism in One Country? Switzerland in the International Economy," *International Organization* 34 (Autumn 1980), pp. 507–40.

24. On jurisdictional disputes in general see Misawa, "An Outline of the Policymaking Process," p. 27; Johnson, "MITI and Japanese International Economic Policy," pp. 231–32; and FECL Article 52 cited in Ozaki, *Control of Imports*, p. 155.

25. See Fukui, "GATT," p. 106. As noted in Chapter 5, most analysts of the Japanese textile industry treat silk as a separate issue area.

authority of ministries in price-based restrictions, however, quantitative restrictions on imports fall under MITI jurisdiction.[26]

In addition to the type of policy under consideration, the international scope of trade policy deliberations often leads to jurisdictional overlap. In the multilateral trade negotiations carried out under the Tokyo Round, MITI officials from the ministry's International Trade Policy Bureau represented textile and other industry interests as part of an interministerial negotiating team. This team consisted of representatives from each of the ministries that constitute what Chalmers Johnson has termed Japan's "economic bureaucracy."[27] In narrower negotiating forums such as in the case of the Multi-Fiber Arrangement, MITI officials tended to receive less input from other ministerial actors. Thus, although MITI officials must share jurisdiction with the Ministry of Foreign Affairs in international trade disputes, they have played the dominant role in resolving textile trade disputes between the United States and Japan.[28]

In contrast to the divisions of authority over tariff and quota issues, MITI and the Ministry of Finance share jurisdiction over enforcing antidumping and countervailing duty policy.[29] The actual relationship between the two ministries is difficult to determine, however, because these measures have never been fully used. The actions raised and subsequently withdrawn by the Japan Spinners Association in 1982 were the first in the sixty-two-year history of Japan's antidumping law

26. The Customs and Tariff Bureau plays an instrumental role in drafting modifications in tariff rates and legislation. These modifications require approval by the Tariff Council and the Diet (Fukui, "GATT," pp. 89, 121). MITI's authority over quantitative restrictions is based on MITI Notification No. 170 (1966) "issued and amended from time to time by MITI pursuant to Article 3 of the Import Trade Control Cabinet Order (1949)" (Kawakami, "Foreign Trade Regulations," pp. 32–33).

Ministry authority also overlaps in the cases of several administrative restrictions on imports. Administrative restrictions such as testing, health, and safety standards are set and administered by the Ministry of Health and Welfare, Industrial Technology Agency, Ministry of Transport, and Environmental Agency. Fukui notes that in the Tokyo Round "the legal work involved in changing the existing conditions of existing nontariff barriers fell within the Finance Ministry's jurisdiction." The Ministry of Finance also negotiated on behalf of these ministries and agencies (Fukui, "GATT," pp. 132–33).

27. The economic bureaucracy consists of the Ministry of Finance, MITI, Ministry of Agriculture, Forestry and Fisheries, Economic Planning Agency, Ministry of Transportation, and Ministry of Construction (Johnson, "MITI and Japanese International Economic Policy," p. 229). The Ministry of Foreign Affairs played a coordinating role and held exclusive authority to draft proposals for the Japanese negotiating team (Fukui, "GATT," pp. 81–82, 103, 114–36).

28. Fukui, "GATT," pp. 86–88; Johnson, "MITI and Japanese International Economic Policy," pp. 232–33; and Destler et al., *Managing an Alliance*, pp. 78–79.

29. *Wall Street Journal*, 16 December 1982. This relationship in discussed in greater detail in the third Japanese case study.

and in the ninety-two-year history of the countervailing duty statute.

MITI officials also share authority with other state actors over adjustment assistance measures. Through its public corporations, the ministry can grant monetary adjustment assistance in the form of loans and grants. The resources available for these measures, however, are shaped by the budgetary authority of the Ministry of Finance and the Diet. In addition, through its supervisory powers over the Bank of Japan, the Ministry of Finance can offer low-interest loans and ease loan burdens for Japanese producers. Since the Ministry of Finance's Tax Bureau is responsible for formulating and administering tax policy, MITI officials must deal with Finance officials to obtain tax exemptions for specific industries.[30] Finally, MITI officials share jurisdiction with the Fair Trade Commission in granting exceptions to Japan's Anti-Monopoly Law. Commission approval is required for the granting of recession and rationalization cartels to hard-pressed domestic industries.[31] Commission approval is not required, however, in cases of "special cartels authorized by special laws" and of MITI "guidance cartels." Under the latter, MITI officials rely on meetings with individual firms or consult with producer associations to promote industry compliance with ministry projections concerning industry prices, production, or investment trends.[32]

## West Germany, 1963–1969

West German state policy makers concerned with textile trade policy issues during the 1960s consisted of the minister, state secretaries, and

---

30. MITI's financial influence over societal actors is wielded for the most part through the Japan Development Bank and the Small Business Finance Corporation (Medium and Smaller Enterprises Credit Fund) (Johnson, "MITI and Japanese International Economic Policy," pp. 229–46, 256–57; interview held in Tokyo, Japan, April 1984; Fukui, "GATT," pp. 92–94; and Haitani, *Japanese Economic System*, pp. 50–52). For a detailed analysis of the Japanese budgetary process, see John C. Campbell, *Contemporary Japanese Budget Politics* (Berkeley and Los Angeles: University of California Press, 1977). For additional detail on tax policy, see Toshi Miyatake et al., "Taxation," in Zentaro Kitagawa, ed., *Doing Business in Japan*, vol. 5, chap. 10 (New York: Mathew Bender, 1985), pp. 16–17.

31. Recession cartels allow producers to fix prices and/or output to overcome industry hardships. Rationalization cartels allow placing restrictions on the competitive use of new technology or on limiting product lines to facilitate cost reduction, technical efficiency, or product quality improvements (Article 24–3 and Article 24–4 of the Anti-Monopoly Law; Haitani, *Japanese Economic System*, pp. 132–34; and Mitsuo Matsushita, "The Anti-Monopoly Law of Japan," *Law in Japan: An Annual* 11 [1978], p. 66).

32. Under the special cartels only the approval of the "competent minister" is required. The guidance cartel procedure "deliberately avoids...interfirm negotiations" to achieve an exemption from antimonopoly regulations (Haitani, *Japanese Economic System*, pp. 133–34).

key division heads of the Federal Ministry of Economics (Bundesministerium für Wirtschaft—BMWi). As in Japan, state policy makers in West German trade policy were located in the economic bureaucracy. Despite this roughly similar location in state institutions, Japanese and West German state policy makers faced different patterns of potential institutional access.

Compared to the relationship between the LDP and MITI in Japan, political parties have made more extensive inroads into BMWi. Japanese political appointees in MITI are limited to the minister and parliamentary vice-minister. In BMWi these appointees can extend beyond the minister down to the division-head level. In this respect West Germany is closer than Japan to approximating the "layers of presidential loyalists" that characterize the U.S. bureaucracy. Political appointments in the United States and West Germany reflect both internal party factions and key interest groups. In West Germany, however, these appointments also reflect the attempt by the chancellor to balance the demands of the major and minor parties belonging to the ruling coalition.[33]

More extensive political appointments do not necessarily indicate that state policy makers are more vulnerable to political pressures. The tenure of political appointees is one consideration. In contrast to the long LDP control of the Japanese Diet and Prime Minister's Office, ruling parties in West Germany have experienced considerable turnover. The ruling coalition in the 1950s of the Christian Democratic Union (CDU), Christian Social Union (CSU), and Free Democratic Party (FDP) gave way to the Grand Coalition of the CDU-CSU and the Social Democratic Party (SPD) in 1966. In 1969, the CDU lost control over the chancellorship to the SPD with the emergence of a new SPD-FDP ruling coalition. This coalition remained in power until the resurgence of the CDU in the 1983 federal elections.[34]

Yet turnover in ruling coalitions can be misleading. First, despite changes in the identity of West Germany's ruling parties, political appointees to the West German bureaucracy have had a longer tenure than political appointees in Japan. The average tenure of individual BMWi ministers from 1949 to 1983 exceeded that of their MITI counterparts by more than a factor of five. Second, coalition changes

33. Renate Mayntz and Fritz W. Scharpf, *Policy Making in the German Federal Bureaucracy* (Amsterdam: Elsevier Scientific Publishing, 1975), pp. 39–40, 86–90; K. H. F. Dyson, *Party, State, and Bureaucracy in West Germany* (Beverly Hills: Sage, 1977), pp. 20–34; Pempel, "Japanese Foreign Economic Policy," p. 147; and Edinger, *Politics in West Germany*, pp. 269–70.

34. See Hans Georg Lehmann, *Chronik der Bundesrepublik Deutschland: 1945/49 bis 1983* (Munich: C. H. Beck, 1983), pp. 204–7.

are not totally reflected in the political penetration of the bureaucracy. From 1966 to 1972 the SPD controlled the BMWi's minister position. Since 1972, FDP officials have headed BMWi. By the mid-1970s, SPD members tended to dominate the state secretary positions in the West German bureaucracy while CDU members dominated division-head positions. Currently, within BMWi, FDP appointees are still numerically overshadowed by SPD members.[35] Thus, although the ruling party changes more frequently in West Germany, the presence and tenure of political appointees among state policy makers has been greater in West Germany than in Japan.

One should still not overemphasize the actual influence that these political appointees have on ministry policy making. Below the level of the minister, long-standing political appointees have tended to focus more on issues than on political orientation. This practice reinforces the dominant role of career bureaucrats in BMWi. At the level of the minister, appointees are less reliant on career bureaucrats than their Japanese counterparts and thus more able to play an active role within the broad political guidelines on policy set out by the chancellor.[36] This ministerial influence, however, is partially restricted by the role of bureaucrats at the division-head level.

Division heads handle external relations and relations with other divisions and ministries.[37] Within the ministry, division heads also mediate between officials at the subdivision and section level and officials at the minister and state secretary levels. Specifically, the division head seeks to integrate the day-to-day "specific issue initiatives" of the lower levels of the ministry with the top-level focus on short-term political controversies and party pressure. Although section and division heads "generally try to avoid developing initiatives and making proposals which they know deviate from the minister's intentions," Renate Mayntz and Fritz W. Scharpf have argued that this does not equal unconditional compliance with ministerial directives. Thus, in contrast to the ideal-typical Japanese pattern of consensus building among state policy makers from the bottom up, and the subordinate-superior relations in the United States, West Germany appears to offer

35. Tenure calculations are based on Lehmann, *Chronik der Bundesrepublik*, pp. 204–7; Dyson, *Party, State, and Bureaucracy*, pp. 33–34; Nevil Johnson, *Government in the Federal Republic of Germany: The Executive at Work* (Oxford: Pergamon Press, 1973), p. 155; and interview with Bundestag member in Ithaca, New York, October 1985.

36. Interview held in Bonn, West Germany, May 1985; and Mayntz and Scharpf, *Policy Making*, p. 38.

37. In this paragraph I rely heavily on the analysis of Mayntz and Scharpf, *Policy Making*, pp. 71–84, 86–92, 95; and interviews conducted in Bonn, West Germany, May and June 1985.

a third pattern of policy formation: division heads mediating and shaping the policy initiatives flowing from bottom to top and from top to bottom.[38]

In textile trade policy, these initiatives are shaped by the structure of BMWi's seven divisions.[39] BMWi divisions are organized by broad economic issues rather than by industry or groups of industries as in MITI. For example, general adjustment assistance issues including tax and competition policy as well as broad trade issues fall under Division I: Economic Policy. The domestic economic concerns of specific industries are addressed in the sections (Referate) of Division IV: Industrial Economics, Economic Promotion—Berlin. The textile industry falls under Division IV: Subdivision C; Section 3. The subdivision's competence covers consumer goods, iron and steel, and economic promotion for West Berlin. Reflecting the weak integration of West German man-made fiber and textile production, issues involving man-made fiber fall under the chemical industry section (IV:B;7) within the capital goods, construction, and chemical subdivision. Trade and economic issues related to the European Community are addressed in sections under Division E: European Policy. Bilateral and multilateral trade issues in the Community and beyond are addressed by sections under Division V: Foreign Economic Policy and Development Assistance. Textile trade policy in the context of GATT and the Multi-Fiber Arrangement, for example, falls under the competence of Division V's basic trade policy section (Subdivision A; Section 2). These breakdowns of section competence reveal that, similar to the United States and Japan, textile trade policy issues are addressed in the context of broader concerns of domestic and foreign economic policy.[40]

Textile trade policy issues are the concern of a number of different sections and divisions. In contrast to MITI's standing intraministry committees, in BMWi the nature of the issue determines which minis-

38. Mayntz and Scharpf (*Policy Making*, p. 100) refer to this pattern as a "dialogue model." The day-to-day business of the ministry is handled by sections (Referate), and the more important the issue the greater the tendency to inform higher levels. Division heads play a key role in this interchange. Among other factors, a minister may be concerned about the electoral health of his party. Under West German electoral law, for example, a minimum of 5 percent of the electoral vote is required to acquire seats in the parliament and to receive federal financing. Larger parties are also interested in maintaining the support of large interest blocs.

39. This paragraph is based on a 1985 organizational chart obtained from BMWi as well as *Jahresbericht Der Bundesregierung, 1978*, Herausgeben vom Presse und Informationsamt der Bundesregierung, pp. 204–5; and Hans-Peter Schwarz, "Die Bundesregierung und die auswärtigen Beziehungen," in Schwarz, ed., *Handbuch der deutschen Aussenpolitik* (Munich: R. Piper, 1975), pp. 84–88.

40. Interview held in Bonn, West Germany, June 1985.

try officials participate and which divisions and sections play a leadership role in subsequent meetings.[41] This trend is reinforced by the structure of advisory councils attached to BMWi. For example, although the BMWi's Foreign Trade Advisory Council provides a formal contact between key business, labor, and banking representatives and the ministry on foreign economic policy issues, no council comparable to the Textile Industry Council in Japan exists for specific industries. Instead, ad hoc meetings between BMWi officials and interested association representatives occur only when specific problems arise.[42] The relative importance of textile issues and the officials concerned exclusively with them within BMWi appears to be less than that within MITI.

How are power and authority over textile issues distributed across state institutions? In contrast to the United States and Japan, the West German Basic Law implicitly gives authority over international commerce to the executive branch.[43] Of the state institutions that make up

41. For example, representatives from Division V are responsible for conducting deliberations on foreign trade issues (interviews held in Bonn, West Germany, May 1985).

42. Michael Kreile, "West Germany: The Dynamics of Expansion," in Katzenstein, ed., *Between Power and Plenty*, p. 202. Advisory councils on a broader level also existed under the government's "concerted action" program during the early to mid-1970s. Concerted action consisted of "a consultive body in which representatives of the government, unions, business, the federal bank, and scientific institutions met to discuss their mutual assessment of the economic situation as well as policies and strategies to be followed by various sectors of society." See Werner Menden, "Industrial Policy in the Federal Republic of Germany," in Margaret E. Dewer, ed., *Industry Vitalization: Toward a National Industrial Policy* (New York: Pergamon Press, 1982), p. 198.

Societal actors can also appeal to BMWi without invitation through letters and visits directed at all levels of the ministry. If rebuffed at the section level, representatives of societal organizations may turn to a higher level within the ministry. Appeals to the BMWi minister on basic issues do not often occur. Instead, industry representatives will try to get a broad "yes or no" of consideration from the minister (interviews held in Bonn and Frankfurt, West Germany, May and June 1985).

43. I make this determination in part by a process of elimination. Under Article 32 of the Basic Law, relations with foreign states are to be conducted by the federal government. Article 73, section 5, places the authority to legislate over international commercial policy within the exclusive authority of the federation. In contrast to the United States and Japan, the legislative branch is not singled out as either the primary lawmaking body or the holder of authority over international commerce. (The only clear delegation of constitutional authority over a specific issue area between the executive and legislative branches is under Article 65a, which places the power of command over the armed forces in the hands of the federal minister of defense.) Under Article 65 the chancellor determines and is held responsible for general policy guidelines. Finally, "within the limits set by these guidelines each Federal minister shall conduct the affairs of his department autonomously and on his own responsibility." Therefore, I conclude that formal authority over international commerce implicitly lies within the executive branch. For the West German Basic Law, see "Basic Law: The Constitution of the Federal Republic of Germany" in Bernd Rüster, ed., *Business Transactions in Germany*, App. 1 (New York: Mathew Bender, 1983), pp. 25, 28–29.

this branch, BMWi "occupies the commanding heights of foreign economic policy."[44] As in the case of Japan, however, ministry primacy in policy initiation does not mean that the West German bureaucracy can entirely ignore the legislative branch.

Parliamentary input in the trade policy-making process takes several forms. The upper house of the West German parliament (Federal Council or Bundesrat) consists of representatives appointed by the regional (Länder) governments. In areas of concurrent jurisdiction between the federal and regional governments, such as internal "economic matters," the Bundesrat is constitutionally authorized to review executive initiatives and ordinances.[45] The directly elected representatives to the lower house (the Federal Diet or Bundestag) are empowered to pass legislation in areas of exclusive federal jurisdiction such as the ratification of international treaties. Since BMWi initiatives in these areas can be delayed in parliamentary committees, the ministry will often send a representative to attempt to "shepherd" measures through committee deliberations.[46] In addition to these formal reviews, ministry policy can be challenged in question and answer periods (Fragestunde) held during legislative sittings. Bundestag representatives can also request that a ministry representative respond to a set of specific questions before a plenum of the Bundestag or before a legislative committee (Kleine or Grosse Anfrage). Finally, parliamentary representatives can appeal to the chancellor to shape the guidelines within which the BMWi conducts policy.[47]

44. Kreile has argued that the ministry was both the "steering agency of Ordnungspolitik" and "the driving force behind the installation of a liberal regime of foreign trade." Johnson has noted that more than 80 percent of all measures passed in the legislature originate in the federal ministries. Edinger, by contrast, sets the figure at 85 percent for the period 1949–73. He argues that this figure reflects the legislators' "lack of expertise, information, and support services" (Kreile, "West Germany," pp. 195, 198; Johnson, *Government in the Federal Republic,* p. 85; and Edinger, *Politics in West Germany,* p. 274).

45. The number of representatives is based on regional population and can range from three to five per region for a total of forty-one. For areas of concurrent jurisdiction see Article 74 of the Basic Law. Following Bundesrat approval, the initiatives are sent to the Bundestag. Executive ordinances must be approved by a majority of the Bundesrat (Edinger, *Politics in West Germany,* pp. 17–18).

46. The frequent changes in the West German ruling coalition suggest that BMWi shepherds face a greater threat from opposition party representatives than their Japanese counterparts face from the LDP-dominated Diet. Yet these coalition changes have also adversely affected the ability of German parliamentarians to acquire the expertise in issue areas held by their LDP counterparts in Japan and senior congressional officials in the United States. In sum, West German parliamentarians are less able to play an extensive role in constraining state policy makers than their Japanese or American counterparts (ibid., pp. 24, 275, 281; and interview held in Bonn, West Germany, May 1985).

47. An absolute majority of Bundestag representatives is necessary to pose a serious

Similar to MITI, BMWi's formal postwar authority over trade policy has been gradually eroding.[48] Yet, in contrast to MITI, this erosion has taken place both on the national and supranational levels. During the mid-1950s, BMWi surrendered its role as negotiator of trade protocols and agreements to the Foreign Office (Auswärtiges Amt) to resolve a jurisdictional dispute between the two ministries over foreign economic policy making. As part of the bargain, BMWi officials were left with control over relations with domestic actors and over the chairmanship positions of a number of key interministerial foreign economic policy committees.[49] Because the cabinet plays a limited role in policy making and efforts are being made among ministerial representatives to avoid raising disputes to the chancellor's level, these interministerial committees along with informal meetings have served to coordinate policy making.[50] Meetings dealing with textile trade policy have most often

threat to the chancellor's position. The chancellor is elected by the Bundestag and can be removed only by a "positive vote of no confidence." For details on this procedure see Edinger, *Politics in West Germany*, p. 21. The seriousness of such a threat being sparked by the textile industry is not great. One official I spoke with noted that textile industry influence was decreasing in the Bundestag because the number of Bundestag representatives who also represented the industry was decreasing. One industry official noted that direct industry appeals to the chancellor are rare because the chancellor tends to pass the issue down to the relevant ministry. Industry representatives will at times use a reverse strategy. Rather than appealing to parliamentary representatives to place pressure on the chancellor, industry representatives will try to get public relations exposure by getting the chancellor to visit a textile firm (interviews held in Bonn and Cologne, West Germany, June 1985).

48. BMWi authority has also been declining in areas other than trade policy. For an analysis of trends in monetary and development policy see Andrew P. Black, "Industrial Policy in West Germany: Policy in Search of a Goal?" (Berlin: IIM/Industrial Policy, n.d.), pp. 5–6; Schwarz, "Die Bundesregierung," p. 84; and David Childs and Jeffery Johnson, *West Germany: Politics and Society* (New York: St. Martin's Press, 1981), p. 59.

49. Kurt P. Tudyka, "Ökonomische Dimensionen auswärtiger Beziehungen," *Atomzeitalter* 6–7 (June–July 1968), pp. 341–42. For the shift of authority over East-West trade between the two ministries, see Angela Stent, *From Embargo to Ostpolitik: The Political Economy of West German–Soviet Relations* (Cambridge: Cambridge University Press, 1981), pp. 36–37. Although BMWi officials share the chairmanship with the Foreign Office over the Trade Policy Committee (Handelspolitische Ausschuss), Schwarz argues that this committee has not met for some time. Other interministerial committees have included the Committee for Development Questions, Committee for Export Questions, and Committee for Import Questions. In the early 1960s, BMWi officials also assumed the chairmanship roles of interministerial committees concerned with European issues (Tudyka, "Ökonomische Dimensionen," pp. 341–42; and Schwarz, "Die Bundesregierung," pp. 71–73).

50. Mayntz and Scharpf, *Policy Making*, pp. 42–44; and interviews held in Bonn, West Germany, May and June 1985. Jack Knott argues, however, that to be successful interministerial committees require the support of the "inner circle" consisting of the chancellor, Finance Ministry, BMWi, Foreign Office, and key party and parliamentary leaders. See Knott, *Managing the German Economy: Budgetary Politics in a Federal State* (Lexington, Mass.: D. C. Heath, 1981), pp. 31–32. For a more recent discussion of

been convened informally at the section level by the relevant section officials of BMWi.[51]

The conditions of the jurisdictional compromise between the Foreign Office and the BMWi were altered by the formation of the European Economic Community under the 1957 Treaty of Rome. Article 113 of the treaty required Community members to set in place a common commercial policy vis-à-vis third countries following a transition period from 1958 to 1969. Building on a common external tariff, Community competency over commercial policy was to include authority over tariff and trade agreements, export policy, and dumping and countervailing duty measures. Article 111 of the Treaty of Rome required that during the transition period to a common commercial policy in these areas, member nations were to "coordinate" their policies regarding nonmembers in areas such as tariff agreements, quantitative restrictions on imports, and the drafting of "lists of liberalization" on imports, exports, and transfers of payments.[52] By the end of the transition period, BMWi's negotiating authority over tariff policies and trade treaties, which was originally surrendered to the Foreign Office, would be shifted to the policy-making institutions of the EEC. More important, the content of these negotiations would no longer be determined solely by the compromise positions drafted in interministerial committees directed by BMWi.[53] Instead, the divergent member nations of the EEC would have to reach a compromise.

---

ministerial responsibilities, see Simon Bulmer and William Paterson, *The Federal Republic of Germany and the European Community* (London: Allen & Unwin, 1987), pp. 31–41.

51. When disagreement occurs, the issue is kicked up to subdivision level (interviews held in Bonn, West Germany, May and June, 1985).

52. Article 113 states that the common commercial policy would apply "particularly in regard to tariff amendments, the conclusion of tariff or trade agreements, the alignment of measures of liberalization, export policy, and protective commercial measures including measures to be taken in cases of dumping and subsidies" (Werner J. Feld, *The European Community in World Affairs: Economic Power and Political Influence* [Port Washington, N.Y.: Alfred Publishing Co., 1976], pp. 21–23; Geoffrey Denton and Theo Peters, "The European Community," in Wilfred L. Kohl, ed., *Economic Foreign Policies of Industrial States* [Lexington, Mass.: D. C. Heath, 1977), p. 195; and Schwarz, "Die Bundesregierung," p. 73). The focus of this book does not permit me to address the introduction of the Common Agricultural Policy of 1966 or measures under the European Steel and Coal Community of 1952.

53. Because of the increasing importance of European issues, in 1963 the State Secretary Committee for European Questions was created to coordinate West Germany's relations with the EEC. Although a representative from the Foreign Office has chaired this committee since 1972, since 1963 a representative from BMWi has always held the secretary position. More important, under this committee, BMWi officials chair the key subcommittee of representatives from divisions concerned with the EEC. This subcommittee serves as an information source as well as a forum for reaching interministerial

The relationship among the primary institutions in trade policy at the Community level has been discussed elsewhere in considerable detail.[54] Briefly, the European Commission and the Council of Ministers act as the two most important Community-level institutions in the formation and implementation of the EEC's trade policy. Along with overseeing national compliance with European Community treaties and practices, commissioners initiate action and legislation in their areas of competence (directorate generals) based on discussions with national and industry officials. National representatives to the Council of Ministers and its attached committees, by contrast, rule on commission proposals by attempting to reach compromise positions ("consensus or at least tacit agreement") in the face of national differences.[55] In other words, although competency over commercial policy lies with the EEC under Article 113, compromises between major EEC members "must be found in Brussels."[56]

The 1961 West German Foreign Trade Act (Aussenwirtschaftsgesetz— AWG) grants the force of law to Community regulations.[57] Because of the need for compromise, the development of EEC authority over trade policy—and thus the development of supranational institutional pressures on West German state policy makers—has been uneven. The EEC has had its greatest success in tariff policy. Following agreement among member countries on a basic framework for tariff equalization

---

consensus on EEC-related policy issues. For a detailed analysis, see Schwarz, "Die Bunderegierung," p. 73; and Bulmer and Paterson, *Federal Republic of Germany*, pp. 31–41.

54. For example, see Helen Wallace et al., eds., *Policy Making in the European Community* (New York: John Wiley, 1983); and Juliet Lodge, ed., *Institutions and Policies of the European Community* (New York: St. Martin's Press, 1983).

55. Commissioners are fairly independent from their national governments in that once they are appointed to their four-year terms they cannot be recalled. Yet the commissioners' desires to serve additional terms may dampen independent action. Commissioner portfolios are distributed upon appointment, and distribution is subject to some degree of national lobbying. Commissioners are supported in their directorate generals by directorates as well as divisions under the directorates. See Stanley Henig, "The European Community's Bichephalous Political Authority: Council of Minister– Commission Relations," in Lodge, ed., *Institutions and Policies of the European Community*, pp. 10–12, 15–18.

56. Interview held in Bonn, West Germany, May 1985.

57. Sections I and V of the AWG discuss West German obligations arising out of international treaties which require domestic legislation and those in which rules of supranational organizations carry the "force of law." See Ulf R. Siebel assisted by Ronald U. Siebel, "Foreign Trade Law," in Bernd Rüster, ed., *Business Transactions in Germany* vol. 1 (New York: Mathew Bender, 1985), pp. 11, 23. For a less trade-specific discussion of the legislative relationship between the EEC and West Germany, see Bulmer and Paterson, *Federal Republic of Germany*, pp. 165–84.

in early 1960, West German state policy makers participated in the removal of internal EEC tariffs.[58]

The pace of tariff equalization set during the 1960s, however, was not matched in the coordination of other protectionist policies. As a result, BMWi officials continued to exercise authority over a number of areas in international commercial policy with limited threats of institutional access through the EEC. Faced with slow progress in introducing dumping and countervailing duty measures at the Community level, for example, West Germany adopted new price-testing procedures and a modified antidumping law in 1966.[59] The failure of the EEC to recognize Eastern Europe also left a considerable opening for West German state policy makers. Up until the end of 1972, for example, Article 113 regulations "did not acknowledge state trading countries." In practice, though EEC tariff policy affected exports from Eastern Europe, individual Community members could set quantitative restrictions on Eastern European goods.[60] In West Germany, authority for

58. The customs union was achieved in 1968. For the most part, West German industry benefited from the equalization formula in that the relatively lower German tariffs were increased while the relatively higher French and Italian tariffs were decreased (Feld, *European Community in World Affairs*, pp. 24–25).

59. In contrast to regulations in the United States, the measures threatened the collection of duties from the importer in cases of suspected dumping. If no dumping was found, the importer would be repaid. These measures were administered by a subordinate office to BMWi—the Federal Office for Industrial Economics (Bundesamt für gewerbliche Wirtschaft). Administration of the textile quota and daily problems are handled by the same office. If more complex problems arise, the office turns to BMWi (Wolfgang von Lingelsheim-Seibicke, *Kooperation mit Unternehmen in Staatshandelsländern Osteuropas: Einführung in die Praxis*, Deutscher Wirtschaftsdienst [Cologne: John von Frey and KG, 1974], p. 162; Hans-Jörg Bauer, "Die deutsche Baumwollindustrie in der europäischen Wirtschaftsgemeinschaft" [Inaugural-dissertation zur Erlangung der Wurder eines Doktors der Wirtschaftswissenschaften der Universität Mannheim, 1968], pp. 242, 178; Hans Tietmeyer, Oberregierungsrat, BMWi, "Die ordnungspolitischen Aspekte des Ost-West-Handels," in Bundesverband Bekleidungsindustrie, *Die Deutsche Bekleidungsindustrie Morgen: Kongress der Bekleidungsindustrie 1968*, October 1968, p. 61; and interview held in Bonn, West Germany, June 1985).

For a detailed analysis of current EEC dumping and countervailing duty measures, see Ivo Van Bael and Jean-Francois Bellis, *International Trade Law and Practice of the European Community: EEC Anti-Dumping and Other Trade Protection Laws* (Bicester: CCH Editions, 1985). In September 1984, the Community also adopted a rough equivalent to the United States's Section 301 regulations on fair trading practices. The New Commercial Policy Instruments (NCPI) allows the assessment of retaliatory import duties and/or quantitative restrictions in the event of discriminatory foreign trade practices. See Joan Pearce and John Sutton with Ray Batchelor, *Protection and Industrial Policy in Europe* (London: Routledge & Kegan Paul, 1985), pp. 45–46; and Anjaria et al., *Trade Policy Issues*, p. 20.

60. Lingelsheim-Seibicke, *Kooperation mit Unternehmen*, pp. 152–53; Deutsches Institut für Wirtschaftsforschung, "Textilimporte der Bundesrepublik Deutschland im Rahmen

setting such restrictions stemmed from Sections 6, 10, and 12 of the Aussenwirtschaftsgesetz, which when combined empowered state policy makers to restrict imports "to prevent or counteract any effects on the Federal Republic from foreign systems with different concepts from the liberal order of the Federal Republic."[61] As the EEC's role in Eastern European trade policy increased, existing bilateral trade arrangements were allowed to run conditionally through 1974.[62]

Yet an increasing portion of Eastern European trade also consisted of outward processing arrangements between Community members (especially West Germany) and Eastern European exporters. These arrangements allowed goods to be exported for low-cost processing and assembly abroad and then imported back by the original exporting country. In an attempt to "harmonize" national regulations on outward processing, the Council of Ministers released a directive in December 1975 (Directive 76/119) setting guidelines on outward processing tariffs and requesting information from the national governments on the magnitude of outward processing. Questions on quantitative limits in textiles, however, were not resolved at the Community level until the conclusion of negotiations over MFA III (1981–86).[63] Thus, during

der EG-Politik: Entwicklungsländer erhöhen ihre Importanteile," *Wochenbericht 38/77,* 22 November 1977, p. 331.

61. Specific restrictions on imports are addressed in Section 10 of the AWG. According to Section 12 of the AWG, the authority to determine which imports are required to have licenses lies with the BMWi and the Ministry of Food and Agriculture in cooperation with the Federal Reserve Bank (Bundesbank). Authority to grant exemptions to existing import restrictions on manufactured goods according to Section 28 of the AWG lies with the Bundesamt für gewerbliche Wirtschaft (Siebel, "Foreign Trade Law," p. 23; and Heinz Freidrich Schulz, *Aussenwirtschaftsgesetz,* vol. 5, Kundendienst für den Aussenhandel der Girozentralen und Sparkassen [Stuttgart: Deutscher Sparkassenverlag, GmbH., 1967], pp. 77–78, 87, 128–29).

62. Lingelsheim-Seibicke, *Kooperation mit Unternehmen,* pp. 152–53. Once negotiating competence had been transferred to the Community during 1974, individual members of the EEC were still allowed to communicate 1974 quota levels to state trading countries in writing after Community approval (West Germany, Bundestag, *Der Parlamentarische Staatssekretär,* BMWi, Antwort der Bundesregierung auf die Kleine Anfrage, 7. Wahlperiode, Drucksache 7/2635, 11 October 1974, pp. 1–3). Recognizing that the transfer of negotiating competence would not be immediate, the EEC Council of Ministers also "approved unilateral arrangements for imports" in March 1975 (Pierre Maillet, *The Economy of the European Community,* Periodical 1–2/1982 [Luxembourg: Office for Official Publications of the European Communities, 1982], p. 9).

63. This is an example of what the West German Tariff Law (Zollgesetz) terms *"passiv Veredelung." "Activ Veredelung"* refers to goods purchased abroad for finishing at home. West German tariffs on outward processing are covered by Sections 46–52 of the Zollgesetz. Quantitative restrictions would be covered under the relevant paragraphs of Section 10 of the AWG. When such goods were reexported to other EEC members, Article 115 of the Treaty of Rome allowed these members to invoke import restrictions to

the period under analysis in this study, West German state policy makers retained control over restrictions on outward processing trade.

The need for compromise in Brussels was clearly evident in other discussions on quantitative restrictions. The EEC's recommendations on textile import restrictions under MFA I (1974–77) were delayed in part because of disagreements among national representatives in the Council of Ministers. The negotiating mandate eventually passed by the council made agreement to the MFA conditional on the outcome of bilateral negotiations under the arrangement; however, the negotiations of these bilaterals were delayed by the commission's lack of experience and low prioritization.[64] Agreements on subsequent versions of the MFA have also been plagued by delays in decision making at the Community level. These delays reflect the continued resistance of West German representatives to the protectionist demands of their French and British counterparts. Aside from deadlock in the Council of Ministers, the commission's dependence on the national governments for information as well as enforcement of the MFA has increased the difficulty of policy making at the Community level.[65] Thus West German state policy makers are not totally subject to the EEC. By coordinating the policy positions taken by West German representatives to Community institutions, state policy makers can clearly influence Community pressures for action on overt types of protectionist policy.

In contrast to the EEC's authority over overt protectionist policies, the potential for strong levels of institutional access has been less extensive on the exercise of adjustment assistance measures. In this area, the EEC has focused primarily on competition policy (cartels) and on state subsidies. Article 85 of the Treaty of Rome allows the forma-

avoid "important market disturbances" (Lingelsheim-Seibicke, *Kooperation mit Unternehmen*, p. 164; Siebel, "Foreign Trade Law," pp. 34–35; and Foreign Trade Association, *Report 1984/85* [Brussels, 1985], p. 18). For a detailed discussion on the role of outward processing in the West German economy, see Folker Fröbel, Jurgen Heinrichs, and Otto Kreye, *Umbruch in der Weltwirtschaft: Die globale Strategie: Verbilligung der Arbeitskraft, Flexibilizierung der Arbeit, Neue Technologien* (Hamburg: Rowohlt Taschenbuch Verlag, 1986). For the MFA III restrictions on outward processing, see Michael B. Dolan, "European Restructuring and Import Policies for a Textile Industry in Crisis," *International Organization* 37 (Autumn 1983), pp. 600–601.

64. Chris Farrands, "Textile Diplomacy: The Making and Implementation of European Textile Policy," *Journal of Common Market Studies* 18 (September 1979), pp. 24, 26.

65. The most common split among Community members on textile protection has been Britain, France, and Ireland calling for trade restrictions versus West Germany, Denmark, and the Netherlands opposing calls for trade restrictions. See Loukas Tsoukalis and Antonio da Salvia Ferreira, "Management of Industrial Surplus Capacity in the European Community," *International Organization* 34 (Summer 1980), p. 365; Pearce and Sutton, *Protection and Industrial Policy*, pp. 60–65; and Farrands, "Textile Diplomacy," p. 32.

tion of cartels to limit and share production when direct benefits accrue to the consumer and interfirm competition is not eliminated. Action under West Germany's antitrust laws therefore must also comply with EEC regulations to avoid action by the commission.[66]

Under the Treaty of Rome, Community officials are authorized to regulate monetary adjustment assistance measures at the national level only if "damage to the common market can be shown."[67] Based on this authority, the commission released guidelines on sectoral aid in textiles to the Council of Ministers and member governments in July 1971, February 1977, and July 1978. The guidelines stressed private initiatives and prohibited state promotion of increases in capacity and the manipulation of costs or prices. In 1977, the commission imposed a two-year ban (extended in 1979) on state investments in synthetic fibers.[68] In addition to placing restrictions on the actions of state policy makers, Community institutions have gradually emerged as new sources of monetary assistance. Furthermore, the commission introduced a

66. Dolan, "European Restructuring," p. 584; Maillet, *Economy of the European Community*, pp. 30–31. Commission rulings on violations (authority granted under Article 86) take precedent over rulings by the Federal Cartel Office when both offices are conducting investigations. In the absence of a commission investigation and ruling, the Federal Cartel Office "can prohibit the pertinent merger as far as it affects the German market" (Martin Heidenhain, "Anti-Trust Law," in Bernd Rüster, ed., *Business Transactions in Germany*, vol. 3, chap. 36 [New York: Mathew Bender, 1983], pp. 58–59).

As in Japan, state policy makers in West Germany have recourse to a number of exceptions from West Germany's Cartel Law (1957 Gesetzes gegen Wettbewerbsbeschrankungen-GWB). Section 5a of the GWB allows the formation of cartels to facilitate specialization in production among small and medium-sized producers. Section 5b inserted in 1974 allows binding arrangements among small and medium-sized producers in areas ranging from production to retailing and distribution. Section 5 (subsections 2 and 3) allows the formation of Rationalisierungskartell cooperatively to reduce costs in areas such as distribution and freight. Finally, Section 4 of the GWB allows the formation of structural crisis cartels to regulate production and prices to facilitate concrete capacity reduction plans ("Merkblatt: Uber die Kooperationserleichterungen für kleine und mittlere Unternehmen nach 56 des Kartellgesetzes vom 15 April 1975," received from the Bundeskartellamt, Berlin; and Professor Kartte, President des Bundeskartellamtes, "Bekanntmachung Nr. 37/38 über Verwaltungsgrundsatze des Bundeskartellamtes für die Beurteilung von Strukturkrisen- und Rationalisierungskartellen vom 31. Marz 1978", received from the Bundeskartellamt, Berlin; and phone interview with official in Berlin, West Germany, June 1985.

67. Articles 92–94 of the Treaty of Rome, cited in Dolan, "European Restructuring," p. 592; and Maillet, *Economy of the European Community*, pp. 32–33.

68. For example, temporary investment subsidies were allowed under the 1971 guidelines only with commission approval, the presence of "severe social conditions" in the area, and a focus on firms with "difficult restructuring problems" (Jean Paul Chauvet with Brigitte Vanderveken, *Textiles and the EEC (Annexes)* [Brussels: Agence Européenne d'Informations, 1980], p. 14; and Jose de la Torre and Michael Bacchetta, "The Uncommon Market: European Policies Towards the Clothing Industry in the 1970s," *Journal of Common Market Studies* 19 [December 1980], pp. 101–2, 118–19).

series of assistance measures aimed at reducing capacity and increasing competitiveness. In 1975 and 1979, the commission, acting with the approval of the Council of Ministers, established narrow research and development programs in textiles at the Community level.[69] Efforts in 1978 substantially to expand the commission's role in regional and social policies, however, ran into considerable resistance from the Council of Ministers. The unwillingness of member countries to shift extensive "political and economic power to Brussels" limited the commission's efforts at taking on an increasingly regulatory role.[70]

In addition to these EEC guidelines and regulations, BMWi officials face sources of institutional access at home when deciding on the use of indirect protectionist policies. Although BMWi officials address the "political and economic aspects of antitrust policies," the Federal Cartel Office (Bundeskartellamt) is responsible for the actual administration of West German cartel law. Appeals of the Federal Cartel Office's rulings, albeit rare, can be made to BMWi or the judiciary.[71] At the federal level, the funds available for BMWi assistance measures to import-competing industries are shaped by interministerial budget deliberations conducted by the Ministry of Finance. Before the 1969 finance reform, these funds were also limited by Article 115 of the West German Basic Law, which prohibited deficit spending on the part of the federal government.[72] In practice, federal assistance measures in the form of tax rebates, low-interest loans, and grants have covered a number of industries and regions. State subsidies for specific sectors of the economy have been limited to those characterized by either large firms in severe decline such as shipbuilding, the supply of "important raw materials," or involvement in high technology. Regional policy has targeted economic assistance at relatively backward areas primarily through investment-promotion and cost-relief measures. Other areas of assistance include measures for small and medium-sized firms and for technological research and development. Although federal assis-

69. For detail on the research and development programs, see de la Torre and Bacchetta, "The Uncommon Market," pp. 103, 119. In 1971 the commission had also revamped European Social Fund assistance measures to facilitate retraining and mobility of workers (Malcolm James MacMillen and John Stanley Chard, "European Social Fund Aid to Textile Workers: The Early Experience," *European Economic Review* 11 [1978], pp. 269–71).

70. Edwards, "Four Sectors," p. 87; and Tsoukalis and Ferreira, "Management of Industrial Surplus Capacity," p. 367.

71. Phone interview with official in Berlin, West Germany, June 1985; and Black, "Industrial Policy in West Germany," pp. 5–6.

72. In 1969, Article 115 of the Basic Law was modified to allow "credit financing up to the officially designated level of investment expenditures or beyond in the event of economic necessity" (Knott, *Managing the German Economy*, pp. 21, 35–37).

tance has primarily been the responsibility of BMWi, authority on research and development–related measures has overlapped with the Ministry for Research and Technology. In addition, the European Recovery Program Fund, set up in 1952 to administer Marshall Plan aid to West Germany, still functions as a "para-fiscal institution" offering low-interest loans. In general, federal funds are primarily distributed through "the major federal bank (Kreditanstalt für Wiederaufbau) ... via the private banking system."[73]

Finally, the ability of BMWi officials to regulate the use of state subsidies can also be constrained by the Länder governments. Since 1969, regional policy has been defined as a "common task" under Article 91a of the Basic Law.[74] Under Article 74 of the Basic Law, Länder governments also hold concurrent authority to legislate on domestic economic matters. Thus, in addition to reviewing federal proposals through the Bundesrat, Länder governments can provide

73. Ernst-Jürgen Horn, *Management of Industrial Change in Germany* (Brighton: University of Sussex European Research Center, 1982), pp. 15, 24–26, 38–39; Jeffery S. Arpan et al., *The U.S. Apparel Industry: International Challenge, Domestic Response*, Research Monograph no. 88 (Atlanta: College of Business Administration, Georgia State University, 1982), pp. 162–63; "Millionen für Grenzlandbetrieb," *Textil-Mitteilungen/Textil-Zeitung*, 24 March 1966, cited in Bauer, "Die Deutsche," pp. 231–32; Alan Whiting, "Overseas Experience in the Use of Industrial Subsidies," in Whiting, ed., *The Economics of Industrial Subsidies* (London: Her Majesty's Stationery Office, 1976), cited in Melvyn Krauss, "Europeanizing the U.S. Economy: The Enduring Appeal of the Corporatist State," in Chalmers Johnson, ed., *The Industrial Policy Debate* (San Francisco: ICS Press, 1984), Table 3; and interviews held in Münster and Bonn, West Germany, May and June 1985. Financial assistance for direct foreign investment also exists (for example, through the Deutsche Entwicklungsgesellschaft). See Folker Fröbel, Jurgen Heinrichs, and Otto Kreye, *The New International Division of Labor: Structural Unemployment in Industrialized Countries and Industrialization in Developing Countries* (Cambridge: Cambridge University Press, 1980), pp. 167–69.

Horn (*Management of Industrial Change*) does not discuss the role of the Finance Ministry in tax assistance measures. Other analysts of tax policy tend to focus more on authority over tax legislation and interpretation of existing legislation than on its use as a possible tool to assist industry. In the case of the former, the Finance Ministry and the Länder finance ministries play the primary roles. See, for example, Reinhard Pöllath, "Taxation," in Bernd Rüster, ed., *Business Transactions in West Germany*, vol. 2, chap. 32 (New York: Mathew Bender, 1983).

74. Horn argues that in practice federal and regional authorities have shared the costs of regional policy measures. Glismann and Weiss argue that a large proportion of adjustment assistance funds is channeled through "various regional development programs," of which the jointly financed federal-Länder programs are the most important. Criteria for assistance are "jointly determined"; however, the federal government's voting weight is set equal to that of the sum of the Länder governments. The forms of assistance through these programs include subsidies, low interest loans, and loan guarantees on individual investments (Horn, *Management of Industrial Change*, p. 25; and H. H. Glismann and F. D. Weiss, "On the Political Economy of Protection in Germany," *World Bank Staff Working Paper No. 427* [Washington, D.C.: World Bank, 1980], pp. 16–17).

assistance to small and medium-sized firms, promote investment, and provide emergency financial relief even in the face of opposition from state policy makers.[75]

## CONCLUSION

Neither the extent of fragmentation nor the potential for high degrees of institutional access is readily apparent from the broader conceptualization of states as being strong or weak. In all three countries, state power and authority are fragmented across state institutions. This fragmentation provides multiple points of access to the policy-making process for societal actors and their state supporters. More important, however, is the nature of the access that these points provide.

The United States, Japan, and West Germany illustrate three different patterns of state fragmentation in the area of trade policy. In the United States, the divisions of state power and authority primarily lie with the executive and legislative branches on the national level. Despite fragmentation between the executive and the legislative branches in Japan, the major splits on trade policy occur within the executive bureaucracy. In West Germany, the predominant divisions operate on a number of levels. Fragmentation between the executive and legislative branches appears to be slightly less than in Japan. In addition, the fragmentation of state power and authority within the executive branch is much greater in West Germany and Japan than in the United States. The presence of an extensive interministerial committee network in West Germany suggests that on paper the fragmentation of the executive branch may be slightly greater in Japan than in West Germany. Finally, because of the expanding authority of the EC, West German state policy makers face a level of fragmentation that is not replicated in either the United States or Japan.

What does the analyst gain from noting such patterns of fragmentation? On a broad level, these patterns illustrate the respective roles of legislative and executive actors in policy making. For scholars seeking to account for broad policy choices, a more refined continuum based on such patterns may prove more useful than a continuum based on state strength. More important for the narrow focus taken in this book,

75. Horn argues that the state governments prefer the exercise of loan guarantees on loans granted by regional banks (Länder-controlled Landesbanken) and savings banks, "which are controlled by the local governments" (*Management of Industrial Change*, pp. 39–40).

however, these patterns may provide a starting point for predicting the sources of high degrees of institutional access in a given country.

The patterns suggest that direct appeals by industrial alliances to state policy makers are unlikely to be more successful than indirect appeals through state officials. State policy makers in all three countries appear to be able to place narrow demands into a broader context, as seen in the president's broader constituency, MITI's consensus building from the bottom up, and the mediating function of BMWi division heads. Although indirect access channels offer greater prospects for binding influence, the specific access channels that offer the greatest degree of institutional access differ cross-nationally. Thus both industrial alliances and state policy makers should be wary of lessons based on the experiences of other countries.

In the United States, industrial alliances in the textile industry are likely to have the greatest success if they are able to invoke Congress's power of unilateral action. In Japan, the presence of overlapping jurisdictions and interministerial rivalry suggest that the greatest chance for exerting binding influence on MITI lies through other ministries. Predictions for West Germany are more difficult given the ad hoc nature of interministerial committees in textiles, the Bundestag's lack of explicit jurisdiction, and the dynamics of compromise in the EC. If industrial alliances are unable to invoke these access channels, state policy makers will avoid full concessions to alliance demands. The first step, however, is that strong industrial alliances must emerge.

CHAPTER THREE

# Beyond Societal Structure: Societal Actors and the Strength of Industrial Alliances

A predominant theoretical premise in the field of political science is that interest groups can influence foreign economic policy. Scholars who focus on interest groups disagree, however, on the way these groups shape policy. Those who follow the pluralist tradition link policy choices to the constellation of interest group coalitions within a given country. Countries characterized by strong coalitions of interest groups have the greatest difficulty with economic adjustment as policy makers are forced to take into account the protectionist demands of stronger societal coalitions. Scholars rooted in the corporatist tradition also look at societal structure but draw different conclusions. Societies characterized by weak coalitions of interest groups fall prey to paralysis and protection instead of economic adjustment. Strong—specifically, organized and inclusive—interest groups, rather than disrupting policy making, facilitate "accommodation at the top" by bargaining among peak associations of business and labor and the state.[1]

This chapter is based on the premise that neither argument is suited for the analysis of trade policy choices among types of protectionist policy. First, overall patterns of societal structure may not necessarily be replicated on the sectoral level. According to the comparative literature on advanced industrial countries, the United States, Japan, and West Germany illustrate three patterns of societal structure. On indexes of centralization and concentration (inclusiveness), private interests are weak in the United States, strong in West Germany, and, with the

1. For arguments incorporating a societal structural focus rooted in the pluralist tradition, see Olson, *Rise and Decline of Nations*; and Gourevitch, "Breaking with Orthodoxy," pp. 98–99, 103–4. For the role of societal structure in corporatist arguments, see the discussion in Katzenstein, *Small States*, pp. 32–33, 209–10.

64

exception of organized labor, strong in Japan. This chapter reveals that this pattern is only partially replicated for the textile industries in these three countries. Second, even a narrower structural focus is not the key to accounting for trade policy choices since the strength of societal actors is not adequately captured by structural attributes alone. By identifying the potential members, supporters, and opponents of in-dustrial alliances, this chapter illustrates that under certain conditions, structural weaknesses can be offset by the convergence of interests among alliance members. Similarly, structural strength can be offset by weak convergence of interests. Tracing the impact of strong industrial alliances, therefore, requires a more integrated conceptualization of the strength of industrial alliances.[2]

## UNITED STATES

### Business Associations

The structural characteristics of business organizations in the United States suggest that strong industrial alliances at the sectoral level should fail to emerge. The representation of American business is more concentrated (inclusive) than centralized. According to the National Association of Manufacturers (NAM), member companies account for roughly 75 percent of manufacturing employment. In contrast, Katzenstein has argued that NAM and the Chamber of Commerce illustrate the "weak" centralization of the American corporate sector. Instead of forming a single business peak association during the 1950s and 1960s, NAM's twenty-two thousand company members overlapped with the Chamber's membership of companies, business organizations, and local and state associations.[3] In trade policy disputes, weaknesses in centralization have not been offset by convergence of interests. The mix of import-competing and export-oriented members limited the role of

2. For an example of the societal comparison of the United States, Japan, and West Germany, see Katzenstein, *Small States*, pp. 33, 209; and Katzenstein, "Conclusion: Domestic Structures," pp. 324, 311. Katzenstein also implicitly raises a similar argument on the inappropriateness of a purely structural focus by defining democratic corporatism as including the presence of a shared ideology linking state and society (*Small States*, pp. 30–37).

3. Katzenstein, "Conclusion: Domestic Structures," p. 311; "Trade Battle Featured Unique Lobby Alliances," *Congressional Quarterly Almanac 1962*, p. 262; and Bauer et al., *American Business*, pp. 334, 336. As a result of mergers, NAM's membership has fallen to 13,500 firms. According to a phone interview (1987) conducted with a representative from NAM, the association does not measure the percentage of industrial production accounted for by association members.

*Table* 2. U.S. textile industry inclusiveness, by key producer association, 1954–1962 (in percent)

| Association | 1954 | 1958 | 1962 |
|---|---|---|---|
| Man-Made Fibers Producers Association | 4.7 | 5.0 | 6.0 |
| American Cotton Manufacturers Institute | 11.2 | 15.4 | 14.2 |
| National Federation of Textiles | 3.0 | – | – |
| National Association of Cotton Manufacturers/ Northern Textile Association | 5.3 | 5.9 | 5.4 |
| National Association of Wool Manufacturers | 2.1 | 2.5 | 2.2 |
| Apparel Industry Committee on Imports, Committee for the Apparel Industry[a] | 57.2 | 57.2 | 57.2 |
| Total textile industry inclusiveness (key producer associations) | | Average = 85% | |

*Sources:* Production and employment figures for industry subsectors calculated from U.S. Bureau of the Census, *United States Census of Manufacturers, 1954, 1958, 1963* (Washington, D.C.: U.S. Government Printing Office, 1957, 1961, 1966). The 1962 figures are from the 1963 census. The proportion of the subsector accounted for by individual producer associations is derived from the following sources: U.S. Congress, Senate, *Trade Agreements Extension, Hearings before the Committee on Finance,* 84th Cong., 1st sess., 1955, pp. 1695, 1635, 1547–48, 1657; U.S. Congress, Senate, Committee on Interstate and Foreign Commerce, *Problems of the Domestic Textile Industry, Hearings before the Subcommittee of the Committee on Interstate and Foreign Commerce,* 85th Cong., 2d sess., 1958, pp. 12–32, 217, 187, 1149; U.S. Congress, Senate, *Problems of the Domestic Textile Industry, Hearings before a Subcommittee of the Committee on Interstate and Foreign Commerce,* 87th Cong., 1st sess., 1961, pp. 110, 443, 394–400; Denise S. Akey, ed., *Encyclopedia of Associations 1985,* 19th ed. (Detroit: Gale Research, 1985), pp. 188–89; Craig Colgate, Jr., *National Trade and Professional Associations of the US 1982, 1983* (Washington, D.C.: Columbia Books, 1982, 1983).
Note: Inclusiveness equals the proportion of total industry employment and production represented by the producer association.
[a]The three most active apparel associations before 1961 were the National Association of Blouse Manufacturers, the Underwear Institute, and the Southern Garment Manufacturers Association, each accounting for less than 3.0 percent of total textile industry production and employment.

general business organizations in the 1950s and continued to constrain their activities during the 1980s.[4]

To what extent are these general characteristics of inclusiveness and organization reflected at the sectoral level? Among textile producer associations from 1954 to 1962, representation of total employment and production stood at roughly 85 percent (Table 2). Because of the

4. "Trade Battle," *Congressional Quarterly Almanac,* p. 292; Bauer et al., *American Business,* pp. 334, 336; and Destler, *American Trade Politics,* p. 161. Dissatisfaction with NAM and the Chamber of Commerce during the early 1970s prompted the rise of the Business Round Table as an alternative lobbying organization. The Round Table consisted of several hundred top executives from large and medium-sized companies.

absence of a major industrywide textile federation and of extensive integration between fiber, mill product and apparel producers, however, producer associations in the textile industry were not well centralized. The absence of centralization increased the importance of those associations which controlled relatively major portions of the industry. Based on indicators of organization and inclusiveness, the American Cotton Manufacturers Institute (ACMI) stood as the single strongest producer association in the U.S. textile industry, even though during the 1950s and early 1960s the ACMI represented an average of only 13.6 percent of total textile production and employment.

The ACMI was a product of numerous key mergers of midstream (spinning, weaving) producer associations. The institute was established in 1949 through the merger of southern and northern textile associations.[5] The new association claimed to represent 85 percent of the spindles and looms in cotton processing and a membership that "extended from Maine to Texas." By the mid- to late 1950s, major cotton textile producers had expanded into the synthetics field and into the membership of the synthetic and silk textile association: the National Federation of Textiles.[6] In 1958, "to achieve a more unified representation over silk and manmade fiber fabric production," the ACMI absorbed the National Federation of Textiles. ACMI's expansion increased its representation to 80 to 85 percent of cotton, man-made fiber, and silk spinning and fabric weaving capacity in the United States. The increasingly noncotton focus of the institute was eventually recognized by a name change in 1962 from the American Cotton Manufacturers Institute to the American Textile Manufacturers Institute.[7]

Despite its broad geographical coverage, over 75 percent of the seats on ACMI's governing board of directors were held by representatives from Georgia, North Carolina, South Carolina, and Alabama.[8] The

5. ACMI linked together the southern-based American Cotton Manufacturers Association and the New York–based Cotton Textile Institute. See Craig Colgate, Jr., ed., *National Trade and Professional Associations of the United States, 1983* (Washington, D.C.: Columbia Books, 1983), p. 80; *Pastore Hearings 1958*, pp. 12–32; and U.S. Congress, Senate, *Trade Agreements Extension, Hearings before the Committee on Finance*, 84th Cong., 1st sess., 1955 (hereafter cited as *TAE 1955*), pp. 1547–48.

6. John Lynch, *Toward an Orderly Market: An Intensive Study of Japan's Voluntary Quota on Cotton Textile Exports* (Tokyo: Sophia University, 1968), p. 34, n. 84; and *Pastore Hearings 1958*, pp. 12–32. The National Federation of Textiles served as the primary representative association for producers of silk and man-made fiber fabric across the same areas of the country as the ACMI. *TAE 1955* (p. 1657) sets the federation's representation at 75 percent while Lynch (p. 81) sets the figure at greater than 80 percent.

7. Colgate, *National Trade and Professional Associations, 1983*, p. 80; and *Pastore Hearings 1958*, pp. 5, 12–32.

8. *Pastore Hearings 1958*, pp. 5, 30–32.

predominant influence of southern capital in the producer association may have accounted for the continued presence of a third major midstream association: the Northern Textile Association (NTA). Despite an overlap in membership with ACMI estimated at 10 to 12 percent, the NTA remained separate from the institute, representing textile producers in New England.[9] The NTA was established in 1956 to reflect the shift of the membership of its predecessor—the National Association of Cotton Manufacturers—into cotton and synthetic spinning and weaving. The NTA had also absorbed northeastern wool manufacturers through the formation of a semiautonomous Wool Manufacturers Council. By 1958, the NTA represented approximately 27 percent of the U.S. cotton and synthetic spinning and weaving production and approximately 30 percent of wool spinning and weaving. The remainder of wool spinning and weaving production was organized under the fourth key midstream association, the National Association of Wool Manufacturers (NAWM).[10] By 1971, NAWM had been absorbed into the American Textile Manufacturers Institute (ATMI), thereby establishing ATMI as a single, merged association covering the bulk of textile mills across a full range of fiber types.

Compared with these midstream associations, the associations for man-made fiber and apparel producers appeared as opposite extremes. Producers of man-made fibers were primarily represented by the Man-Made Fibers Producers Association, formed in 1933 and consisting of fourteen major companies (out of an industry total of forty-four), accounting for the "great bulk" of U.S. man-made fiber production.[11] Members included industry leaders such as Dow, Union Carbide, and Allied Chemical. The absence of extensive formal and informal linkages with mid- and downstream producers characteristic of the Japanese man-made fiber industry, however, limited the Man-Made Fibers Producers Association's role in subsequent textile alliances.

9. The membership of the association and the institute overlapped by an estimated 10 to 12 percent (ACMI members belonging to the NTA). I base this estimate on a comparison of the congressional testimony of association representatives and 1958 employment figures. For the testimony, see *TAE 1955*, pp. 1547–48; and *Pastore Hearings 1958*, p. 217. For detail on the NTA's expansion, see Craig Colgate, Jr., *National Trade and Professional Associations of the United States, 1982* (Washington, D.C.: Columbia Books, 1982), p. 242; *TAE 1955*, p. 1561; and *Pastore Hearings 1958*, pp. 12–32, 187.

10. NAWM membership consisted of "70 percent of American manufacturers producing textiles of wool and other fibers on the woolen and worsted systems measured in terms of employment, production, or sales (not including carpet and rug manufacturing)" (*Pastore Hearings 1958*, p. 187; and U.S. Congress, Senate, *Problems of the Domestic Textile Industry, Hearings before a Subcommittee of the Committee on Interstate and Foreign Commerce*, 87th Cong., 1st sess., 1961 [hereafter cited as *Pastore Hearings 1961*], p. 110).

11. Four association members also comprised the Rayon Staple Fiber Producers

In contrast to the organization of fiber and midstream producers, producer associations in the apparel subsector were highly fragmented by product and geographical location. The National Association of Blouse Manufacturers, the Underwear Institute, and the Southern Garment Manufacturers Association each accounted for less than 3.0 percent of total textile industry production and employment.[12] The Apparel Associations Inter-Association Committee, by contrast, was a weak federation of thirteen major New York–based men's and women's apparel producer associations. In 1961, the members of the committee joined forces with a national, emergency, apparel peak association—the Apparel Industry Committee on Imports—to represent apparel producers on the issue of textile imports. In total, twenty-three diverse apparel associations representing roughly 57.2 percent of the textile industry's production and employment participated in or lent support to the two apparel committees.[13]

In 1962, two major associations instrumental in forming the Apparel Industry Committee on Imports—the Southern Garment Manufactur-

Association, accounting for over 95 percent of rayon staple fiber production (*Pastore Hearings 1961*, p. 433, 541–43).

12. Based on participation in tariff reduction hearings, RTA authority hearings, and hearings devoted to textile trade issues, these associations were the most active apparel associations in textile trade policy before 1961. The percentages are calculated from U.S. Bureau of Census, *United States Census of Manufacturers, 1954, 1958, and 1963* (Washington, D.C.: U.S. Government Printing Office, 1957, 1961, 1966); *TAE 1955*, pp. 1695, 1635; and *Pastore Hearings 1958*, p. 1149.

13. Membership of the Committee for the Apparel Industries (formed in 1947) consisted of the following by 1961: National Association of Shirt, Pajama, and Sportswear Manufacturers; Corset and Brassiere Association of America; Boys Apparel and Accessories Manufacturers Association, Inc.; Infants' and Children's Garment Association; National Skirt and Sportswear Association; International Association of Garment Manufacturers; Lingerie Manufacturers Association of New York; Manufacturers of Snowsuits, Novelty Wear and Infants Coats, Inc.; National Association of Blouse Manufacturers; National Knitted Outerwear Association; Underwear Institute; and United Infants and Children's Wear Association.

Membership of the Apparel Industry Committee on Imports (AICI) consisted of the following associations: National Association of Shirt Pajama and Sportswear Manufacturers; Corset and Brassiere Association of America; Southern Garment Manufacturers Association; Association of Corset and Brassiere Manufacturers; National Skirt and Sportswear Association; International Association of Garment Manufacturers; and Trouser Institute of America. Nonmembers authorizing the AICI as proxy spokesgroup consisted of the following associations: National Outerwear and Sportswear Association, Inc.; National Association of Knitted Outerwear; House Dress Institute; Boy's Apparel and Accessories Manufacturers Association, Inc.; American Knit Handwear Association, Inc.; National Association of House and Daytime Dress Manufacturers; United Infants and Childrenswear Association; and National Association of Knitted Outerwear (*Pastore Hearings 1961*, pp. 394, 397–98, 400, 557, 559; and Denise S. Akey, ed., *Encyclopedia of Associations 1985* [Detroit: Gale Research, 1985], pp. 188–89).

ers Association and the National Association of Shirt, Pajama, and Sportswear Manufacturers—merged to form the American Apparel Manufacturers Association (AAMA). Through a series of additional mergers during the 1960s and 1970s, the AAMA has become the most powerful apparel producer association in the U.S. textile industry. The AAMA currently accounts for nearly two-thirds of total apparel shipments in the United States.[14] Knitted apparel producers, however, remain in separate organizations.

The absence of an industrywide federation linking man-made fiber, midstream, and apparel producers has required industrial alliances to rely heavily on convergence of interests among member producer associations. As illustrated in Chapter 4, the divergent demands of individual producer associations have often complicated this task. Recognizing that formal centralization can contribute to the building of interest convergence, industry representatives met under the auspices of the Textile/Apparel Import Steering Group from 1965 to 1983. Since 1983, nineteen producer associations and two labor unions have sought to coordinate action on trade policy issues through the American Fiber, Textile, Apparel Coalition (AFTAC).[15]

## Labor Associations

Organized labor in the United States is structurally weak. Overall concentration rates of roughly 25 percent have traditionally been split between a number of independent unions such as the Teamsters and the AFL-CIO.[16] Similarly, organized labor in textiles has been characterized by low inclusiveness and centralization. From the mid-1950s to

14. Akey, ed., *Encyclopedia of Associations*, p. 188; and Arpan et al., *The U.S. Apparel Industry*, pp. 291–92.
15. Susan B. Martin and Karin Koek, eds., *Encyclopedia of Associations 1987*, vol. 1, *National Organizations of the U.S.* (Detroit: Gale Research, 1986), p. 157. In the 1985 testimony before the Senate on the Textile and Apparel Trade Enforcement Act, AFTAC representatives (here referred to as Fiber, Fabric, and Apparel Coalition for Trade) noted that their association included the Man-Made Fibers Producers Association, ATMI, American Apparel Manufacturers Association, Clothing Manufacturers Association, and National Cotton Council (U.S. Congress, Senate, *Textile and Apparel Trade Enforcement Act, Hearing before the Subcommittee on International Trade of the Committee on Finance*, 99th Cong., 1st sess., 1985, p. 86).
16. Robert H. Salisbury, "Why No Corporatism in America?" in Schmitter and Lehmbruch, eds., *Trends*, p. 217. In 1987, the Teamsters were readmitted into the AFL-CIO. See Kenneth B. Noble, "Teamsters Gain a Readmittance to A.F.L.-C.I.O.," *New York Times*, 25 October 1987, pp. 1, 26.

the mid-1960s, the representation of organized labor in the textile industry was split between five associations accounting for only 37.9 percent of the total textile labor force.[17] This low unionization rate reflected weak unionization among southern textile workers (15 to 20 percent) compared to their northern counterparts (95 percent). The five labor associations were primarily divided by production process. The Textile Workers Union of America (TWUA) represented workers in man-made fiber and textile mill production. The smaller, competing United Textile Workers Association primarily represented mill product workers. The remaining three associations acted as national representatives for workers engaged in different spheres of apparel production. Men's and boys' apparel workers belonged to the Amalgamated Clothing Workers of America (ACWA) while women's apparel workers turned to the International Ladies Garment Workers Union. The third and smallest association was the United Garment Workers Association of America. The fragmentation within organized labor decreased slightly in 1976 with the merger of the TWUA and the ACWU. Renamed the Amalgamated Clothing and Textile Workers Union, the new association was the first to link fiber, mill product, and apparel workers together in a single association. The union's membership, however, still covered less than one-sixth of the total textile labor force.

*Other Societal Actors*

Aside from textile producer and labor associations, other societal actors involved in U.S. textile trade policy during the 1950s and early 1960s included importers, natural fiber producers, general business associations, and national lobby organizations. The American Importers of Japanese Textiles, Inc., representing 70 percent of all Japanese textiles imported into the United States, served as the most vocal

17. I list the associations here along with the percentage of textile employment represented for 1955 and 1965 respectively: Textile Workers Union of America (8.7 percent and 5.4 percent); United Textile Workers Union of America (2.1 percent and 1.6 percent); American Clothing Workers Union of America (9.2 percent and 12.6 percent); International Ladies Garment Workers Union (16.9 percent and 15.9 percent); and United Garment Workers of America (1.8 percent and 1.5 percent). This paragraph is based on Colgate, *National Trade and Professional Associations, 1983*, pp. 23, 173, 297, 301; Gary M. Fink, ed., *The Greenwood Encyclopedia of American Institutions: Labor Unions* (Westport, Conn.: Greenwood Press, 1977), pp. 456–73, 491–95; U.S. Department of Labor, *Bureau of Labor Statistics Bulletin 1312-11, Employment and Earnings, U.S.: 1909–1978* (Washington, D.C.: U.S. Government Printing Office, 1979), pp. 504–8, 547–51; and *Pastore Hearings 1958*, pp. 376–79, 545, 559–60, 726, 1009.

importers association.[18] Although lacking an extensive domestic constituency, the association appeared repeatedly before congressional committees stressing the domestic problems of the U.S. textile industry. During the early 1960s, the U.S.-Japan Trade Council also supported the importers association's efforts. Although the council represented Japan-oriented export, import, and shipping interests as well as Japanese producers located in the United States, the council still lacked a domestic constituency comparable to that of associations representing the textile industry. By the 1980s, the textile alliance found itself faced with a more extensive countercoalition in the Retail Industry Trade Action Coalition (RITAC). In the 1985 congressional hearings over textile trade policy, for example, RITAC representatives prefaced their remarks by claiming a membership of companies employing approximately 1 million workers located in fifty states.[19]

In contrast to the role of the importer and retail associations, growers of natural fibers have primarily acted as a source of support for the protectionist forces in the domestic textile industry. The raw cotton industry is represented by the National Cotton Council, whose interests were initially divided between the domestic textile industry and an extensive foreign market for raw cotton exports that included Japan. As imports of cotton textiles began seriously to challenge domestic consumption of raw cotton in the late 1950s, however, cotton growers began to support the textile industry's efforts to restrict imports. As John Lynch has argued, despite extensive exports of raw cotton, the domestic textile industry was still the cotton producer's "main source of bread and butter."[20] In contrast to the informal relations between growers and textile producers in cotton, the National Association of Wool Growers maintained formal relations with the NAWM and the American Wool Council.[21]

General business associations and lobby organizations at the national level were only indirectly involved in textile trade policy. Through

18. See, for example, the association's participation in the RTA and Pastore hearings. In addition, see American Importers of Japanese Textiles, Inc., "The Importation of Cotton Textiles from Japan," in U.S. Congress, Committee on Ways and Means, Subcommittee on Foreign Trade Policy, *Foreign Trade Policy: A Compendium of Papers on United States Foreign Trade Policy* (Washington, D.C.: U.S. Government Printing Office, 1957), pp. 917–98. For detail on the U.S.-Japan Trade Council, see "Trade Battle," *Congressional Quarterly Almanac*, p. 294.

19. U.S. Congress, *Textile and Apparel Trade Enforcement Act*, p. 260.

20. "Trade Battle," *Congressional Quarterly Almanac*, p. 294; Lynch, *Toward an Orderly Market*, p. 64; and *Pastore Hearings 1961*, p. 79.

21. *Pastore Hearings 1961*, p. 236; and Bauer et al., *American Business*, p. 339. This distinction disappears in the current organization of AFTAC.

varying degrees of participation in the debates over the extension of presidential trade-negotiating authority, these actors at times placed additional pressure on state policy makers concerning the broad directions of U.S. trade policy. Divisions among export-oriented and import-sensitive members of both NAM and the U.S. Chamber of Commerce limited the role each played in the trade policy debates of the 1950s and 1960s. Conflicts among NAM members were reflected in a divided board of directors and a neutral stance on continued liberalization of imports, and the Chamber's membership was only slightly less divided in favor of its export-oriented members.[22] The fragmentation of both national business associations offered the textile alliance little in the way of either support or opposition. Similarly, the broad focus of lobby organizations resulted in little direct support for or opposition to the textile alliance. The three most active lobbies during this period consisted of the Committee for National Trade Policy, the Trade Relations Council, and the Nationwide Committee on Import-Export Policy.[23] During debates over the Reciprocal Trade Act, however, the major textile associations were conspicuously absent from the lists of industry associations "unofficially coordinated" by these organizations.[24]

JAPAN

*Business Associations*

In contrast to the United States, Japan's societal structure reflects both high concentration (inclusiveness) and high centralization among producers at the overall industry level. Encompassing 812 corporate members and 100 associations representing financial, commercial, and industrial interests, Japan's Federation of Economic Organizations (Keidanren) is the "most important and powerful of the postwar Zaikai [collective business leaders organizations]."[25] Although Keidanren is primarily concerned with the industrial and financial interests of big

22. "Trade Battle," *Congressional Quarterly Almanac*, p. 292.

23. Based in Washington, D.C., these organizations relied on public relations and lobbying to disseminate information and coordinated protectionist and antiprotectionist interests. See "Trade Battle," *Congressional Quarterly Almanac*, pp. 293–94.

24. See, for example, "List of Groups for and against Reciprocal Trade," *Congressional Quarterly Almanac, 1958*, p. 176.

25. Keidanren, *Keidanren* (Tokyo: Keidanren, 1983), pp. 1–9; and Ward, *Japan's Political System*, pp. 77–78. Three other major peak associations have played a lesser role in trade policy issues: the Japan Chamber of Commerce and Industry (Nissho), the Committee for Economic Development (Keizai Doyukai), and the Federation of Employers Organizations (Nikkeiran).

*Table 3.* Japanese textile industry inclusiveness, by key producer association, 1974–1980 (in percent)

| Association | 1974 | 1977 | 1980 |
|---|---|---|---|
| Japan Textile Federation | 83.4 | 84.1 | 82.8 |
| Japan Chemical Fibers Association | 12.5 | 10.5 | 10.4 |
| Japan Spinners Association | 9.5 | 8.3 | 7.8 |
| Japan Cotton Staple Fibers Weavers Association | 9.6 | 10.2 | 8.8 |
| Japan Silk and Rayon Fibers Weavers Association | 5.2 | 4.8 | 5.0 |
| Japan Knitting Industry Association | 10.2 | 10.7 | 10.6 |
| Federation of Clothing Manufacturers/ All Japan Apparel Federation | 21.9 | 25.7 | 27.0 |
| Total textile industry inclusiveness (key producer associations)  Average = 83.4% | | | |

*Sources:* Production and employment figures for industry subsectors calculated from Japan Chemical Fibers Association, *Man-Made Fibers of Japan, 1978/79* (Tokyo: JCFA, 1978); Japan Spinners Association, *Annual Statistical Review, 1974, 1982/83* (Osaka: JSA, 1974, 1983); and Japan, Ministry of International Trade and Industry, *The Textile and Apparel Industries of Japan, 1981* (Tokyo, 1981). The proportion of the subsector accounted for by individual producer associations is derived from interviews held in Tokyo, Japan (1984); Japan Chemical Fiber Association, *Man-Made Fibers of Japan 1978/79*, pp. 21–23, 205–15; Japan Spinners Association, *Annual Statistical Review; Cotton and Allied Textile Industry in Japan, June 1974*, pp. 14–16; Japan Spinners Association, *Annual Statistical Review, 1982 and Early 1983*, p. 9; Japan, Ministry of International Trade and Industry, *The Textile and Apparel Industries of Japan, 1981*, pp. 29–30; *Daily News Record*, 2 December 1974; *Japan Times*, 28 November 1974, *Japan Economic Journal*, 15 October 1974, 3 December 1974; and Ippei Yamazawa, "Increasing Imports and Structural Adjustment of the Japanese Textile Industry," *Developing Economies* 18 (December 1980), pp. 441–62; "Scrapping of Surplus Equipment in Japanese Textile Industry," *JTN*, November 1977, pp. 14–18.

business, small and medium-sized firms are also included in the federation through subcontract ties to larger companies and through membership in affiliated producer associations.

This pattern of centralization and inclusiveness is partially replicated in the Japanese textile industry. From 1974 to 1983, the proportion of total industry production and employment accounted for by the major textile producer associations averaged roughly 83.4 percent (Table 3). The Japanese textile industry is also centralized through the Japan Textile Federation (JTF), established in 1970 as a counterweight to the vocal American textile coalition led by the American Textile Manufacturers Institute. The JTF currently spans twenty-nine associations covering all portions of the textile industry. Yet, as a voluntary federation bridging several traditionally independent producer associations, the

JTF relies heavily on the unity of its diverse membership. Since its inception, the key task of the JTF has been to transfer the feelings of unity in the industry in opposition to American restrictions on Japanese exports that spawned the federation to unity on other issues. Difficulties in achieving this task have led a number of industry analysts to conclude that the JTF has not been as powerful as its ambitious name would suggest.[26]

In the absence of strong loyalty to the federation, producer associations combine independent action with coordinated protests through the JTF to shape industry demands. The Japan Chemical Fibers Association (JCFA) and the Japan Spinners Association (JSA) represent predominantly large man-made fiber producers and natural and man-made fiber spinners.[27] The JCFA accounts for roughly 99.5 percent of man-made fiber production and, through its spinning division, 90 percent of synthetic and rayon spun-yarn production. In addition, through upstream integration the membership of the JCFA includes ten raw material producers.[28] Thus compared to the Man-Made Fiber Producers Association in the United States, the JCFA has a more direct stake in downstream yarn production.

In contrast to the American Textile Manufacturers Institute's practice of merging with rival associations, the JCFA and the JSA share representation of close to 50 percent of synthetic spun-yarn production and over 65 percent of rayon spun-yarn production.[29] As major cotton

26. Interviews held in Tokyo, Japan, April and May 1984; and Destler et al., *Textile Wrangle.*

27. Respectively, Nihon Kagaku Sen-i Kyōkai and Nihon Boseki Kyōkai. See Ippei Yamazawa, "Increasing Imports and Structural Adjustment of the Japanese Textile Industry," *Developing Economies* 18 (December 1980), pp. 441–62.

28. Fiber production percentage based on calculations derived from 1977 production capacity statistics from JCFA and non-JCFA members. See Japan Chemical Fiber Association, *Man-Made Fibers of Japan 1978/79* (Tokyo: JCFA, 1978), pp. 21–23. Representation of yarn production percentages is based on *Daily News Record*, 2 December 1974; *Japan Times*, 28 November 1974; *Japan Economic Journal*, 3 December 1974; and through a comparison of association membership lists in Japan Chemical Fiber Association, *Fibers 1978/79*, pp. 205–15, and Japan Spinners Association, *Annual Statistical Review: Cotton and Allied Textile Industry in Japan, June 1974*, no. 9 (Osaka: JSA, 1974), pp. 14–16.

29. In spun-yarn production, JCFA members who did not also belong to the spinners association accounted for the minority share of spun rayon and spun synthetic yarn production (24.7 percent and 41.6 percent respectively). The Japan Spinners Association represented 48.4 percent of synthetic spun-yarn production and 65.3 percent of rayon spun-yarn production (90.0 percent minus exclusive JCFA figures). I calculated the proportion of synthetic and rayon spun yarn accounted for by the JSA and JCFA from Japan Spinners Association, *Annual Statistical Review, 1982 and Early 1983*, no. 19 (Osaka: JSA, 1983), p. 9; and MITI, *The Textile and Apparel Industries of Japan* (Tokyo, 1981), pp. 29–30.

spinners diversified into man-made fiber production and processing, producers belonging to the JSA became members of the chemical fibers association. The JSA continues to retain influence over cotton spinning, accounting for 84.1 percent of cotton yarn production.[30] Similar to the American Textile Manufacturers Institute, JSA influence spans both spinning and weaving, although inroads into the latter are minor compared to the weaving portion of the textile industry as a whole. In 1980, for example, JSA members accounted for only 19 percent of cotton fabric and 10.2 percent of synthetic fabric production.[31]

The two major representatives of the small and medium-sized firms that dominate Japan's weaving industry reflect the industry's division between spun-yarn weavers (cotton, rayon, and synthetic) and filament fabric weavers (silk, synthetic silk, and other synthetic filament fabric). The former are located primarily on the Pacific coast of Japan in sixty-four government-designated producing districts while the latter are primarily located on the Sea of Japan coast concentrated in Fukui and Ishikawa prefectures. The Japan Cotton and Staple Fibers Weavers Association represents over 80 percent of spun-yarn weavers through affiliated associations on the district level.[32] Filament fabric weavers are represented by the Japan Silk and Rayon Fiber Weavers Association. Although the latter association's membership accounts for an estimated 90 percent of filament fabric production, filament fabric weaving as a whole makes up slightly less than one-third of total weaving industry production.[33]

30. Based on an average of 1979 and 1980 figures calculated from ibid. Membership in the association is both voluntary and private. As a result, many small and medium-sized spinners are not members. In addition, noncotton natural fiber spinners belong to separate minor industry associations such as the Japan Wool Spinners Association (interview held in Tokyo, Japan, April 1984).

31. Calculated from Japan Spinners Association, *Statistical Review 1982*, p. 9; and MITI, *Textile and Apparel Industries*, pp. 31–32.

32. The spun-yarn weavers association (Nihon Men Sufu Orimono Kōgyō Rengyōkai) consists of 17,000 members and 340,000 registered looms. District-level affiliated associations differ in competitiveness, reliance on trading companies as marketers and contractors, and reliance on major man-made fiber producers and cotton and man-made fiber spinners as contractors ("Scrapping of Surplus Equipment in Japanese Textile Industry," *JTN*, November 1977, pp. 14–18; Yamazawa, "Increasing Imports," p. 454; and interview held in Tokyo, Japan, April 1984). A smaller group of weavers (wool worsted fabric) are primarily (70 percent) located in the Bishu textile center in Aichi Prefecture. For additional information, see *Textile Japan*, 1975, pp. 68-69.

33. Nihon Kinu Jinken Orimono Kōgyō Kumiai Rengō-kai. Yamazawa, "Increasing Imports," p. 454, n. 7. This rough estimate of inclusiveness may be overvalued because of my inability to find information on the percentage of filament fabric production accounted for by members of the Japan Chemical Fibers Association. Actual membership figures for the weaving association were not consistent across sources, with membership ranging

Despite a higher prevalence of small and medium-sized firms as one moves downstream, the representation of producers of knit fabric and apparel and producers of woven apparel was less fragmented in Japan than in the United States during the periods analyzed in the case studies in the following chapters. In the knitting portion of the industry, the shift toward centralization occurred in 1974. Acting on MITI recommendations, three separate producer associations merged to form the Japan Knitting Industry Association (JKIA). The association accounts for approximately 80 percent of the production of knitted goods and slightly over 10 percent of total textile industry production and employment. Yet fragmentation of the knitting industry by production type (circular, flat, and warp knitting) and the relative newness of the JKIA limit the association's influence.[34] In woven apparel, centralization increased in 1973 with the formation of the All Japan Apparel Federation (AJAF) by six major apparel associations. The AJAF currently represents over 80 percent of the production of woven and cut-and-sewn knit apparel.[35]

---

from 3,400 to 30,000. Production capacity figures for the association reveal 300,000 looms, 180,000 producing man-made fiber products. See "Scrapping of Surplus Equipment," *JTN*, November 1977, pp. 14–18; and *Daily News Record*, 22 February, 8 August 1977. I calculated total weaving industry figures from MITI, *Textile and Apparel Industries*, pp. 31–32. For additional detail on filament fabric weavers, see T. Kuroki, "Fukui File: Problems of Small Scale Weavers," *JTN*, November 1978, pp. 24–26.

34. *Japan Economic Journal*, 30 July 1974; interview held in Tokyo, Japan, April 1984; and MITI, *Textile and Apparel Industries*, pp. 22–23. The breakdown of the three types is as follows: circular knitting of jersey materials, apparel, and fine fabric accounts for 60 percent of production; flat knitting of sweaters accounts for 30 percent; and warp knitting of ladies' foundations and products for industrial use accounts for 10 percent. The JKIA's membership is heavily skewed in favor of flat knitting (78.3 percent), followed by circular (19.6 percent) and warp (1.9 percent) knitters. Along with the two major weaving associations, the JKIA and seven other minor industry associations belong to the Small and Medium-Sized Firm Association. Interviews and a review of primary source material, however, indicate that each of the three major associations appears to have been more active individually on trade policy issues than through the association.

35. The AJAF grew out of the Federation of Clothing Manufacturers. As reported by the *Japan Economic Journal* in October 1974, the Federation of Clothing Manufacturers Associations consisted of sixty-eight associations accounting for over 85 percent of apparel production. The AJAF, by contrast, has combined federation members with two additional associations and a number of major producers. The AJAF's primary members include the Japan Export Clothing Manufacturers Association (JECMA) and associations representing producers of men's, women's and children's and industrial apparel. JECMA and the industrial apparel association currently belong to JTF. As of 1986, AJAF's membership also included the Japan Textile Importers Association (International Apparel Federation, *Yearbook 1984 and 1985* [Berlin: International Apparel Federation, 1984 and 1985], pp. 8, 62; and correspondence from Japan Export Clothing Manufacturers Association).

*Labor Associations*

Traditionally, organized labor in Japan has exhibited the low levels of inclusiveness and centralization that characterize unionized labor in the United States, albeit for slightly different reasons. Japanese workers are organized by enterprise instead of by industry or craft as in the United States. Until 1987, the overall unionization rate of less than 30 percent was spread across a number of national-level labor federations, including the General Council of Japanese Trade Unions (Sohyo) and the Japanese Confederation of Labor (Domei). Moreover, the top four labor unions in Japan accounted for less than 70 percent of organized workers.[36] Centralization among Japanese trade unions has changed markedly since 1987. The Japanese Private Sector Trade Union Confederation (Zenminrokyo), established in 1982, had displaced Sohyo and Domei as Japan's largest trade union by 1987. Moreover, declining membership prompted the two rival associations to decide in favor of disbanding and joining Zenminrokyo.[37]

At 43 percent (1981), the inclusiveness of organized labor in the Japanese textile industry appears to be greater than that in the United States and that of the national Japanese labor councils. The Japanese Federation of Textile, Garment, Chemical, Distributive, and Allied Industry Workers' Unions (Zensen) alone accounts for 87.9 percent of organized labor in this sector. Zensen's predominance—and thus the centralization of organized labor in the textile sector—is qualified because labor in Japan is primarily organized along the lines of enterprise unions, and unions at the national level are primarily federations of enterprise unions. Zensen, by illustration, consisted of 1,453 enterprise unions in 1981 with an average of 324 workers per union. As in federations of producer associations, labor's loyalty is to the enterprise union first and the federation second, increasing the difficulty of consensus building in the federation. Consensus building is made much more difficult in Zensen because the proportion of textile workers in the federation has been steadily declining. As a result of declining employment in the midstream portions of the industry and weak unionization in growth areas of apparel manufacturing, by 1981 only 56.7 percent of Zensen-affiliated workers were involved in textile industry production. To compensate for the decline in the number of textile workers, Zensen has turned to chain stores, part-time and temporary

36. Ward, *Japan's Political System*, pp. 78–79.
37. Domei was to join by November 1987 while Soyho's integration was to be complete by 1990 (Haruhiro Fukui, "Japan in 1987: An Eventful Year," *Asian Survey* 26 [January 1988], p. 30).

workers, and new affiliated unions.[38] Although textile production workers remain the dominant force in Zensen, in the future this trend may be reversed, leading to deadlocks between import-competing labor (production workers) and import-oriented labor (distribution workers).

*Other Actors*

Other actors involved in textile trade policy include silk industry associations, trading companies, retailers, and business peak associations. The long tradition of raw silk production and the manufacturing of silk products in Japan, as well as the integration of sericulture and agriculture, has caused textile industry analysts to address the Japanese silk industry separately from the textile industry as a whole.[39] Although this practice will be followed in this study, I include silk associations as relevant societal actors in textile trade policy. In pressing for restrictions on imports of raw silk and silk textiles, for example, the association representing silk producers placed pressure on state actors at the same time as the protectionist alliance in the textile industry began to emerge.

Trading companies and retailers, however, promote textile imports. Japanese trading companies engaged in import and export trade, domestic production, planning and investment coordination, and extensive third-country trade have played an extensive role in the textile industry and in the Japanese economy as a whole. Of the over six thousand trading companies in Japan, nine are termed Sogo Shosha because of their "number of commodities, geographical spread, and economic power."[40] Many of the Sogo Shosha (such as Mitsui, Mitsubishi, and C. Itoh) began as textile traders and were also instrumental in

38. Employment in the textile industry during the 1970s and 1980s decreased in man-made fiber production and textile mill product production and increased in apparel and related product manufacture. Because of the relative predominance of small firms in apparel production, however, organized labor has been the weakest in this growth area of industry employment. In 1981, for example, although 43 percent of total textile industry workers were organized, the percentage for fiber and mill product production stood at 55.5 percent. The percentage for apparel and related product manufacture stood at 29.8 percent. These figures were calculated from MITI, *Textile and Apparel Industries*, p. 22; and Zensen, *Zensen* (Tokyo: International Affairs Bureau, Zensen, 1982), pp. 12–17. For detail on the general structure of Japanese labor, see Pempel, "Japanese Foreign Economic Policy," pp. 173–75.

39. Yamazawa, "Increasing Imports," p. 448.

40. Kunio Yoshihara, *Sogo Shosha: The Vanguard of the Japanese Economy* (Tokyo: Oxford University Press, 1982). The nine are Mitsui and Company, Ltd., Mitsubishi Corporation, C. Itoh & Company, Ltd., Sumitomo Corporation, Marubeni Corporation, Toyo Menka Kaisha, Ltd., Nissho Iwai Corporation, Nichimen Corporation, and Kanematsu-Gosho, Ltd.

establishing and nurturing what have become major textile companies in Japan such as Teijin and Toray.[41] Although the trading interests and economic role of the Sogo Shosha have broadened, as of 1980 the nine companies still carried 51.1 percent of Japan's textile exports and 56.5 percent of its textile imports.[42]

In 1963, with government approval, over 250 companies including Sogo Shosha, other trading companies, textile companies, and textile retailers formed the Japan Textile Importers Association (JTIA). The influence of the JTIA over import flows, although considerable, is limited by the presence of nonmember small and medium-sized trading companies. In 1982, by illustration, JTIA members accounted for 62.5 percent of cotton fabric imports, 60.3 percent of cotton yarns, 40.0 percent of chemical fiber fabric, and 50.0 percent of woven and knit apparel. The JTIA's position on imports is also shaped by its membership in the Japan Federation of Importers Associations.[43]

Finally, in contrast to the business peak associations in the United States, Keidanren is more centralized and a stronger supporter of trade liberalization. Textile industry influence in Keidanren has declined during the postwar period to the point that the federation no longer acts as a spokesgroup for the industry. Current membership by textile interests in the federation stands at four associations (including the JCFA and JSA) and thirty-five companies. Thus, on textile trade issues, textile members will air their views in Keidanren but have "given up a long time ago" on obtaining Keidanren endorsement for restrictive measures such as the Multi-Fiber Arrangement.[44]

## WEST GERMANY

### Business Associations

As in Japan, representation in the West German business community is both centralized and concentrated (inclusive). Approximately eighty

41. Ibid., pp. 14–81 (esp. pp. 31, 52–53). Sogo Shosha and major spinners and fiber producers tend to belong to the major *keiretsu* or industrial grouping networks. In some cases these ties have included bank guidance and/or bank representation in the executive offices of major textile companies. See the appendix in Yoshihara for a breakdown of *keiretsu* networks by major groups. For examples of the role of banks in textile companies see *Daily Yomiuri*, 26 February 1978, and *Mainichi Daily News*, 25 April 1978.

42. Keizai Koho Center, "Sogo Shosha Spearhead a Growth Area: Third Country Trade," *KCC Brief*, no. 15, January 1984.

43. Japan Textile Importers Association, *1983 List of Members* (Tokyo: JTIA, 1983); interview held in Tokyo, Japan, May 1984; statistics provided by the JTIA; and Japan Federation of Importers' Organizations, *Japan Importer's Guide, 1984* (Tokyo: JFIO, 1984).

44. Interview held in Tokyo, Japan, April 1984.

thousand firms are channeled through five hundred trade and region-
al associations into the thirty-seven "parent" associations that make up
the Federation of German Industry (Bundesverband der Deutschen
Industrie, BDI). BDI represents the interests of roughly 98 percent of
West German industry.[45] Through the Joint Committee of German
Trade and Industry (Gemeinschaftsausschuss der Deutschen Gewerblichen
Wirtschaft), BDI is also linked to other business and financial peak

*Table 4.* West German textile industry inclusiveness, by key producer association, 1963–1969
(in percent)

| Association | 1965 | 1970 |
|---|---|---|
| Federation of the Textile Industry (Gesamttextil) | 43.3 | 44.2 |
| Apparel Industry Federation (BBI) | 26.7 | 25.8 |
| Chemical Fiber Industry Confederation | 4.2 | 7.1 |
| Yarn Industry Association | 8.6 | 7.1 |
| Cotton and Other Fiber Weaving Industry Association | 11.7 | 9.5 |
| Federation of the German Knitting Industry | 10.9 | 12.2 |
| Baden-Württemberg Textile Industry Association | 17.5 | 18.1 |
| Northern Bavarian Textile Industry Association/ Southern Bavarian Textile Industry Association | 12.6 | 13.0 |
| North Rhine Textile Industry Association, Westphalia Textile Industry Association | 20.9 | 20.7 |
| Women's Outerwear Industry Association | 15.4 | 15.9 |
| Men's Apparel Industry Association | 8.9 | 8.7 |
| Total textile industry inclusiveness (Gesamttextil + BBI) | Average = 70% | |

*Sources:* Production and employment for industry subsectors calculated from Ulrich Adler
and Michael Breitenacher, *Bekleidungsgewerbe: Strukturwandlungen und Entwicklungsperspectiven*
(Berlin: Dunker and Humblot, 1984), p. 29; Gesamttextil, *Die Textilindustrie der Bundesrepublik
Deutschland im Jahr 1970, 1973, 1976* (Frankfurt: Gesamttextil, 1971, 1974, 1977); Diplom-
Kaufmann Günter Steinau, *Strukturwandel und Konjunktur in der Textilindustrie 1960–1978*,
Forschungsberichte des Landes Nordrhein-Westfalen, Nr. 3021, Fachgruppe Wirtschafts- und
Sozialwissenschaften (Münster: Westdeutscher Verlag, 1981), pp. 212-47; Michael Breitenacher,
"Die Textilindustrie in der Bundesrepublik Deutschland," *Wirtschafts- und Gesellschaftspolitische
Grundinformationen*, no. 54, 1983, Deutscher Institutes-Verlag, GmbH (Cologne: Greven and
Bechtold, 1983), p. 26; and material received from Gesamttextil and BBI. Additional informa-
tion on representation figures obtained from interviews held in West Germany, May–June
1985.

45. Bundesverband der Deutschen Industrie, *BDI*, 1981, p. 1; and Edinger, *Politics in
West Germany*, p. 224. For a detailed analysis of BDI see Gerard Braunthal, *The Federation
of German Industry in Politics* (Ithaca: Cornell University Press, 1965), p. 29.

associations, including the Association of German Chambers of Industry and Commerce and the Federation of German Banks.[46]

From 1963 to 1969, West German textile producer associations illustrated a pattern of concentration and centralization distinct from BDI as well as from associations in the United States and Japan. During this period the proportion of total industry production and employment accounted for by the major industry associations averaged roughly 70 percent (Table 4). This figure is the lowest of the three countries and is almost 30 percent lower than the inclusiveness of the West German business community as a whole. Textile producers are also less centralized than is industry as a whole. Subsectoral and regional associations are combined into two distinct industry federations: the Federation of the Textile Industry in the Federal Republic of Germany (Gesamtverband der textilindustrie in der Bundesrepublik Deutschland e.V., Gesamttextil) and the Apparel Industry Federation (Bundesverband Bekleidungsindustrie e.V., BBI).

Gesamttextil's membership covers approximately 70 percent of the combined man-made fiber production, yarn spinning and processing, weaving and finishing, and knitted apparel production in West Germany.[47] This membership consists of ten regional associations and thirty subsectoral associations defined by product. On paper, the regional associations (Landesverbande) focus primarily on regional policy and labor and social issues while the product associations (Fachverbande) focus on international trade issues. Chapter 6 illustrates that this division has not been adhered to by either group of associations. Gesamttextil was established in 1948, and its tenure and acceptance as a federation were greater by the 1960s than the comparable experience of the Japan Textile Federation during the 1970s. Thus, although Gesamttextil officials still face action by independent member associations as well as resistance from major member associations wary of conceding increased authority to the federation, Gesamttextil remains a more tightly knit federation than the JTF.

The major members of Gesamttextil are listed in Table 4. Gesamttextil's key regional associations reflect subsectoral concentration in the central and southern states of West Germany. The associations representing

46. Other members include the Federation of Wholesale and Foreign Trade (Bundesverband des Deutschen Gross und Aussenhandels) and the Confederation of German Employers Associations (Bundesvereinigung der Deutschen Arbeitgeberverbande e.V.) (Bundesverband der Deutschen Industrie, *BDI*, pp. 5–6).

47. This paragraph is based on interviews held in Frankfurt, West Germany, June 1985; and unpublished material received from Gesamttextil, "The German Textile Industry and Its Representative Organizations," and "List of West German Associations."

North Rhine–Westphalia, Baden-Württemberg, and Bavaria accounted for roughly 50 percent of total man-made fiber and textile mill production and employment from the mid-1960s to the mid-1970s. By 1983 this figure had increased to an estimated 82.5 percent.[48] Among Gesamttextil's major subsectoral associations, the Chemical Fiber Industry Confederation (Industrievereinigung Chemiefaser) represents 95 percent of man-made fiber production.[49] Similar to the Man-Made Fibers Producers Association in the United States, confederation members in West Germany focus primarily on fiber production and play only a limited role in downstream manufacturing. The confederation's role in textile trade policy, however, differs from that of its American counterpart of the 1950s because it is included in Gesamttextil decision making.

The Yarn Industry Association (Industrieverband Garne e.V.) represents 90 percent of cotton, synthetic, chemical, wool, and worsted yarn spinners.[50] As in the case of ATMI, the Yarn Industry Association's coverage reflects the expansion of West German cotton spinners into the use of chemical and synthetic fibers. Wool and worsted yarn spinners associations merged with the cotton spinners in 1967 and 1975 respectively. In contrast to Japan, the spinning association's membership overlaps extensively with that of the spun-yarn weavers association. An estimated 40 percent of Industrieverband Garne e.V. member capacity also belongs to producers engaged in weaving production. These "spinning-weavers" account for roughly one-half to two-thirds of the membership of the Cotton and Other Fiber Weaving Industry Association (Industrieverband Gewebe aus Baumwolle und anderen Fasern e.V.). The weaving association itself represents approximately

48. In the regions themselves, the associations represented an average of 6.7 percent of total industrial production and employment. These figures do not include woven apparel since apparel producers were represented by regional associations attached to the Apparel Industry Federation. If these figures are included, the average percentage of total industry production and employment accounted for by the total textile industry in these regions increases to 10.6 percent. See Ulrich Adler and Michael Breitenacher, *Bekleidungsgewerbe: Strukturwandlungen und Entwicklungsperspectiven* (Berlin: Dunker and Humblot, 1984), p. 29; and Gesamttextil, *Die Textilindustrie der Bundesrepublik Deutschland im Jahr 1970, 1973, 1976, 1979* (Frankfurt: Gesamttextil, 1971, 1974, 1977, 1980). More recent figures were calculated from Gesamttextil, *Jahrbuch der Textilindustrie 1984* (Frankfurt: Gesamttextil, 1984), pp. 5*, 21*.

49. Membership consists of Bayer AG, Deutsche ICI GmbH, Dupont de Nemours (Deutschland) GmbH, Enka AG, Hoechst AG, Norddeutsche Faserwerke GmbH, and Rhodia AG. (Industrievereinigung Chemiefaser e.V., *Die Chemiefaser-Industrie in der Bundesrepublik Deutschland 1983* [Frankfurt, 1983], p. 19; phone interview with association official in Frankfurt, West Germany, June 1985).

50. This paragraph relies heavily on interviews held in Frankfurt, West Germany, June 1985.

100 percent of spun yarn weavers of cotton, synthetics, and wool fibers. Yet, despite the coverage and extensive overlap of the two associations, the midstream portion of the West German textile industry has not produced the merged associations that characterize the U.S. textile industry.[51]

West German knitted fabric and knitted apparel producers, however, are more organized and concentrated than their American or Japanese counterparts.[52] The Federation of the German Knitting Industry (Gesamtverband der deutschen Maschenindustrie e.V., Gesamtmasche) represents approximately 84 percent of knitted goods production. The subsector's mix of capital-intensive (presewing) and labor-intensive production often places Gesamtmasche at odds with Gasamttextil's more capital-intensive spinning and weaving association members. Thus, along with working through Gesamttextil, Gesamtmasche lobbies extensively on its own at the federal and regional government levels. Staff, employment, and production figures indicate that Gesamtmasche is currently the largest single association within Gesamttextil. In a bid to become a more powerful force in the overall textile industry, Gesamtmasche has also attempted to extend its representation to associations of woven apparel producers.

The latter are primarily represented by the second major federation in the West German textile industry: the Apparel Industry Federation (BBI). As in the case of Gesamttextil, BBI has had a long postwar history. It was formed in 1950, and its membership of eleven regional and ten product associations currently represents approximately 70 percent of woven apparel production.[53] In 1983, 75 percent of the woven apparel subsector was located in Bavaria, North Rhine–Westphalia, and Baden-Württemberg. For the most part, however, regional members of BBI have focused on social and wage-related issues whereas product associations have addressed domestic and international eco-

51. With a few exceptions most of West Germany's filament fiber weavers belong to a separate association covering silk and synthetic fiber weaving. The bulk of the weaving industry, however, consists of spun-yarn weavers. Within this subsector, the presence of the "spinning-weavers" is also declining. Seeking to take advantage of cheaper imported yarn, such firms have been moving away from vertical integration.

52. This paragraph relies heavily on an interview held in Stuttgart, West Germany, June 1985. The knitting subsector consists primarily of small and medium-sized firms (75 percent), but larger producers account for roughly 75 percent of industry turnover.

53. This paragraph relies heavily on interviews held in Cologne, West Germany, June 1985. During the period under analysis, producers of woven apparel accounted for only 34.6 percent of the total textile industry. This figure has increased over time (primarily because of the relative rise in apparel employment) to 41.3 percent in 1983 (Gesamttextil, *Jahrbuch*).

nomic policy issues. The two major product associations affiliated with BBI represent producers of women's outerwear and men's apparel. The Women's Outerwear Industry Association (Verband der Damen-oberbekleidungsindustrie e.V., DOB) and the Men's Apparel Industry Association (Verband der Herrenbekleidungsindustrie e.V., HAKA) account for the bulk of production and employment in their respective areas.[54] Like the member associations of Gesamttextil, DOB and HAKA have been active within BBI as well as outside the federation.

*Labor Associations*

In contrast to the representation of business interests, unionized labor in West Germany accounts for approximately 40 percent of the labor force. West German labor, however, is more centralized than its Japanese (pre-Zenminrokyo) and American counterparts. Instead of a system of enterprise unions or the combination of industrial and craft unions that characterizes the AFL-CIO, the German Federation of Trade Unions (Deutscher Gewerkschaftsbund, DGB) combines sixteen industrial unions accounting for over 80 percent of organized labor.[55]

Organized labor in the textile industry is the primary preserve of the Textile-Apparel Union (Gewerkschaft Textil Bekleidung, GTB). During the 1970s, GTB represented an average of just under 40 percent of the textile work force.[56] Although GTB's inclusiveness was less than that in Japan, the association exhibited a higher degree of organization. In the absence of the enterprise union system that characterizes Zensen, West German textile workers belong directly to the national association. Centralization has also been facilitated by the presence of GTB members on factory workers councils and on the "supervisory boards of directors" of those firms required to engage in codetermination. Workers councils are legally empowered to represent a plant's workers in relations with their employers.[57] Codetermination, by contrast, refers to the inclusion of labor representatives on the board of directors of a company that employs more than two thousand workers.[58] In 1978, of

54. I overestimate this figure at 100 percent because of insufficient data.
55. Percentages calculated from Edinger, *Politics in West Germany*, p. 227.
56. Calculated from *Handelsblatt*, 15 September 1978.
57. Edinger, *Politics in West Germany*, pp. 335–38; and Wolfgang Streeck, "Organizational Consequences of Corporatist Cooperation in West German Labor Unions," manuscript, International Institute of Management, 1978.
58. The Codetermination Act of 1951 applied to firms in the iron, coal, and steel industries. These boards were required to contain five employee representatives, five employer representatives, and a neutral member. In other industries, firms with more than two thousand employees were required to fill one-third of the board of directors

the fifteen firms bound by codetermination in the textile industry GTB members held 99.9 percent of the labor positions.[59] Despite labor's centralization, however, the relatively low inclusiveness of organized labor has limited GTB's influence on textile trade policy issues.

### Other Actors

Other actors at the national and supranational levels play an active role in West German textile trade policy. At the national level, Gesamttextil and BBI influence in the business peak association BDI has been decreasing over time. Similar to the case of Keidanren, as technology, and subsequently the relative importance of major economic sectors, has changed, so has the importance of different associations within BDI. Moreover, bigger business interests consistently tend to predominate at BDI's "upper echelons."[60] Despite shifting power coalitions within BDI, however, Gesamttextil's concerns over trade policy issues are not easily dismissed by BDI and as a result still prompt extensive and often difficult negotiations within the business peak association.[61]

Retail, wholesale, and importer associations, by contrast, have consistently rejected calls for increased protection for the textile industry. Textile imports account for between 40 and 60 percent of the total imports by firms belonging to the Foreign Trade Alliance of German Retailers (Aussenhandelsvereinigung des Deutschen Einzelhandels e.V., AVE). The AVE's membership consists of eleven industry and national retailer associations and twenty-six companies and department stores. Because of the importance of textile imports to the peak retail association as a whole, the Federation of German Textile Retailers (Bundesverband des Deutschen Textileinzelhandels) tends to work through the AVE on textile trade policy issues.[62] AVE's interests in opposing textile protec-

---

with employee representatives. Under 1976 legislation, labor's participation was increased to one-half of the board positions, but one labor appointee was slated for white-collar workers selected from a list compiled by top company officials, and the chairmanship fell under the influence of the shareholders (Edinger, *Politics in West Germany*, pp. 335–38).

59. Calculated from *Handelsblatt*, 15 September 1978.

60. Braunthal, *Federation of German Industry*, pp. 35–43; Katzenstein, "Conclusion: Domestic Structures," p. 320; and Kreile, "West Germany," p. 201.

61. Such negotiations, for example, produced a compromise position between BDI and Gesamttextil on the appropriate nature of West Germany's participation in the Multi-Fiber Arrangement. In contrast, because they take similar positions on the issue of federal subsidies, the BDI had little difficulty in supporting Gesamttextil's opposition to such assistance measures (interview held in Cologne, West Germany, June 1985).

62. Interview held in Cologne, West Germany, June 1985; and AVE, *AVE: Aussenhandelsvereinigung des Deutschen Einzelhandels, e.V.* (Cologne: AVE, 1984).

tion are often shared by the eleven regional associations and fifty branch associations that constitute the Federation of German Whole-sale and Foreign Trade (Bundesverband des deutschen Gross- und Aussenhandels e.V., BGA).[63] In addition, the Working Group of German Far East Product Importers (Arbeitsgemeinschaft Deutscher Fernost-Fachimporteure) has actively sought to counter efforts by the textile alliance to restrict imports of East Asian textile goods.[64]

Rather than acting as a supporting or opposing "coalition" to alliances of textile producer associations, the West German banking community has been involved in textile trade policy at the company level. In general, bank leverage over individual companies stems from a combination of sources. Along with stock ownership and proxy holding, bank officials also act as representatives of the bank's interests on company supervisory boards. Through a combination of various forms of stockholding, the banking community votes 70 percent of the shares of the 425 largest corporations in West Germany industry. The West German banking community is so centralized that representatives from the top three commercial banks are members of close to 75 percent of the supervisory boards of the country's top one hundred companies.[65] Among textile companies, banking influence has been greatest in cases of major company bailouts, which began to emerge in the mid-1970s.

In response to the partial shift in authority over trade policy to the European Community, interest groups have emerged to play a role in textile trade policy at the Community level. Gesamttextil belongs to a corresponding European peak textile association: the Coordinating Committee for the European Textile and Clothing Industries (COMI-TEXTIL).[66] COMITEXTIL also acts as a peak federation for subsectoral

63. Interview held in Bonn, West Germany, June 1985.
64. *Textil-Mitteilungen/Textil-Zeitung*, 23, 30 June 1966.
65. Kreile, "West Germany," pp. 211–12; U.S. Congress, Joint Economic Committee, *Monetary Policy, Selective Credit Policy, and Industrial Policy in France, Britain, West Germany, and Sweden* (Washington, D.C.: U.S. Government Printing Office, 1981), pp. 115, 117–18; Katzenstein, "Conclusion: Domestic Structures," p. 320; and Andrew Shonfield, *Modern Capitalism: The Changing Balance of Public and Private Power* (New York: Oxford University Press, 1976), pp. 247–52.
66. The European Commission was initially opposed to dealing directly with the national federations but encouraged COMITEXTIL's formation in 1961. See Emil Kirchner and Konrad Schweiger, *The Role of Interest Groups in the European Community* (Hampshire: Gower Publishing Co., 1981), pp. 29–30; Camille Blum, "The Textile Policy of the European Community," in Steven J. Warnecke and Ezra N. Suleiman, eds., *Industrial Policies in Western Europe* (New York: Praeger, 1975), pp. 209–10; and Chris Farrands, "External Relations: Textile Politics and the Multi-Fibre Arrangement," in Wallace et al., eds., *Policy-Making in the European Economic Community*, p. 301.

producer associations at the EC level.[67] These associations include the European Federation of Garment Industries (AEIH), Eurocotton, Mailleurop (knitting industry), and the Comite International de la Rayonne et des Fibres Synthetiques (CIRFS). COMITEXTIL attempts to coordinate its members to pressure EC institutions. COMITEXTIL also serves these institutions by providing a central source of information on the European textile industry and by acting as a liaison to the national industry associations.[68]

Finally, general industry, labor, and trade organizations at the EC level are less active on textile trade policy issues. The Union of Industries of the European Community (UNICE) consists primarily of national peak business associations such as BDI.[69] The ability of COMITEXTIL and other European textile industry associations to influence UNICE decisions, however, has been constrained by UNICE restrictions that limit sectoral associations to "only a consultative voice in some areas." Similarly, labor unions representing specific sectors at the Community level are not always allowed input in the European Trade Union Confederation (ETUC). Unions that have a focus broader than Europe, as is the case of the textile unions, are not recognized by the ETUC. In contrast, retailers have a voice at the Community level. The Foreign Trade Association, formed in 1977, includes the national peak associations such as AVE as well as West German retail firms such as Kaufhof and Kaufhalle.[70] Finally, wholesalers associations such as the BGA belong to the Federation of European Wholesale and International Trade Associations (FEWITA).[71]

## CONCLUSION

The broad patterns of concentration (inclusiveness) and centralization (organization) that characterize societal actors in the United States,

67. COMITEXTIL, *Progress Report—1984/1985 Financial Year*, Twenty-fifth General Assembly, May 23, 1985. Kirchner and Schweiger (*Role of Interest Groups*, pp. 29–30), by contrast, argue that relations between the intrasector associations and the European-level sector association are informal.

68. Blum, "Textile Policy," pp. 209–10; and Farrands, "External Relations," p. 301.

69. This paragraph relies heavily on Blum, "Textile Policy," and Farrands, "External Relations."

70. FTA, *FTA: Foreign Trade Association* (Brussels: Foreign Trade Association, n.d.).

71. FEWITA has a small staff so the national associations play a predominant role in the running of the federation (interview held in Bonn, West Germany, June 1985; and memo from the Federation of European Wholesale and International Trade Associations, "FEWITA schlagt Deregulierung des Welthandels mit Textilien und Bekleidung vor").

Japan, and West Germany are not fully replicated at the sectoral level. During the 1950s and 1960s, textile producer associations in the United States were more inclusive and less organized than the general business community. In West Germany during the 1960s, such associations were less organized and less inclusive than their general counterparts; and in Japan during the 1970s and 1980s, they were roughly as organized and only slightly less inclusive than producer associations in general.

How accurate are the predictions of the comparative literature on advanced industrial countries? As expected, at both the general and sectoral levels, producer associations appear to be weakest in the United States based on criteria of centralization. On indexes of concentration (inclusiveness), the U.S. textile industry appears to be stronger than the American business community in general (85 percent versus 75 percent) as well as stronger than its counterparts in Japan and West Germany. Although Japan and West Germany have strong general business associations, German textile producers are weaker than their Japanese counterparts at the sectoral level because of the lack of a single overarching federation and lower inclusiveness (70 percent versus 83.4 percent). Relatively low levels of inclusiveness appear to undercut the strength of organized labor on textile trade policy issues in all three countries. West German labor movements emerge as the strongest of the three countries at both the general and sectoral levels.

What do these structural comparisons mean? Strong industrial alliances should be most likely to occur in Japan, followed by West Germany and the United States. Such comparisons implicitly assume, however, that indicators of formal organization can also account for convergence of interests among alliance members. Although formal organization can facilitate coalition building, it does not necessarily lead to consensus. Organizational deadlock often occurs. At the same time, however, convergence of interests among alliance members cannot compensate for low levels of inclusiveness among producer associations. All three components—organization, inclusiveness, and convergence of interests—must be considered as integrated sources of industrial alliance strength.

Given the levels of organization and inclusiveness revealed in this chapter and the role of interest convergence, it is possible for textile producer associations in all three countries to form strong industrial alliances. The previous chapter indicated that the potential exists for such alliances in all three countries to gain high degrees of institutional access. The following chapters explore how these potentials have been met and the impact of the interaction between domestic pressure and international constraints on textile trade policy choices.

# CHAPTER FOUR

# United States Textile
# Trade Policy

The origins of patchwork protectionism lie in the U.S. textile trade policy of the 1950s and early 1960s. Under pressure from industry for relief from competitive imports, the United States disrupted the GATT and Japan's future in the organization by forcing Japan to "voluntarily" restrict the quantity of its cotton textile exports to the American market. After the failed attempt to force similar action by Hong Kong, American state policy makers worked to establish multilateral frameworks for the selective regulation of textile trade through bilaterally negotiated quotas. By 1962, however, the United States was relying on unilateral quotas to pressure textile exporters into restraint agreements.

What explains the choices made by state policy makers among types of protectionist policy during this period? This chapter sets out the international constraints faced by American state policy makers and analyzes three cases in which industrial alliances demanded action contrary to that dictated by such constraints.

## INTERNATIONAL CONSTRAINTS

During the 1950s and early 1960s, international economic constraints on state policy makers' actions were mixed. U.S. dependence on foreign trade, as measured by trade as a percentage of GNP, averaged only 6.7 percent (low −).[1] Constraints based on international economic structure, by contrast, were on the borderline between moderate and high.

---

1. Calculated from International Monetary Fund, *International Financial Statistics*, selected issues.

During the 1950s, the United States was a hegemonic power in an international economic system with France and West Germany as "spoilers" and Great Britain as a "supporter" soon to join the spoiler ranks. By the early 1960s, the British shift had occurred, leaving the United States faced with an international economic structure characterized by three spoilers and not a single supporter. Spoilers prefer to follow protectionist policies over free trade and are strongly opposed to the option of free trade at home and protection abroad. Protection on the part of the United States would, therefore, either run a strong risk of retaliation or force American state policy makers to rely on a greater degree of side payments (or sanctions) to obtain the spoilers' cooperation in maintaining open international trade.[2] Thus, from an economic standpoint, although the United States faced a considerable threat of retaliation, its actual vulnerability to retaliation was rather limited.

Economic constraints were clearly overshadowed by strategic considerations. In the 1950s a new phase of a commitment to the liberal trade principles arose, rooted in the arguments of Cordell Hull and incorporated in the 1934 Reciprocal Trade Act. Hull believed that domestic economic health and world peace depended on the expansion of international trade. The 1947 GATT incorporated Hull's concerns by providing a framework to regulate the use of protectionist measures. In the 1950s, American state policy makers modified Hull's argument by adding the positive role of international economic integration in "stemming the tide of world communism." State policy makers saw liberalization at home as the key to protecting war-torn Western Europe from communist military and economic expansionism. In the Far East, liberalization was necessary to facilitate reconstruction and to prevent Japan from turning to old markets in communist China. Because of the "loss" of China and one-half of Korea to communism by 1953, the United States needed a capitalist Japan for security reasons.[3] The framework for liberalization established under GATT, therefore, became even more important as a tool to achieve political-military ends.

Japan posed a dilemma for American state policy makers. To prevent the spread of communism the United States needed a strong push under the GATT toward trade liberalization. GATT restrictions fo-

2. This section is derived from the operationalization of international economic constraints in the Appendix and Lake's discussion of the "price of compliance" in "Beneath the Commerce of Nations," pp. 151–52, 154–55, 164 (Table 2).

3. Joan Edelman Spero, *The Politics of International Economic Relations*, 2d ed. (New York: St. Martin's Press, 1981), p. 93; Destler, *American Trade Politics*, p. 12; Krasner, "United States Commercial Policy," p. 55; Bauer et al., *American Business*, p. 29; and Aggarwal, *Liberal Protectionism*, pp. 46–47.

cused primarily on reducing tariffs. Quotas were allowed under Article 19 but only on a nondiscriminatory basis. To impose quotas on Japanese exports under the GATT, American state policy makers would have had to restrict as well as compensate other trading partners. Such a step also risked fueling the strong European opposition to American efforts at promoting Japan's full inclusion in the GATT.[4] Moreover, protectionist actions under GATT on the part of the United States would justify similar actions by Western Europe. Yet at the same time, stepping outside of GATT to impose protectionist measures would encourage other countries to bypass GATT regulations and procedures. In short, either step by the United States would cause GATT to lose its effectiveness as a tool for liberalization and, in turn, as a tool for preventing the spread of communism. By the early 1960s, the Japanese dilemma had become even more complex as President Kennedy began to realize that overt protectionist action against Japan was undercutting American ties to the European Economic Community.[5] American efforts to open the European market to international trade with the United States and Japan would be more sympathetically received by the Europeans if the United States was not simultaneously closing its own markets to Japan.

In sum, international economic constraints against adopting overt protectionist policies were mixed. Vulnerability to retaliation was overshadowed by the structural threat of retaliation. More important, economic considerations were nested in broader political-military concerns. Avoiding protectionist measures would contribute to the security of Western Europe and Japan, thereby preventing the loss of support from strategic allies. Tensions within the Western alliance over the framework for liberalization would also be avoided if American state policy makers remained consistent in their push for an open international system.

The moderate to high level of political-military constraints suggests that state policy makers should have avoided protectionist policies that were likely to provoke retaliation and disrupt imports. This does not necessarily mean that state policy makers favored less overt types of protectionist policy. Until Kennedy's tenure as president, postwar state policy makers had tended to oppose direct government involvement in the day-to-day operation of producers. According to Andrew Schonfield, this position reflected a weak interventionist tradition characterized by an ingrained "hostility to public initiative." State subsidies and production cartels were not in line with the post–New Deal opposition to

4. Aggarwal, *Liberal Protectionism*, pp. 46–47; and Bauer et al., *American Business*, p. 76.
5. Aggarwal, *Liberal Protectionism*, pp. 46–47.

government budget deficits and strong antitrust bias. With Kennedy's election in 1960, however, the government role in the domestic economy began to increase.[6]

CASES

In 1954, faced with rapid increases in cotton textile imports, primarily from Japan, producer associations in the textile industry began to demand government assistance. In part because of the size of the domestic market, the industry's export and foreign investment positions—and therefore concern with foreign retaliation in the event of protectionist action—were rather weak.[7] In addition, producer associations were strongly opposed to government intervention at the sectoral and subsectoral levels. The textile alliance's first strong challenge to the dictates of international constraints emerged during the 1955 extension of the Reciprocal Trade Agreements Act and culminated in the 1957 Japanese voluntary export restraint. The second U.S. case study addresses the events leading up to the Eisenhower administration's attempt to impose a similar restraint agreement on Hong Kong. The third case study addresses Kennedy's Seven Point Textile Plan, the 1962 Trade Expansion Act, and the Short and Long Term Arrangements in Textiles.

*Case 1: 1954–1957*

The protectionist alliance in textiles emerged in late 1954 when producer associations appeared before the Committee for Reciprocity Information (CRI) to voice their concerns over upcoming reciprocal tariff negotiations with Japan. The prospect of increases in labor-intensive imports threatened a U.S. textile industry already characterized by overcapacity and displaced workers.[8] Despite the American

6. Schonfield, *Modern Capitalism*, pp. 299–329.

7. In cotton cloth, the main area of competition from imports, for example, exports as a percentage of production reached only 5.6 percent in 1954. This was the highest level of export orientation achieved by any subsector from 1954–1961 (calculated from Hunsberger, *Japan and the United States*, p. 298). Among producers of noncellulosic man-made fibers (the dominant force in the Man-Made Fiber Producers Association), however, exports surpassed imports by a factor of five until 1959 (*Pastore Hearings 1961*, pp. 425–97).

8. Aggarwal, *Liberal Protectionism*, pp. 44, 46–47. On industry conditions, see Vinod K. Aggarwal with Stephan Haggard, "The Politics of Protection in the U.S. Textile and Apparel Industries," in John Zysman and Laura Tyson, eds., *American Industry in International Competition: Government Policies and Corporate Strategies* (Ithaca: Cornell University Press, 1983), pp. 254–59.

Cotton Manufacturers Institute's strident call to prepare for the "battle against imports," only a weak protectionist alliance appeared before the CRI. This industrial alliance consisted of a fragmented group of producer associations accounting for less than 20 percent of the industry's employment and production.[9] Since the CRI was not bound to act on the industry's recommendations, the textile alliance failed to gain more than a low degree of institutional access. Thus American negotiators began secret tariff negotiations with Japan under extremely low levels of domestic pressure.

In 1955, the president's authority to conduct reciprocal tariff reductions came up for renewal under the Reciprocal Trade Act (HR 1). As the debate over the extension of presidential negotiating authority raged between national lobby organizations, affiliated business groups, administration spokesmen, and concerned congressmen, the textile alliance sought to limit the pace of import liberalization. Despite an expanding membership, the industrial alliance's strength continued to be plagued by internal conflicts of interest and weak organization. In testimony before the House and Senate, the four major midstream associations were split between advocating total or partial rejection of HR 1, and apparel manufacturers were divided over the broader issue of trading with Japan.[10]

In contrast, Congress's power of approval over the extension of negotiating authority acted as a moderate source of institutional access

9. Of the major up- and midstream producers associations only the ACMI and the National Association of Wool Manufacturers participated, each in a separate hearing. The former was concerned primarily with moderating the rate of tariff decreases, and the latter had waged a campaign since 1950 for countervailing duties on semimanufactured products from Latin America and for exemption of wool products from tariff reductions. The ACMI was joined by minor associations representing velveteen producers and textile finishers and a representative from the New England Governors and New England Textile Committee. This representative also appeared with the wool manufacturers at the wool product hearing. A number of apparel associations (four separate outerwear associations) also participated but, for the most part, not in the wool hearings. Of the five labor unions in the U.S. textile industry, only one participated in the CRI hearings (Lynch, *Toward an Orderly Market*, p. 81; *Pastore Hearings 1958*, pp. 1738–39; and *TAE 1955*, p. 1695).

10. The four midstream associations were the National Federation of Textiles, ACMI, the National Association of Cotton Manufacturers, and NAWM. The only apparel associations appearing before the House were the Underwear Institute and the National Knitted Outerwear Association. In testimony before the Senate these associations were joined by the National Association of Blouse Manufacturers (*TAE 1955*, pp. 855–60, 1548–54, 1561–73, 1636–37, 1653–57, 1695–96; and U.S. Congress, House, Committee on Ways and Means, *Trade Agreements Extension, Hearings before the House Committee on Ways and Means on H.R. 1*, 84th Cong., 1st sess., 1955 [hereafter cited as *HTAE 1955*], pp. 1612–29, 1637, 1707, 1753, 1892).

on state policy makers' action. State policy makers were, in effect, held hostage by Senate supporters of the industrial alliance. ACMI officials had found themselves faced with a worst-case scenario in which the ongoing secret negotiations with Japan would lead to extensive tariff reductions with Japan and, in turn, would provide a new and unreasonable baseline for additional negotiations under HR 1 authority. As a result, ACMI officials opposed acting on HR 1 until the industry was made aware of the tariff agreements being negotiated with Japan. To afford the industry some degree of security, ACMI officials demanded that HR 1 be based on January 1955 tariff levels. This position was taken up by Senate supporters of the producer association and incorporated into an amendment calling for a shift in the base period for HR 1 from June back to January 1955.[11]

In addition to the ACMI protests, the Northern Textile Association had protested against the weakness and lack of clarity of the escape clause during House and Senate testimony. Figures presented by the association and others also illustrated that imports were adversely affecting some portions of the textile industry more than others. Once again, association testimony did not go unnoticed. Senators representing large textile constituencies in the Northeast introduced an amendment to HR 1 calling for the modification of the escape clause to cover portions of an industry rather than the industry as a whole.[12] In the final compromise over HR 1, the Eisenhower administration verbally committed itself to exercise quota-fixing powers and to avoid future reductions in textile tariffs. More important, Eisenhower accepted the Senate amendments modifying the base period for reductions in textile tariffs and allowing subsectors of the industry to appeal for escape clause relief.[13]

These limited concessions did not pacify the textile alliance. At the ACMI annual convention in April 1955, the institute's president advocated the use of quantitative restrictions on textile imports on a "global

11. Lynch, *Toward an Orderly Market*, p. 75; *HTAE 1955*, pp. 1612–29; Bauer et al, *American Business*, pp. 67–70; and *TAE 1955*, pp. 1548–54.

12. *TAE 1955*, pp. 1561–73; and *HTAE 1955*, p. 1637. For example, trade figures in early 1955 revealed that although textile import penetration stood at only 2 percent overall, in narrow categories of goods such as gingham, velveteen, and cotton blouses, import penetration was approaching 60 to 65 percent. See Hunsberger, *Japan and the United States*, pp. 305–7; and Yoffie, *Power and Protectionism*, p. 45. The measure was introduced by Senators John Pastore (Democrat from Rhode Island) and Henry Bridges (Republican from New Hampshire) (Bauer et al., *American Business*, pp. 67–70). For NTA testimony, see *HTAE 1955*, p. 1637; and *TAE 1955*, pp. 1561–73.

13. "Reciprocal Trade Amendments," *Congressional Quarterly Almanac*. 1955, pp. 294, 296; Bauer et al., *American Business*, pp. 67–70; and Lynch, *Toward an Orderly Market*, p. 85.

basis" to ensure the industry's survival.[14] His speech signaled the beginning of a shift in the alliance's orientation from concern over minimizing reductions in protection to concern with increasing protection for the industry. But because the industry had limited institutional access outside of the completed HR 1 deliberations, state policy makers did not respond favorably to the ACMI's demands. On June 6, Secretary of State John Foster Dulles expressed his opposition to import quotas on Japanese textiles, claiming that such a move would threaten the "trade and economic vitality" of Japan as a source of free world strength. Three days later, the State Department announced the results of the secret tariff negotiations with Japan. The department's press release noted that in making concessions to Japan, negotiators had avoided yielding on products of industries that paid substandard wages and had "operated under statutory safeguards to avoid injury" to domestic producers. In contrast, the actual bilateral agreement with Japan included extensive textile tariff cuts such as 20 percent reductions in gray goods and 48 percent reductions in finished fabrics. Labeling the tariff concessions a "staggering blow," the ACMI began campaigning for the United States to impose quantitative restrictions on textile imports.

In August 1955, the ACMI rejected overtures by Japanese textile industry representatives for interindustry negotiations on export restraints. Instead, ACMI officials demanded administrative or legislative action by the United States as a precondition for interindustry discussions.[15] Legislative support for the textile alliance was slowly reemerging after the HR 1 campaign. As congressional officials began to threaten a new push for protectionist relief for the industry, Secretary of State Dulles sought to dissuade congressional action before it could gather momentum.[16] Dulles slightly compromised his opposition to import

14. This paragraph draws heavily from Lynch, *Toward an Orderly Market*, pp. 75–76, 92–93, 100; and "Reciprocal Trade Amendments," *Congressional Quarterly Almanac*, p. 300.

15. The ACMI's stance was rather ironic. The April 1955 decision to call for quantitative restrictions was based on dealings with Japan before World War II. In 1937, the United States and Japan accepted interindustry negotiated quantitative restrictions as a means to resolve a textile trade dispute between the two countries. This earlier concession was seen by ACMI officials as indicative of a willingness by the Japanese to agree to some form of quantitative restraint. In August 1955, the Japanese acted as they had in 1937. This time, however, the American industry was not satisfied with the Japanese response. ACMI officials argued that such steps would be in violation of Justice Department interpretations of free trade (Lynch, *Toward an Orderly Market*, pp. 75–76, 94–96, 101, 104; and Aggarwal with Haggard, "Politics of Protection," p. 273).

16. Dulles's actions came following a letter by Senator Margaret Smith (Republican from Maine) in which she threatened to support restrictive legislation in the absence of a curtailment of Japanese exports (Yoffie, *Power and Protectionism*, pp. 46–47).

restrictions by secretly advising the Japanese government to restrain its textile exports. Heeding the secretary's advice, MITI officials imposed a ban on all textile exports in November and proposed unilateral restraints on selected textile products in December.[17]

Rejecting the idea of Japanese control over United States textile imports, the textile alliance all but ignored the Japanese offer of restraint and redoubled efforts to force state policy makers to increase protection for the industry. In late December, the ACMI filed a petition with the Department of Agriculture to implement textile import quotas under Section 22 of the 1933 Agricultural Adjustment Act. Although the ACMI petition was rejected the following February, in the first three months of 1956 velveteen producers, blouse manufacturers, and pillowcase manufacturers all filed escape clause petitions with the Tariff Commission.[18] The textile alliance gained strength in early March, when the ACMI, the National Federation of Textiles, and the National Association of Wool Manufacturers closed ranks to form the National Council of Textile Industries to testify before the House Ways and Means Committee hearings on the Organization for Trade Cooperation (HR 5550). Spokesmen for the council introduced themselves as direct representatives of the "national textile industry" and indirect representatives of garment manufacturers, "who don't have an organization of this kind that can make a presentation for them."[19]

Although only temporary, the national council was a stark contrast to the organizational and interest fragmentation that had characterized the protectionist alliance during the HR 1 hearings. The lone apparel association participating in the HR 5550 hearings endorsed the position of the council, lending credence to the council's claims of representation and interest orientation. In addition, the Northern Textile Association, although not included in the council's membership, did not reject its claims of representation in its own presentation against HR 5550. Faced with a powerful textile alliance and opposition to HR

17. The proposed restraint was to cover export of ginghams, velveteen, blouses, and fabrics (Aggarwal, *Liberal Protectionism*, p. 50).

18. ACMI officials also petitioned the State Department requesting an American quota set at 150 percent of 1953 and 1954 import levels (equivalent to a 25 percent reduction in import levels). See Lynch, *Toward an Orderly Market*, p. 105; Aggarwal, *Liberal Protectionism*, p. 50; and *Pastore Hearings 1958*, pp. 1259–61. For detail on the escape clause petitions, see Hunsberger, *Japan and the United States*, pp. 270, 311–13, 318; and *Pastore Hearings 1958*, pp. 1259–61.

19. Lynch, *Toward an Orderly Market*, p. 87; and U.S. Congress, House, Committee on Ways and Means, *Organization for Trade Cooperation: Hearings before the House Committee on Ways and Means on H.R. 5550*, 84th Cong., 2d sess., 1956 (hereafter cited as *OTC*), pp. 984–1006.

5550 from the U.S. Chamber of Commerce and national lobby organizations, the administration backed down and the proposed bill "was never brought up for a vote."[20]

The failure of efforts at increasing the internationalization of trade negotiations and a growing protectionist alliance during a presidential election year caused state policy makers to strengthen presidential authority to negotiate voluntary restraint agreements with foreign exporters and introduce subsidies to promote textile exports.[21] Yet these efforts did little to dissuade congressional inquiries, unsuccessful "textile quota" bills and amendments, escape clause petitions, and state-level regulations. The threat of severe institutional access reflected in the narrow defeat of the protectionist Green Amendment in the Senate, the onset of trade policy hearings by the Boggs Subcommittee in the House, and upcoming rulings on earlier escape clause petitions forced state policy makers to respond to the textile alliance by increasingly compromising Eisenhower's support of trade liberalization.[22]

In September 1956, state policy makers began to try to extract trade concessions from Japan. In contrast to Dulles's secret advice to MITI the previous year, U.S. representatives attempted to hammer out a "voluntary" agreement with Japan.[23] Japanese resistance to American

20. For testimony by the Underwear Institute and the Northern Textile Association, see *OTC*, pp. 1030–31, 1326. For the outcome of HR 5550, see Aggarwal with Haggard, "Politics of Protection," pp. 272–73.

21. Presidential authority was strengthened under Section 204 of the Agricultural Adjustment Act (Hunsberger, *Japan and the United States*, p. 318). The export program called for reimbursing domestic producers for the difference between the price of American cotton sold at home and abroad (Seymour E. Harris, "The Cotton Textile Industry and American Trade Policy," in U.S. Congress, *Foreign Trade Policy*, pp. 903–4).

22. In the House, HR 8658 restated an ACMI request for limiting cotton textile imports to 150 percent of 1953 and 1954 levels. HR 9170 called for setting import quotas based on a comparison of foreign wages. Senate Resolution 236 called on the Tariff Commission and the president to consider the impact of imports on the textile industry and to accelerate investigations under the escape clause. The Green Amendment to a foreign aid bill before the Senate called for quantitative restrictions on textile imports. The amendment failed by two votes. See Lynch, *Toward an Orderly Market*, pp. 87–88, 90; Yoffie, *Power and Protectionism*, pp. 43, 47–49; Brandis, *Textile Trade Policy*, p. 10; "Four Year Extension of Reciprocal Trade," *Congressional Quarterly Almanac*, 1958, p. 167; U.S. Congress, Senate, Committee on Foreign Relations, *Imports of Cotton Textiles from Japan, Hearing before the Committee on Foreign Relations on the Green Amendment to the Mutual Security Act of 1956*, 84th Cong., 2d sess., 1956; "Major Legislation," *Congressional Quarterly Almanac*, 1956, p. 424; and U.S. Tariff Commission, *Operation of the Trade Agreements Program*, 9th Report (Washington, D.C.: U.S. Government Printing Office, July 1955–June 1956), pp. 115–17.

23. To maintain the image of voluntary concessions, congressmen were told that "no US formal requests, recommendations, bargaining or agreements were being negotiated" (Lynch, *Toward an Orderly Market*, p. 106; and Yoffie, *Power and Protectionism*, pp. 53–55, 65).

proposals prompted President Dwight Eisenhower to invoke the Geneva Resolution allowing the United States to restrict wool fabric imports. The measure served a dual purpose by offering a concession to the administration's most consistent critic in the textile alliance (wool manufacturers) and by providing the Japanese with proof of the Eisenhower administration's resolve to act on imports.[24] To maintain the threat of unilateral action, Eisenhower delayed the escape clause hearings on gingham products and postponed a response to the Tariff Commission's positive ruling on an escape clause petition by velveteen producers. Faced with the possibility that American state policy makers would be forced to take unilateral action against Japan to satisfy domestic political pressures, Japanese officials agreed to a five-year voluntary export restraint (VER) on cotton fabric, apparel, and selected other made-up goods in early 1957.[25]

## Case 2: 1957–1960

Warren Hunsberger has argued that the 1957 VER "largely calmed the storm of American producer protest."[26] A more accurate description would be that from the imposition of the Japanese VER in early 1957 to the end of the year, state policy makers faced the eerie calm of the eye of the protectionist hurricane. During this period, the textile alliance consisted of only two associations pursuing two separate aims. The wool manufacturers association sought to defend its concessions obtained under the Geneva Resolution against State Department efforts at liberalization. ACMI officials, by contrast, used the occasion of their association's annual meeting to reiterate demands for reducing presidential authority over trade policy and for increasing quantitative protection for the textile industry.[27]

The textile alliance also lacked the degree of institutional access achieved during 1956. For the first time since 1952, state policy makers

24. The resolution, attached to the U.S. schedule of concessions presented to GATT in 1947, reserved the right to increase "ad valorem duty (from 20–45 percent) on certain categories of woolen and worsted fabrics when these imports...[were greater than (by weight)]...five percent of the average annual production of similar fabrics in the US during the three preceding years." The National Association of Wool Manufacturers had been pressing for the Geneva Resolution since 1953. See Yoffie, *Power and Protectionism*, p. 55; *Pastore Hearings 1958*, pp. 195, 199; Aggarwal, *Liberal Protectionism*, p. 52; and *TAE 1955*, pp. 858–60.

25. Aggarwal, *Liberal Protectionism*, p. 52; Yoffie, *Power and Protectionism*, pp. 51, 55–59; and Hunsberger, *Japan and the United States*, p. 323.

26. Hunsberger, *Japan and the United States*, p. 319.

27. Aggarwal with Haggard, "Politics of Protection," pp. 274–75; and *Pastore Hearings 1958*, p. 198.

were free from national elections and hearings over the extension of
RTA authority. In the face of a weak protectionist alliance and limited
institutional access, they began to retract earlier concessions to the
textile industry. Having made his point with Japan in late 1956, for
example, Eisenhower eased the impact of the Geneva Resolution by
reducing the tariff rate on a narrow group of wool product imports
and by authorizing a study of possible alternatives to the resolution
itself.[28]

This temporary reprieve from protectionist pressure was short-lived.
In 1958, Congress began a new set of hearings on the merits of
extending the Reciprocal Trade Act. In contrast to the congressional
hostility of the 1955 hearings, however, the 1958 extension went
smoothly. Eisenhower's tariff-negotiating record since 1955 and his
willingness to concede to congressional concerns on the escape clause
issue diminished congressional opposition to the act's extension. In the
1958 RTA hearings the textile alliance also lacked the inclusiveness and
interest cohesion that had characterized the 1955 HR 1 hearings as well
as the organization that had emerged in the 1956 HR 5550 hearings.[29]

Following the renewal of RTA authority, the textile alliance shifted its
attention to the upcoming congressional elections and the rise of Hong
Kong as a new source of import competition in cotton textiles. Recognizing the political importance of the textile industry during an election
year, the Senate established a special subcommittee staffed by senators
from textile constituencies to study the industry's "situation." The
subsequent hearings held by the Pastore Subcommittee of the Committee

28. *Pastore Hearings 1958*, p. 198.
29. Bauer et al., *American Business*, p. 73; and Thomas B. Curtis and John Robert
Vastine, Jr., *The Kennedy Round and the Future of American Trade* (New York: Praeger, 1971)
p. 7. Spokesmen for the ACMI noted the "burden" of the RTA on existing industry
difficulties and called for a two-year extension of presidential authority in a modified
form. This modification explicitly exempted the textile industry. Representatives of the
Northern Textile Association and the National Association of Wool Manufacturers,
however, explicitly opposed the RTA. The Northern Textile Association cited low duties,
lack of protection for wool products, absence of a VER framework, and the need for
binding Tariff Commission rulings. The wool manufacturers representative was more
succinct, arguing that RTA extension was not "expanding trade in a manner consistent
with economic welfare, defense, and the Constitution." The lone apparel participant, the
National Knitted Outerwear Association, based its opposition to the RTA on the absence
of adequate safeguards while the lone labor association (Textile Workers Union of
America) expanded this complaint into a request for "safeguard levels of protection."
The TWUA, however, rejected the Northern Textile Association's demand for binding
tariff commission rulings (U.S. Congress, House, Committee on Ways and Means, *Renewal
of the Trade Agreements Act*, 85th Cong., 2d sess., 1958, pp. 758, 766, 771–72, 855, 2452–57,
2466–70, 2487, 2489, 2529; "Four Year Extension," *Congressional Quarterly Almanac*, pp.
168–69; and *Pastore Hearings 1958*, p. 80).

on Interstate and Foreign Commerce offered the textile alliance a receptive forum to air its displeasure with the administration's textile trade policy. Needless to say, the textile alliance rose to the occasion. Testifying before the Pastore Subcommittee, the Northern Textile Association and the National Association of Wool Manufacturers joined ACMI for the first time in calls for category-specific quotas on imports. This image of unity, however, did not extend to other types of protectionist measures. The three associations offered conflicting testimony on reciprocal tariff reductions and on institutional changes in the trade policy process. Statements by NAWM, the Southern Garment Manufacturers Association, and the Textile Workers Union of America also conflicted on the nature and appropriate use of indirect protection through measures to assist the industry. Despite this weak convergence of interests, the Pastore Subcommittee's report released in February 1959 stressed the image of industry unity and called for tightening the Japanese VER and protecting "existing textile capacity" through category-specific textile quotas.[30]

Faced with an increasingly cohesive core in the textile alliance and the threat that the subcommittee's report would spark protectionist action in the Senate, state policy makers decided to seek voluntary export restraint from Hong Kong. Aggarwal has argued that economic and strategic concerns ruled out the use of unilateral quotas against Hong Kong just as such concerns had done three years earlier with Japan.[31] Yet these same concerns also weighed against the use of nonunilateral quotas. Both voluntary export restraints on shipments to the United States and unilateral American quotas would divert Hong Kong's exports to Western Europe. Strategically, Hong Kong's role as a listening post and "capitalist showcase" next to China would not be enhanced by voluntary export restraints. In addition, British officials were not in favor of discriminatory trade agreements against their colony by other countries. Although international constraints weighed

30. This subcommittee was based on Senate Resolution 287 and chaired by Senator John Pastore from Rhode Island. Other portions of the final Pastore report included calls for the elimination of export subsidies for American raw cotton (two-price system), modifications in International Cooperation Administration procurement practices, and the establishment of a committee at the cabinet level to study textile trade issues. The Pastore report did not include points raised by the Textile Workers Union of America and the Union of Textile Workers of America decrying the lack of business efforts to cope with industry problems (Aggarwal with Haggard, "Politics of Protection," pp. 275–77; *Pastore Hearings 1958*, pp. 1–2, 8, 86, 199–201, 217–31, 280, 283, 320, 322, 473, 475, 482, 1202; and Hunsberger, *Japan and the United States*, p. 322).

31. Aggarwal, *Liberal Protectionism*, pp. 54–64; and Hunsberger, *Japan and the United States*, p. 325.

against the use of either type of quantitative restriction, Eisenhower dispatched the assistant secretary of commerce for international affairs to Hong Kong less than two weeks following the release of the Pastore Subcommittee's report.[32]

Assistant Secretary Henry Kearns was unsuccessful, however, both in persuading Hong Kong to accept a VER and, upon his return, in acting to "contain protectionist demands" by textile industry forces.[33] As a result, in June, cotton textile producer associations led by the ACMI again attempted to gain relief under Section 22 of the Agricultural Adjustment Act of 1933. In contrast to the 1955 appeal, the textile alliance joined forces with the National Cotton Council. This time the secretary of agriculture forwarded the petition to the president, who authorized the Tariff Commission to study the case. Eisenhower also announced that he was considering the possibility of imposing a duty on imports of cotton textile goods produced from cotton originally purchased from the United States at subsidized prices.[34]

Despite this implicit threat of unilateral action against Hong Kong, state policy makers were unable to cajole Hong Kong into a voluntary export restraint agreement. Negotiations between the two countries collapsed when industry associations on both sides failed to approve proposed restraints by the Hong Kong government. By early 1960, strong congressional threats of action against Hong Kong as well as Eisenhower's import duty measures had yet to appear. Following a narrow interpretation of Section 22, the Tariff Commission had rejected the National Cotton Council's petition for import restrictions. Thus, although Hong Kong had failed to comply with American demands, domestic pressure on the Eisenhower administration had begun to abate. Without the threat of severe institutional access by congressional supporters of the textile alliance, state policy makers limited their concessions to the failed attempts at obtaining a VER from Hong Kong. In addition, to avoid the future prospect of being pressured into overt unilateral action on imports, the Eisenhower administration continued to support efforts begun in October 1959 to develop an international

32. Aggarwal, *Liberal Protectionism*, p. 68. For a detailed analysis of the U.S.–Hong Kong trade dispute, see Yoffie, *Power and Protectionism*, pp. 65–79.

33. Yoffie, *Power and Protectionism*, pp. 68–69.

34. Hunsberger, *Japan and the United States*, pp. 312–13; and Brandis, *Textile Trade Policy*, pp. 13–14; *Pastore Hearings 1961*, p. 16. Aggarwal has argued that Eisenhower complied with the secretary of agriculture's request to enhance Kearns's bargaining power in Hong Kong. Yet Kearns was in Hong Kong because of domestic political pressure (Aggarwal, *Liberal Protectionism*, p. 70).

consensus among GATT members on "market disruptions" and on appropriate action in the event of such disruptions.[35]

## Case 3: 1960–1962

The poor showing of the textile alliance by mid-1960 and the upcoming presidential election prompted textile industry forces to redouble their efforts to obtain relief. As in the previous cases, however, increased activity did not immediately take the form of cohesive action. The National Association of Wool Manufacturers appealed to the Department of the Treasury to study how Japanese assistance to wool textile producers was adversely affecting producers in the United States. ACMI officials demanded that the Department of Commerce take action on "foreign discrimination" against U.S. exports. A surge in imports of man-made fibers during 1959 also incited the Man-Made Fiber Producers Association to protest against the Eisenhower administration's textile trade policy before the Tariff Commission and the Committee for Reciprocity Information. In addition to the demands by producer associations, the Amalgamated Clothing Workers Union threatened that its members would cease to work with Japanese cloth unless something was done about the pace of apparel imports. Yet, despite the number of protesting voices, the industrial alliance's strength was undercut by the wide range of interests reflected in the demands of alliance members.[36]

Faced with the prospect of another Republican administration unable or opposed to offering substantial concessions to the textile alliance, industry forces and their supporters did not limit their appeals to the Eisenhower administration or Republican candidate Richard M. Nixon. Thomas Curtis and John Robert Vastine, Jr., have argued that industry forces waged a "tough political campaign to elicit assurances" from the Democratic party candidate, John F. Kennedy.[37] What the *New Republic*

35. Yoffie, *Power and Protectionism*, pp. 67, 69–76, 78–79; and Aggarwal, *Liberal Protectionism*, p. 71.

36. The ACMI request was made in cooperation with the Textile Export Association. The Man-Made Fiber Producers were joined in their demands by the Rayon Staple Fiber Producers Association (*Pastore Hearings 1961*, pp. 17, 33, 106, 425–97; and Hunsberger, *Japan and the United States*, p. 326).

37. Responding to South Carolina Governor Ernest Hollings, Kennedy pledged vigorous use of "Congressionally established procedures," such as the escape clause and Section 22 of the Agricultural Adjustment Act, while working "within the framework of our free trade policies." The following month, as a show of resolve to both candidates, the Southern Governors' Conference adopted a resolution calling for quotas and "other

termed his "artful and ambiguous allusions to textile problems" gained Kennedy the support of key textile states such as North Carolina, South Carolina, and his home state of Massachusetts in the November elections.[38]

Kennedy, a supporter of "free trade policies," quickly sought to repay—remove the constraints of—his electoral debt to the textile alliance. One method of repayment was through incorporating into his administration top politicians who had represented textile alliance interests. In a major step, Kennedy appointed former textile manufacturer and North Carolina Governor Luther Hodges to the post of secretary of commerce. In February 1961, Kennedy appointed Hodges as chairman of a new cabinet group created to study textile problems and to recommend alternative policies. Although the committee's formation delayed the likelihood of immediate action on textile imports, the prospect of a cabinet-level audience for the textile alliance and its supporters stimulated a second round of Pastore Subcommittee hearings in the Senate.[39]

The protectionist alliance that emerged during the early 1961 Pastore hearings was stronger than its counterpart in 1958 and the election year alliance in 1960. The rapid spread of import competition beyond fabrics into apparel and man-made fibers affected the industrial alliance in a number of ways. The growth of imports prompted the participation of two overlapping apparel federations in the textile alliance. The Committee for the Apparel Industries and the Apparel Industry Committee on Imports represented twenty-five apparel producer associations. The large-scale participation by the apparel subsector enlarged the textile alliance's inclusiveness to approximately 85 percent. The combination of apparel federations, merged mill product associations (such as ACMI), and separate fiber associations also increased the overall organization of the textile alliance. Finally, the convergence of interests among alliance members reached its highest point since the inception of the alliance in 1954. Fiber, mill product, and apparel associations all explicitly demanded quotas on textile

restrictive measures" (Curtis and Vastine, *Kennedy Round*, p. 165; *Pastore Hearings 1961*, p. 79; and Pastor, *Congress and the Politics*, pp. 108–9).

38. Pastor, *Congress and the Politics*, p. 108; and *New Republic*, 24 July 1961, p. 8. The agreement by the GATT contracting parties a few weeks later on a definition of "market disruption" came too late to aid the cause of Republican candidate Nixon (Hunsberger, *Japan and United States*, p. 328).

39. The establishment of a cabinet-level committee had been suggested by Hodges and recommended in the 1958 Pastore Subcommittee report. See "Other Major Developments Related to the 1962 Trade Act," *Congressional Quarterly Almanac*, 1962, p. 287; Pastor, *Congress and the Politics*, pp. 108–9; and Aggarwal with Haggard, "Politics of Protection," pp. 275–77.

imports "by category and by country." Alliance supporters such as the International Ladies Garment Workers Union, the Amalgamated Clothing Workers Union, and the Textile Workers Union of America went one step further by demanding that quotas be linked to domestic production. On the issue of state financial assistance, alliance members either rejected industry "aid" measures such as "handouts, subsidies, [or] favored treatment" or avoided taking a stance.[40]

Following the Pastore hearings, congressional action on behalf of the textile alliance began in earnest. In March, ten senators led by Senator John Pastore argued on the Senate floor in favor of import quotas and threatened to withhold support for the 1962 extension of the Reciprocal Trade Act. In late March, sixty representatives from the House sent a committee of fifteen members to the White House urging textile quotas. Less than three weeks later, this committee organized a bipartisan group of seventy representatives to speak out in favor of import quotas on textile goods.[41] Although strong threats of congressional action comparable to the Green Amendment of 1956 failed to emerge, the potential for such steps clearly existed.

On May 2, Kennedy began to take action based on the recommendations of his cabinet committee on textiles. Kennedy responded to the textile alliance and its supporters with a Seven Point Textile Plan. In the absence of extensive institutional access on the textile alliance's behalf, however, the plan appeared to offer little that dealt directly with textile imports in a new manner. Direct action on imports was limited to requests for the Department of Agriculture to study "eliminating" the two-price system in cotton, requests for the Department of State to arrange conferences between major textile importers and exporters to

---

40. *Pastore Hearings 1961*, pp. 10, 13, 64–66, 109, 233–34, 286–88, 328, 394, 400–402, 432–33, 497, 543, 545, 547, 557–59, 561–62. Once again free trade arguments were in the minority at the hearing. Although the textile alliance garnered the support of natural fiber producer associations, the appeals of associations such as the U.S.-Japan Trade Council and the Association of Japanese Textile Importers fell on deaf ears (ibid., pp. 80–82, 236, 526).

Producers of both man-made fibers and apparel stressed the close links between their portion of the industry and other stages in the textile production process in testimony before the Pastore Subcommittee. Aggarwal and Haggard have argued that the man-made fiber producers participated in the hearings to divert the attention of other portions of the textile industry away from possible interfiber competition (Aggarwal with Haggard, "Politics of Protection," p. 269). This argument is weakened because the textile spinning and fabric producer associations had already moved into man-made fiber products. As noted in Chapter 3, for example, ACMI had merged with the National Federation of Textiles in 1958 because their memberships overlapped.

41. Pastor, *Congress and the Politics*, p. 109; "Other Major Developments," *Congressional Quarterly Almanac*, p. 287.

avoid "undue disruption," and promises by the Kennedy administration to engage in "careful consideration" of escape clause and national security claims by textile producers.[42]

The plan's reference to the two-price system acknowledged that export subsidies on raw American cotton had forced domestic textile producers to pay a relatively higher price for American cotton than that paid by foreign textile producers.[43] Yet Kennedy's directive to the Department of Agriculture looked disturbingly similar to Eisenhower's promise to consider the imposition of import duties on selected cotton goods in late 1959, as well as to Eisenhower's support for efforts at reaching a GATT consensus on "market disruption." And Kennedy's pledge for the "careful consideration" of industry claims was as yet untested. Kennedy's plan also introduced adjustment assistance measures, a concept that many textile alliance members had opposed ever since Kennedy broached the idea as a senator in 1958.[44] Despite opposition from the textile alliance, the plan addressed imports indirectly by offering depreciation allowances to textile producers, Small Business Administration financing, and future federal assistance.[45]

The textile alliance responded to Kennedy's new plan by ignoring all that was new and immediately petitioning for relief under the national security clause that had been introduced in the 1955 extension of the RTA. On May 15, ten associations including the five major producer associations, filed a demand with the Office for Civilian Defense and Mobilization for import quotas to remove a threat to national security.[46] Faced with this new tactic and the textile plan's poor reception, Kennedy attempted to fragment the textile alliance by targeting the interests of its primary associations. In June, as part of the textile plan, Kennedy

42. Pastor, *Congress and the Politics*, p. 109; and Bauer et al., *American Business*, p. 76.
43. Harris, "Cotton Textile Industry," pp. 902–3.
44. Adjustment assistance bills introduced in 1958 included HR 1105 and HR 9505 and were supported by members of the House and by Kennedy in the Senate. See U.S. Congress, House, *Renewal of the Trade Agreements Act, 1958*, p. 771. For the origins of these proposals in the Council of Foreign Relations during the 1940s and the Randall Commission in 1953, see Destler, *American Trade Politics*, pp. 21–22.
45. These measures included increased Department of Commerce research on textile products and markets, a Department of Treasury review of depreciation allowances on textile machinery, and Small Business Administration assistance for cotton textile firms requiring financing for modernization (Hunsberger, *Japan and the United States*, p. 327).
46. The ten associations included ACMI, NAWM, Northern Textile Association, Man-Made Fiber Producers Association, and Apparel Industry Committee on Imports. Despite this showing of concern, the application was never granted (Hunsberger, *Japan and the United States*, pp. 327–28, 336; "Other Major Developments," *Congressional Quarterly Almanac*, p. 287; and Brandis, *Textile Trade Policy*, pp. 19–20).

authorized the under secretary of state for economic affairs to hold discussions in the United States and abroad on the potential for international action based on the 1957 Japanese voluntary export restraint agreement. As an alternative to more extensive import quotas, the restraints were to cover only cotton yarn, fabric, and apparel, using 1960 as a base year.[47]

Kennedy's efforts were "denounced" as inadequate in a congressional letter to the White House and as "completely unsatisfactory and unacceptable" by ACMI.[48] Despite these protests, by late July the under secretary's efforts had culminated in a sixteen-nation GATT conference approving the text for a Short Term Arrangement on Textiles (STA). The one-year agreement (October 1961–September 1962) empowered importing countries to "request . . . [through bilateral arrangements] . . . that exporters limit exports in any of 64 product categories of cotton textiles."[49] Unilateral action, within limits, was also allowed, but only if a bilateral agreement with the exporting nation could not be reached.

The STA provided an internationally sanctioned means of responding to pressures from the textile alliance.[50] With the support of key Western European nations for the STA, Kennedy had partially reduced the threat that American action on cotton textiles would lead to strained relations with the EEC. In the Far East, Japan's gradual shift away from cotton textile exports meant that the STA would not be a major impediment to Japan's economic development and ability to resist communism. Action on noncotton textiles, price-based restrictions, or improper use of the STA, however, would still be potential sources of tension between the United States and its major allies. Specific restrictions under the STA, however, risked disrupting relations with minor allies and neutral countries that relied on textile exports to the United States (suggesting a low level of political-military constraint).

By the end of December, U.S. negotiators acting under the STA had made forty-three requests to seven countries covering thirty-one prod-

47. Hunsberger, *Japan and the United States*, p. 328; and "Other Major Developments," *Congressional Quarterly Almanac*, p. 287.
48. Association officials argued that the 1960 import levels were too high to consider that year a base period for determining quantitative restrictions and that restrictions were needed on all textile products (Brandis, *Textile Trade Policy*, pp. 20–21; "Other Major Developments," *Congressional Quarterly Almanac*, p. 287; Hunsberger, *Japan and the United States*, p. 328; and Pastor, *Congress and the Politics*, p. 109).
49. Hunsberger, *Japan and the United States*, p. 328; and Pastor, *Congress and the Politics*, p. 109.
50. Hunsberger, *Japan and the United States*, pp. 324–25.

uct categories of cotton goods.[51] Despite alliance opposition to "aid" measures, the Tariff Commission also began studying a cotton price equalization scheme and the Department of Treasury began modification of depreciation allowances on weaving and spinning equipment.[52] Not surprisingly, this was the equipment used primarily by the core, midstream membership of the textile alliance.

In December 1961, with the beginnings of a multifaceted package of concessions to the textile alliance in place, Kennedy began his campaign for a "new and bold" trade bill to replace the Reciprocal Trade Act.[53] Yet Kennedy's concessions still had not produced support within the textile industry for a new trade bill. ACMI's board of directors viewed the STA as a "first step" requiring rigorous administration and extension to noncotton textiles to meet the industry's needs. Yet after a three-day debate with administration representatives in late March 1962, ACMI unanimously decided to support the 1962 Trade Expansion Act.[54] This about-face occurred for two reasons. First, the previous month the GATT Cotton Textile Committee had completed a long-term agreement (LTA) on cotton textiles, which allowed a two-year freeze on textile import quotas and allowed countries to take action against nonsignatories. In contrast to the earlier admonishment over the events leading up to the STA, seventy-four representatives sent a letter to the White House conveying their thanks for the president's efforts and asking for similar action on noncotton textiles.[55] Second, the *Congressional Quarterly* noted that the "administration reportedly dropped hints" linking U.S. acceptance of the LTA to the ACMI's support of Kennedy's new trade act.[56] Thus, not only was the ACMI losing support but the producer association was caught on the same hook it had used so effectively in the past. Instead of state policy makers needing only support from the textile alliance for an extension of

51. U.S. Tariff Commission, *Operation of Trade Agreements Program*, 14th Report (Washington, D.C.: U.S. Government Printing Office, 1960–1962), pp. 76–79, cited in Mark Hansen, "The Politics of Persuasion: An Examination of Government Policy in the Domestic Textile Industry," unpublished paper, Cornell University, 1978.

52. "Other Major Developments," *Congressional Quarterly Almanac*, p. 288. The depreciation modifications were extended to apparel producers in January, knitwear producers in February, and the rest of the industry in July (Hunsberger, *Japan and the United States*, p. 334).

53. Pastor, *Congress and the Politics*, p. 107; and Bauer et al., *American Business*, p. 73.

54. Brandis, *Textile Trade Policy*, p. 22; Bauer et al., *American Business*, p. 79; Pastor, *Congress and the Politics*, p. 109; and "Other Major Developments," *Congressional Quarterly Almanac*, p. 285.

55. Pastor, *Congress and the Politics*, pp. 109–10; Hunsberger, *Japan and the United States*, p. 330; and "Other Major Developments," *Congressional Quarterly Almanac*, p. 288.

56. "Other Major Developments," *Congressional Quarterly Almanac*, p. 285.

negotiating authority, in this case the alliance needed the support of state policy makers to gain an extension of the STA. Rather than holding Kennedy's trade act and concern with Western Europe hostage for an even greater textile concession, however, the ACMI backed down after three days of negotiations. The ACMI's pledge of support for the new trade act showed that Kennedy had successfully begun to fragment the protectionist alliance in textiles.

In June 1962, at Kennedy's request, Congress passed a bill allowing the president to restrict cotton textile imports from nonsignatories to the LTA.[57] The bill was introduced into the House at the same time ACMI's three-day debate with administration officials began, possibly serving as a means for increasing pressure on ACMI officials to agree to Kennedy's proposal. By late September, Congress had passed the 1962 Trade Expansion Act. Meanwhile, administration representatives continued to make vague promises of relief to man-made fiber and wool textile producer associations.[58] In contrast, within three months of the LTA's implementation, U.S. negotiators had reached agreement with eight countries covering "39 cotton textile categories in 71 separate restraint actions."[59]

U.S. action under the LTA, however, was not entirely in line with the policies sanctioned by the LTA. According to Article 3, an importing country can impose unilateral quotas in two instances: either during the period of negotiation if exceptional market disruption exists, or in the event of a lack of agreement after sixty days between contracting parties to the LTA. U.S. negotiators violated these rules by imposing unilateral restrictions on eighteen countries to increase bargaining leverage. Only eight of these had been changed to bilaterals by December.[60] Kennedy appeared to be acting in the face of international constraints to make sure that the cotton textile industry would remain supportive of the 1962 Trade Act. In sum, by 1963 cotton

57. The bill amended Section 204 of the Agricultural Act of 1956. See "Other Major Developments," *Congressional Quarterly Almanac*, p. 285; Brandis, *Textile Trade Policy*, p. 26; and "Cotton Textile Imports," *Congressional Quarterly Almanac*, 1962, p. 346.

58. For example, on September 20, the assistant secretary of commerce informed the Northern Textile Association that "the government will soon have a plan that will please you all" ("Other Major Developments," *Congressional Quarterly Almanac*, p. 288). Brandis has argued that a presidential directive also existed which stated that wool imports would be frozen at "zero growth" (*Textile Trade Policy*, p. 26).

59. Yoffie, *Power and Protectionism*, p. 96. Brandis has also argued that a presidential directive was released before the LTA began which stated that cotton textile imports were to be capped at 6 percent of domestic consumption. Subsequent ATMI efforts to achieve such a goal raise questions about the accuracy of this argument (*Textile Trade Policy*, p. 26).

60. Aggarwal, *Liberal Protectionism*, pp. 90–91.

textile producers had their quota protection, Kennedy had his trade act, and the remainder of the fragmented alliance was left with promises.

## CONCLUSION

From 1954 to 1962, state policy makers and industrial alliances engaged in three major disputes over textile trade policy. All three cases support the hypothesis that when faced with increasing domestic pressure, state policy makers will act against the dictates of international constraints. Using the indexes developed in the Appendix, Table 5 traces the interaction between domestic pressure and international constraints.

*Table 5.* U.S. textile trade policy, case summary

| Case | Domestic Pressure | | International Constraint | | |
|------|------|------|------|------|------|
| | IAS | DIA | Vulnerability | Threat | Political-military |
| *Case 1* | | | | | |
| 1954 | Low+ | Low | Low− | High−/Mod+ | High−/Mod+ |
| 1955 | Mod | Mod | Low− | High−/Mod+ | High−/Mod+ |
| 1956 | High− | High−/Mod+ | Low− | High−/Mod+ | High−/Mod+ |
| 1957 | High− | High−/Mod+ | Low− | High−/Mod+ | High−/Mod+ |
| Outcome: Nonunilateral quotas (1956–57) | | | | | |
| *Case 2* | | | | | |
| 1957 | Low | Low− | Low− | High−/Mod+ | High−/Mod+ |
| 1958 | Mod | Mod | Low− | High−/Mod+ | High−/Mod+ |
| 1959 | Mod | Mod+ | Low− | High−/Mod+ | High−/Mod+ |
| 1960 | Mod | Low+ | Low− | High− | High−/Mod+ |
| Outcome: Nonunilateral quotas attempted (1959) | | | | | |
| *Case 3* | | | | | |
| 1960 | Low+ | Mod | Low− | High− | High−/Mod+ |
| 1961 | High/High− | Mod+ | Low− | High− | High−/Mod+[a] |
| 1962 | High/High− | Mod | Low− | High− | High−/Mod+[a] |
| Outcome: Unilateral quotas (1962) | | | | | |

*Note:* The indicator scores are based on the highest level reached in a given year. Abbreviations are used here for industrial alliance strength (IAS) and degree of institutional access (DIA). The policy outcomes are the most overt type of protectionist policy adopted in the given case study period. For more detail on ranking procedure, see Appendix.

[a]This is the level of political-military constraint for those actions not sanctioned by the STA and LTA. Political-military constraints on sanctioned actions would range between low− and low+.

During the time of Case 1, international constraints remained constant. Trade as a percentage of GNP hovered between 6.4 and 7.4 percent, suggesting limited vulnerability to retaliation. As hegemon surrounded by spoilers and a single supporter (Great Britain), by contrast, the United States faced a much greater threat that trading partners would retaliate in the event of overt protectionist action. This mixed combination of international economic constraints was overshadowed by political-military considerations. Of primary concern was the potential that overt protectionist steps would injure or at a minimum increase tension with key allies. Despite the consistent levels of international constraint, state policy makers were not consistent in their policy choices. Limited concessions under HR 1 in 1955 and strong administration opposition to textile quotas gave way to administration-backed nonunilateral quantitative restrictions in 1956–57. International constraints had not changed; domestic pressures had.

Domestic pressures on state policy makers rose dramatically from 1954 to 1957. Japanese textile exports sparked increases in the alliance's inclusiveness and interest convergence. By the 1956 congressional hearings on HR 5550, all aspects of the industrial alliance's strength had increased. Although actual inclusiveness stood at under 30 percent, the midstream associations claimed before Congress that they were also acting as the spokesgroup for the apparel subsector. Since this position was reinforced by the supporting claims of the few apparel associations active at that time, the textile alliance appeared to be speaking for roughly 85 percent of the industry. The level of interest convergence reflected alliancewide opposition to further internationalization of authority over trade, selective cries for escape clause relief from adverse tariff concessions, wool manufacturers' demands for steps under the Geneva Resolution, and an ACMI-led push for unilateral quotas on Japanese exports of cotton textiles. Finally, the temporary National Council of the Textile Industries slightly increased alliance organization by coordinating three out of four key midstream associations into a single federation.

Institutional access on the alliance's behalf also increased during this period. In contrast to the nonbinding Committee for Reciprocity Information consultations held in 1954, state policy makers were held hostage during the 1955 HR 1 deliberations. The degree of institutional access increased in 1956 as threats of congressional action against Japan became more and more likely. Yet the narrowly defeated Green Amendment, which called for unilateral quotas, was the closest the textile alliance and its supporters came to binding input on the action of state policy makers. Thus, although state policy makers faced considerable domestic pressures, the combined impact of industrial alliance strength and institutional access was not extensive enough to force the use of unilateral quantitative restrictions.

In Case 2, the level of political-military constraints remained unchanged. British opposition to foreign restrictions against Hong Kong and the strategic importance of the crown colony contributed to political-military constraint. Protectionist forces in Congress bemoaned the State Department's concerns over the spread of world communism. As Senator Pastore argued, such concerns turned the topic of import restrictions into a "big political question."[61] Political-military factors continued to outweigh economic concerns, although the threat of retaliation increased slightly in 1960 as Great Britain shifted from supporter to spoiler status in the international economic structure. In contrast to the pattern of international constraints, the decrease in domestic pressures from early 1957 prompted state policy makers to begin to undercut earlier concessions to the textile alliance. Although by 1958 the industrial alliance's strength had increased to 1955 levels, these levels were never surpassed. The 1958 Pastore Subcommittee hearings reveal that the interest convergence of alliance members was never narrowed down to the level it held during the dispute over Japan in 1956. The absence of industry federations linking merged and separate associations also adversely affected the industrial alliance's strength. Institutional access during the second case study peaked in 1959 with the Pastore Subcommittee recommendations. Yet strong threats of quota legislation based on these recommendations failed to materialize in Congress. As a result, the Eisenhower administration avoided major concessions to the textile industry.

At the time of Case 3, political-military concerns with communism were a primary source of international constraint. By the early 1960s, developments in Cuba and Southeast Asia were pressing concerns. Although the fears of a missile gap of the 1950s had dissipated under the Kennedy administration, state policy makers faced the Bay of Pigs failure in 1961, the Cuban missile crisis in 1962, and the rising U.S. commitment to South Vietnam. Although political-military constraints continued to turn import policy into a "big political question," the STA decreased these constraints in the area of cotton textiles. From 1961 on, by contrast, political-military constraints on actions not sanctioned by the STA and its long-term successor remained unchanged.

By establishing the STA in 1961, however, Kennedy acted against international constraints. He sacrificed the long-run openness of the

61. Statement from the 1958 Pastore hearings (p. 1717) cited in ibid., p. 78.

international trading system to promote short-run gains in openness and reduced tensions between the United States and Western Europe. The creation of a limited, multilateral textile regime sanctioned the use of nonunilateral quantitative restrictions on cotton textiles and, in turn, alleviated the prospect that such action by American state policy makers would lead to tension between the United States and its major allies. Since the textile alliance could prevent passage of Kennedy's mandate for extensive tariff liberalization, concessions would be necessary to buy industry support. Thus domestic political considerations led state policy makers to act against the dictates of international constraints in 1961.

Kennedy's violation of the Long Term Arrangement in 1962, however, is less clear. Whereas Eisenhower operated during the gradual rise and fall of the textile alliance during the 1950s, Kennedy faced a strong industrial alliance his first year in office. The strong textile alliance combined inclusiveness, increased organization, and high interest convergence. In the 1961 Pastore hearings, the alliance's participation had grown to include fiber producers and the apparel subsector. Alliance organization had increased because of the presence of overlapping apparel federations. The common call for specific quantitative restrictions linked the participants of the expanded alliance. Institutional access on the textile alliance's behalf, however, fell short of that reached at the time of the Green Amendment in 1956. The threat of quota bills emerging in Congress, as well as Congress's ability to hold Kennedy's 1962 Trade Expansion Act hostage, were clear sources of concern for the Kennedy administration. The combination of industrial alliance strength and institutional pressure led Kennedy to promote the STA.

The reasons for the Kennedy administration's extensive use of unilateral quotas under the LTA are not immediately clear. The creation of the STA and ACMI's March decision to support the 1962 Trade Expansion Act reduced congressional opposition to Kennedy's liberalization efforts. Despite the decrease in the textile alliance's institutional access, the Kennedy administration chose a more overt form of protection not sanctioned by international constraints. One possible explanation is that an early resolution of LTA quotas would quiet the textile alliance during the initial stages of the Kennedy Round of multilateral tariff reductions. The more drawn out the negotiations for bilateral restrictions under the LTA, the less satisfied and more active the textile alliance could become in its appeals to Congress. Thus, by turning to unilateral restrictions, the Kennedy administration could forestall a resurgence of institutional access on the textile alliance's behalf.

Finally, these three case studies raise several questions for the predominant theoretical approaches in the political economy literature. Arguments based on the international economic structure would suggest that the United States as a hegemonic power should have avoided the overt steps of quantitative restrictions given the composition of the international system. International regime approaches also have difficulty with the steps taken by the United States against Japan and Hong Kong. With both countries, American state policy makers violated the rules and procedures of dispute resolution and the norms and principles of nondiscrimination set out by the GATT regime. Regime approaches are more successful in explaining the use of bilateral quotas under the STA and LTA. Yet, the initial push for the STA (as a violation of the GATT) and the extensive use of unilateral quotas that were not warranted according to regime regulations during the early 1960s, still raise difficulties for regime arguments.

According to statist arguments, the "weak" American state should have been forced by strong societal groups to adopt types of protectionist policies more overt than nonunilateral quotas in the first two case studies. The introduction of unilateral quotas in the third case study, by contrast, supports the statist prediction. The domestic structure argument faces the least difficulty in explaining the U.S. textile cases. As predicted, the United States emphasized strategies of protection (overt) over strategies of adjustment (less overt). The integrative approach, however, offers better understanding of the variation among specific types of overt protectionist policy that characterizes these three cases.

CHAPTER FIVE

# *Japanese Textile Trade Policy*

The status of the Ministry of International Trade and Industry as the gatekeeper to Japan was under serious attack by 1973. MITI officials' influence was declining and the ministry's trade and economic policies were criticized by both domestic and foreign sources. Top ministry officials responded to these concerns by calling for structural changes in the Japanese economy. Instead of the rapid growth of light industry in the 1950s and heavy industry during the 1960s, MITI officials advocated a new "knowledge-intensive" industrial structure. Older "smokestack" industries would be gradually replaced by high technology sectors.[1]

A key component of this transition was for a reorganized MITI to promote the structural shift while leading the "campaign toward internationalization" of the Japanese economy. Ministry officials emphasized the role that the new MITI would play in addressing issues of market friction and Japan's responsibility as a world economic power. Liberalization at home was vital to the proposed changes in Japan's economic structure. Phasing out "smokestack" industries would require Japan to turn abroad for standardized goods, especially in heavy industry products. Import growth would also reduce foreign criticism over lack of access to Japan's domestic market. In turn, Japan would be able to

1. The new policy direction was embodied in a structural reorganization of the ministry revealed in 1973 and reaffirmed in 1974 (Johnson, "MITI and Japanese International Economic Policy," pp. 273–74). For a detailed analysis of the development of this policy position from the Second Amaya Thesis of 1969 (Basic Direction of New International Trade and Industrial Policy) to the Industrial Structure Council's report in 1971, see Johnson, *MITI*, pp. 289–91.

export the new knowledge-intensive goods to the United States and Western Europe.[2]

Despite the potential costs that adopting protectionist measures would have for this vision of Japan's future, state policy makers jeopardized Japan's international trade relations when faced with pressure from the textile industry. In contrast to policy choices made by the United States, Japanese state policy makers relied less on quantitative restrictions and more on administrative restrictions and production cartels. What explains the types of protectionist policy chosen during the 1970s and early 1980s? This chapter sets out the international constraints faced by Japanese state policy makers and analyzes three cases in which industrial alliances demanded action contrary to that dictated by such constraints.

## INTERNATIONAL CONSTRAINTS

Japan faced greater international economic constraints than did the United States of the 1950s and early 1960s. Japan's foreign trade as a percentage of GNP stood at 23.5 percent (low +), compared to 6.7 percent for the United States.[3] Moreover, since Japan relied on export earnings to meet the costs of extensive raw material imports, this figure may underestimate the extent of Japan's actual vulnerability to retaliation. In addition to vulnerability, Japanese state policy makers faced a clear threat of retaliation if Japan adopted overt protectionist measures. In a historical analysis of the postwar international economic structure, David Lake has classified Japan as a "spoiler" in a system characterized by a "multilateral supportership."

Yet this argument is misleading. Spoilers face a high threat of retaliation from trading partners but prefer this mutual closure to mutual free trade. This description does not intuitively apply to Japan. Disaggregating Lake's average productivity scores reveals that Japan was on a par with West Germany and France in manufacturing productivity and was surpassed only by the United States during the 1970s.[4]

2. Johnson, "MITI and Japanese International Economic Policy," p. 274. The relationship between Japanese export and import patterns is addressed in greater detail by Kiyoshi Kojima in his analysis of Kaname Akematsu's models of the product cycle, *Japanese Direct Foreign Investment* (Tokyo: Charles E. Tuttle, 1979).

3. Calculated from International Monetary Fund, *International Financial Statistics*, selected issues.

4. Lake, "Beneath the Commerce of Nations," pp. 155–56, 164 (Table 2). For a comparison of relative productivity by agricultural, manufacturing, and service sectors, see Keizai Koho Center, *Japan 1983: An International Comparison* (Tokyo: Keizai Koho Center, 1983), p. 65; also Keizai Koho Center, *Japan 1987: An International Comparison*

In effect, Japan can be accurately classified as a "marginal supporter," a country with a selective stake in the continued openness of the world economy (at least in manufacturing). More important, because Japan was a highly productive country in manufacturing, mercantilism (domestic protection and export promotion) would be a much greater threat to supporters in the international economic system than a mercantilist stance taken by the average spoiler. The price of Japan's selective support for the open international economy, therefore, was a greater threat of retaliation (high+) than other major trading countries as the latter sought to ensure Japanese compliance in limiting protection.

In contrast to the United States, Japanese state policy makers faced few political-military constraints in selecting types of protectionist policy. America's crusade against world communism had no real counterpart in Japan. Japan's relations with East and Southeast Asia were for the most part economically oriented, rather than being nested in broader concerns with intermediate and strategic allies.[5] In Japan's overtures to the People's Republic of China, for example, political normalization was used to promote an economic relationship rather than vice versa. During the early 1980s, the South Korean government stressed that its contribution to the broader defensive interests of Japan merited extensive economic assistance and trade concessions. Japanese officials recognized the importance of a stable South Korea but were not moved to comply fully with the Korean request.

Japanese restrictions on American exports clearly served as a source of tension between the two allies, especially as Congress began to draw linkages between low Japanese defense spending and economic competitiveness in 1981. Yet, since the American textile industry had not emphasized exports to Japan, Japanese policy on textile imports was not a major sticking point in the broader political-military relationship between the two countries. During the 1970s and 1980s, congressional ire focused instead on sectors such as agriculture, automobiles, and telecommunications.[6] Thus during the first major postwar period

---

(Tokyo: Keizai Koho Center, 1987), p. 71. For a response to Lake's contention that Japan is a spoiler, see Takashi Innoguchi, "Japan's Images and Options: Not a Challenger, but a Supporter," *Journal of Japanese Studies* 12 (Winter 1986), pp. 98–99.

5. On the economic focus of Japan's regional interests, see Bernard K. Gordon, "Japan and the United States and Southeast Asia," *Foreign Affairs* 56 (April 1978), pp. 579–600.

6. On Congressional linkages between trade and defense spending, see Japan Economic Institute, "Japan's Defense Spending: A Reaction from the U.S. Congress," *JEI REPORT*, No. 4A, 29 January 1982. For trade disputes on other industrial sectors, see I. M. Destler and Hideo Sato, eds., *Coping with U.S.-Japanese Economic Conflicts* (Lexington, Mass.: D. C.

in which the Japanese textile industry faced competition from imports, international economic constraints overshadowed political-military constraints on state policy makers' action.

These economic concerns suggest that state policy makers should have avoided protectionist policies that were likely to provoke retaliation and disrupt imports. In contrast to their American counterparts, Japanese state policy makers did not rule out less overt measures. This difference stems, in part, from MITI's reorientation in 1973. If the ministry was to take a leading role in transforming Japan's industrial structure, state subsidies and production cartels would be vital tools in alleviating barriers to structural change. MITI's plans for a more active role in restructuring industry reflected a long tradition in Japan. Postwar restructuring measures in textiles began with an informal production cartel for cotton spinners in 1952 and with the 1956 Law on Extra-Ordinary Measures for Textile Industry Facilities.[7] Support for state subsidies declined during the 1970s, however, because of a combination of budgetary constraints and questions concerning the adverse structural effects of continued monetary assistance to portions of the industry.[8]

## CASES

In 1974, textile producer associations began to demand government assistance in response to rapid surges in textile imports from countries such as South Korea and China. The uneven international competitiveness of portions of the Japanese textile industry, however, led the chemical fiber association to remain in the background until the late 1970s amid calls from other associations for overt protectionist measures. Similarly, the decline in protectionist activity by segments of the apparel subsector

Heath, 1982). In contrast, Japanese textile exports to the United States have long been a point of contention between the two countries at the political-military level. For example, see Destler et al., *Textile Wrangle*; and U.S. Congress, Senate, *Textile and Apparel Trade Enforcement Act*.

7. The textile cartel was legitimized by cartel regulations included in the 1952 Special Measures Law for the Stabilization of Designated Medium and Smaller Enterprises and the Exports Transactions Law (Johnson, *MITI*, pp. 224–25; and Brian Ike, "The Japanese Textile Industry: Structural Adjustment and Government Policy," *Asian Survey* 20 [May 1980], p. 539).

8. Outstanding public debt as a percentage of GNP, for example, increased from 7 percent in 1974 to 39 percent in 1983. Public debt service cost as a percentage of GNP increased from 0.6 percent to 2.9 percent during this same period. These figures were calculated from Keizai Koho Center, *Japan 1983*, p. 72.

during the 1980s can be traced to improving international competitiveness. In contrast to their American counterparts, Japanese producer associations demanded direct and indirect assistance to deal with competition from imports. Producer associations made up of larger, more competitive producers, however, requested only limited nonmonetary assistance.

The textile alliance's first strong challenge to the dictates of international constraints culminated in the formulation of the 1976 Textile Policy Guidelines. The second Japanese case study details the events leading to the 1981 exemption of cotton textile products from Japan's Generalized System of Preferences (GSP). The third case study addresses the origins and outcomes of Japan's first dumping and countervailing duty actions and the new import guidelines contained in the 1983 "Vision" proposal for the textile industry.

### Case 1: 1974–1976

Textile producer associations in Japan had accepted the gradual increase of international competition as a natural consequence of industrialization abroad and Japan's trade liberalization that began in the 1960s. In late 1973, however, a surge of imports resulted in a 121 percent increase of imports and an increase in the industry's import penetration ratio of almost 6 points to 16.2 percent. Noting the sharp increase in textile and other imports and reports of rumblings in industrial circles concerning potential injury, MITI officials began to consider safeguards as well as investigating the industrial impact of textile imports.[9] Despite the surge in imports and MITI's concern, the overt protests from the industry that emerged in 1974 had little impact on state policy. The spinning and weaving associations that joined together in May 1974 to protest the import surge represented less than a quarter of the textile industry. The associations demanded that state policy makers ensure "orderly imports"; yet the Japan Spinners Association's call for an industry import council was the alliance's only specific suggestion as to how "order" was to be achieved. The combination of a weak industrial alliance and low institutional access met with predictable results. MITI officials repeatedly refused the alliance's demands on the grounds that such measures would "incite exporting nations."[10]

9. *Japan Economic Journal,* 23 October 1973; and Yamazawa, "Increasing Imports," p. 446. The import statistics are calculated (in tons), from Japan Chemical Fibers Association, *Fibers 1978/79,* pp. 82–83.
10. The alliance consisted of the Japan Spinners Association, the Japan Cotton and Staple Fibers Weaving Association, and the Japan Silk and Rayon Fiber Weavers Association.

The textile alliance expanded in October to include associations representing producers of woven and knit garments. These associations improved the textile alliance's inclusiveness and organization but did little to increase the convergence of interest among alliance members. Instead of demands for "orderly imports," the garment producers explicitly petitioned the Diet and MITI for increases in low-interest loans, tariff increases to pre–Kennedy Round levels, and the restriction of garment imports. To lend credence to their demands for assistance, the garment producers argued that imports were interfering with the long-run shift to knowledge-intensive integration and high value-added production encouraged by MITI's 1974 Textile Law. MITI's vice-minister, however, reiterated that the government would "not support a move for import restrictions" and rejected the garment producers' petition. Having failed in a direct appeal to MITI, the garment producers attempted to sidestep the ministry by discussing voluntary export restraints with industry counterparts in Taiwan. These discussions came to naught as the Taiwanese associations saw no threat of pending action by the Japanese government to restrict imports.[11]

Alliance requests for less overt relief measures were only slightly more successful. Confronting a decline in cotton yarn prices, the Japan Spinners Association requested monetary adjustment assistance to facilitate voluntary curtailment of cotton yarn production. MITI's initial response was an offer to freeze 16 percent of existing stocks of unsold cotton fabric. Although the resulting price increases in cotton fabric would indirectly spur the rise of cotton yarn prices, this was not the relief the spinners association had in mind. Through the remainder of 1974, the Japan Spinners Association reiterated demands for relief

---

In Osaka the following month, the MITI vice-minister again rejected the idea of import restrictions (*Daily News Record*, 24 May, 18 June 1974; and *Japan Economic Journal*, 7 May 1974).

11. For detail on the activities of the Federation of Clothing Manufacturers and knitwear producers, see *Japan Economic Journal*, 15 October 1974; *Daily News Record*, 28 May 1974; "How to Reshape Structure as Imports Soar," *Textile Japan*, 1975, pp. 89–91; and *Textile Asia*, December 1974. The 1974 Law on Extraordinary Measures for Structural Improvement of Textile Industry replaced a 1967 textile law that had aimed at restructuring specific portions of the industry through financial assistance. The revised law differed from its predecessor in both the shift to knowledge-intensive integration and the shift in coverage (for loans, tax relief, and measures to reduce capacity) to the entire textile industry. Direct steps against textile imports were not addressed. See MITI, *Textile and Apparel Industries*, p. 13; Toko Hirai and H. Iwasaki, *Seni Gyokai* (Tokyo: Kyoiku-sha, 1982), p. 159; Ike, "Japanese Textile Industry," pp. 444–45; and Bernice M. Hornbeck, *Developments in the Japanese Textile Industry* (Washington, D.C.: U.S. Department of Agriculture, 1975), p. 20.

while also attempting voluntary production cuts by association members. With no government relief in sight by late November, the association joined the Japan Chemical Fibers Association in an application to create a temporary recession (production curtailment) cartel for its partially overlapping membership of spun-yarn producers.[12]

The cartel that eventually emerged in January 1975, however, was a watered-down version of the original application. Instead of a six-month freeze of 35 percent of capacity and the purchase and freeze of one hundred thousand bales of yarn, the Fair Trade Commission (FTC) approved only a two-month production freeze. FTC officials argued that improving market conditions and expectations of increased demand justified only a limited cartel. To ensure the cartel's success, the FTC encouraged MITI in December 1974 to take steps to prevent speculative imports during the run of the cartel. In effect, MITI officials again found themselves dealing with the prospect of direct action against imports. Although the FTC's general recommendation was nonbinding, it coincided with earlier demands from the textile alliance for orderly imports. The strength of the industrial alliance had increased with the limited participation of the Japan Chemical Fibers Association. In this context of slowly rising domestic pressure, the ministry's concession to the textile alliance was minimal. According to one trade journal, MITI representatives advised the chairman of the Japan Spinners Association to request textile importers to exercise restraint. The ministry itself introduced a program of "import surveillance" by encouraging the Japan Textile Importers Association to report the pace of import contracts.[13]

Domestic pressure on state policy makers began to increase in 1975. One noticeable change was the role of the Japan Textile Federation (JTF). The February decision of JTF's Executive Committee to urge government action on textile imports spurred a month of discussions within the federation aimed at consolidating the industry's position. In mid-March the JTF Executive Committee formally requested that MITI study "effective measures...[to] regulate rising imports." Although specific measures were not demanded, the textile alliance was exhibiting

12. "Cotton Textile Industry Eyes Fashion Business," *Textile Japan*, January 1975, pp. 66–67; *Textile Asia*, October 1974; *Japan Economic Journal*, 15 October, 3 December 1974; *Daily News Record*, 17 October, 2 December 1974; *Japan Times*, 28 November 1974; *Mainichi Daily News*, 11 March 1975; Japan Economic Journal, "Natural Fibers," *Industrial Review of Japan 1975*, pp. 102, 104. For detail on recession cartels, see Johnson, *MITI*, pp. 98–99.

13. *Japan Times*, 28 November 1974, 7 April 1975; and *Textile Asia*, February 1975, December 1974.

a greater convergence of interests. In addition, the federation's participation had increased the proportion of the industry represented by the textile alliance. In contrast to the blunt refusals of 1974, the MITI minister "listened" to the JTF's request and "did not take any position." By the end of March, MITI was reportedly studying a plan for relying on bilateral talks to encourage foreign cooperation in decreasing textile exports to Japan.[14]

The apparent thaw in the MITI minister's position reflected concern over increasing pressure from the textile alliance and the Liberal Democratic party for measures to restrict imports. By the end of March 1975, the LDP Textile Committee had responded to textile association "calls for help" by advocating restrictions on textile imports. Previously, the Textile Committee had limited its demands to the narrow and culturally charged issue of protecting Japan from silk imports. A group of LDP officials, concerned with the upcoming national elections, met with representatives from the JTF the following week. The meeting produced a joint statement calling on MITI to introduce an "import control valve" to cover imports from China, Taiwan, and South Korea. The LDP's activity on textiles coincided with pressure from the Diet for the protection of silk imports under the Kennedy Round of multilateral tariff negotiations, which prompted cabinet officials to ask MITI for action on imports. Although both instances of institutional access were limited from the standpoint of pressure on behalf of the textile alliance, state policy makers faced the prospect of strong Diet support spreading from silk to the textile alliance.[15]

As the degree of institutional access increased, MITI officials began more active consideration of the textile alliance's demands. Haruhiro Fukui has argued that growing industry and Diet opposition to textile import trends led MITI's GATT negotiating team to take a harder line against Tokyo Round concessions on textile tariffs.[16] In addition, less than two weeks after the LDP-JTF meeting, MITI officials released a "unified opinion" on the restriction of textile imports. The three basic

14. For detail on the demands raised by key producer associations in the JTF deliberations, see *Daily Yomiuri*, 16 February, 21 March 1975; and *Textile Asia*, April, May, September 1975. For the MITI response, see *Daily News Record*, 17 March 1975; and *Mainichi Daily News*, 30 March 1975.

15. *Daily News Record*, 17 March 1975; *Mainichi Daily News*, 30 March 1975; *Japan Times*, 7 April 1975; and *Textile Asia*, May 1975. For detail on steps taken by cabinet officials, see Fukui, "GATT," p. 106. For details on MITI silk policy during this period, see *Mainichi Daily News*, 30 March 1975, 22 February 1976; *Daily News Record*, 4 April, 28 May, 2, 30 July 1974, 17 March 1975; and *Textile Asia*, May, June 1975.

16. Fukui, "GATT," p. 101.

measures proposed in the MITI opinion clearly represent an attempt to limit the spread of protectionism beyond the silk industry. Although MITI officials pledged to engage in bilateral talks with silk-exporting countries, the opinion explicitly rejected either increases in textile tariffs or the introduction of textile quotas. Overt protectionist action was ruled out on the grounds that such measures would threaten Japan's international relations in general, relations with developing countries, and supplies of raw materials. The MITI opinion's only concession to the textile alliance was a pledge to study the 1974 proposal by the Japan Spinners Association for an import council. This concession failed to ease the concerns of the textile alliance. The same day the MITI opinion was released, JTF representatives turned for the first time to the LDP, MITI, and other ministries with demands for "concrete steps to cope with imports from neighboring countries," including tariff increases on textile goods.[17]

Evidence of efforts within MITI to develop "concrete steps" surfaced in November 1975. Citing requests by the Japan Spinners Association for guidance, the Textile Problem Council, an advisory body to MITI's Consumer Goods Industries Bureau, submitted recommendations for "immediate textile measures." That the Textile Problem Council was established sixteen months after the spinners association's initial request suggests that MITI was not necessarily responding to the merits of the association's demands but rather to increasing alliance strength and to the need for "immediate" measures to calm Diet concern over MITI policies. The Textile Problem Council broke with previous MITI policy by calling for restrictive measures beyond import surveillance for those cases in which imports were "feared to cause considerable damage to domestic industry." The Textile Problem Council also recommended a series of financial relief measures for small textile firms such as a debt moratorium and additional loans. In accordance with MITI's internal decision-making procedure, the minister submitted the bureau-level recommendations to the Textile Industry Council "for discussions on a more concrete direction" at the ministry level before releasing an official position.[18]

17. For detail on the MITI opinion, see summary in *Asahi Evening News*, 18 April 1975. In the textile alliance's response, the JTF and the Japan Spinners Association jointly demanded "restrictions on textile imports as allowed by GATT and the MFA, increased import duties on textiles comparable to those in other countries, and the establishment of a consultative body to review the supply and demand situation" (*Textile Asia*, June 1975).

18. Interview held in Tokyo, Japan, April 1984; *Daily Yomiuri*, 9 November 1975; *Textile Asia*, December 1975; "Proposal for Immediate Textile Measures," *Japan Textile News*, February 1976, pp. 28–29; *Japan Times*, 7 November 1975; *Nihon Keizai Shimbun*, 26

During the Textile Industry Council's deliberations, top MITI officials actively worked to separate the silk industry and the textile alliance
in the minds of Diet supporters. The ministry targeted its efforts at
resolving the emotional issue of silk imports. In early November,
Chinese silk fabrics were placed under an import-licensing program.
MITI officials also invoked administrative guidance on silk importers to
encourage postponement of import deliveries and to delay the signing
of new import contracts. During 1976, MITI extended import controls
on raw silk, modified earlier tariff reductions, and instituted bilateral
restraint agreements with South Korea and China on silk products.[19] In
contrast to these overt protectionist measures granted to silk textile
producers, MITI officials continued to reject the textile alliance's demands for overt import restrictions.[20]

The official guidelines for MITI's textile policy finally released by the
Textile Industry Council in December 1976 represented only a small
victory for the textile alliance. The guidelines finally addressed the
Japan Spinners Association's request for an import council. The committee, located within the Textile Industry Council, was empowered "to
keep watch on rising imports ... [and] to recommend steps in case of
sudden increases in imports in specific categories." These steps included import surveillance, administrative guidance on the pace of import
contracts, unofficial bilateral talks with trading partners, and, finally
temporary restrictions based on GATT rules. Such restrictions would
be allowed only "in cases where import surge is realized and gives
serious damage to Japanese textile production." These new guidelines
offered fewer opportunities for invoking overt protectionist policies
than those proposed by the lower advisory council in 1975. The Textile
Industry Council relegated bilateral negotiations on textile trade to the
unofficial level and tied the proposed tariff modifications to GATT
regulations. In addition, MITI officials borrowed a lesson from the
United States by requiring the domestic industry to prove a state of

December 1975; and Japan Economic Journal, "Natural Fibers," *Industrial Review of Japan
1976*, p. 106.

19. *Mainichi Daily News*, 22 February 1976; *Textile Asia*, December 1975, January,
March, June, July, November 1976; *Japan Times*, 29 January 1976; *Asahi Evening News*, 19
May 1977; and *Women's Wear Daily*, 30 January 1976.

20. In early 1976, for example, Japan's chief GATT textile negotiator rejected the use
of MFA restrictions for the Japanese industry (*Textile Asia*, April 1976). In the fall of
1976, industry officials were told by the old and new directors of the Consumer Goods
Industries Bureau that the textile industry "should make its own efforts to solve its
structural problem" (*Textile Asia*, October 1976).

"serious damage" as a condition for the exercise of overt protectionist policy.[21]

With few exceptions, the Textile Industry Council placed the monetary burden of adjustment on the textile industry. Despite the lower council's recommendations for a debt moratorium and additional loans, the Textile Industry Council recommended that the government avoid financing the industry's problems with surplus capacity. One key exception would be low-interest loans provided to small and medium-sized firms in which scrapping occurred under a "pre-concerted action." Moreover, the council recommended that firms that were going out of business should be assisted by tax and other financial relief measures.[22]

Although negligible when compared to the American case studies, these limited concessions contained in MITI's 1976 Textile Policy Guidelines must also be interpreted in light of the situation before their formulation. Compared to the ministry's 1974 stance on imports, the policy guidelines of 1976 were "concrete" steps. Faced with the rising strength of the industrial alliance and increased institutional access, MITI officials were no longer able to reject industry demands. The absence of more overt protectionist policies, such as quantitative or price-based restrictions, however, reflected strong international constraints on Japanese state policy makers against the use of such measures and a degree of institutional access limited primarily to expressions of increasing concern by Diet officials over MITI policies.

The absence of extensive adjustment assistance during 1975 and 1976 and the limited scope of the adjustment assistance provisions in the 1976 guidelines partially reflect the nature of domestic pressure on this issue. Beginning in 1975, the textile alliance's demands and the focus of textile supporters in the Diet stressed direct action against textile imports. Extensive pressure for state subsidies began to reappear only with the onset of a major industry downturn in 1977. Over the course of the year, 1,328 textile manufacturing and marketing firms

21. *Daily News Record*, 17 December 1976; interview held in Tokyo, Japan, April 1984; *Asahi Evening News*, 11 December 1976; Ippei Yamazawa, "Japan's Adjustment"; and *Textile Asia*, February 1977.

22. One of the council's key recommendations was to phase out the capacity registration system for spinners and especially for weavers. These measures were originally intended to prevent overproduction but had become a source of financial assistance to scrapping programs in the midstream portion of the industry. This issue resurfaced in 1982 as part of the Vision deliberations discussed in Case 3 (*Textile Asia*, December 1976, January, February 1977; *Asahi Evening News*, 11 December 1976).

collapsed.[23] Calls by textile producer associations for financial and cartel relief found a receptive audience among state officials. In March, MITI and the FTC approved requests by spinning associations for recession cartels. By midyear, industry relief plans in the Diet and action by Prime Minister Takeo Fukuda (himself from a textile area) had led to more extensive action by the Ministry of Finance and MITI. By September 1977, producer associations representing knitting, weaving, apparel, and spinning associations had begun to take advantage of a modified low-interest loan program.[24] Compared to the limited results achieved in the three-year battle over direct import restrictions, the textile alliance had achieved a modicum of success.

*Case 2: 1977–1981*

By late 1977, it had become clear that the cooperation over financial relief did not extend to more overt forms of protection. Concerns raised by the chemical fiber producers association over South Korean imports and the spun-yarn weavers association's demands for tariff increases on fabric imports failed to produce concessions from MITI.[25] In the absence of institutional access on the behalf of the weak industrial alliance, MITI officials reduced tariffs on textile products by enlarging the textile quota for goods imported under preferential rates. In contrast, MITI officials coordinated production cuts for man-made fiber producers in late 1977 and a recession cartel in early 1978. By March 1978, MITI was supporting legislation in the Diet (the Law for the Stabilization of Specific Depressed Industries) that designated several industries, including textiles, as eligible for new financial assistance measures.[26]

These measures, however, failed to ease the textile alliance's con-

23. Gary R. Saxonhouse, "Industrial Restructuring in Japan," *Journal of Japanese Studies* 5 (Summer 1979), pp. 289–95; MITI, *Textile and Apparel Industries*, p. 1; and *Textile Asia*, June, July, August 1977.

24. *Daily News Record*, 11, 22 February, 12 April 1977; Japan Economic Journal, "Natural Fibers," *Industrial Review of Japan 1978*, p. 110; *Textile Asia*, May, June, July, August, September, November 1977; Japan Economic Journal, "Synthetic Fibers," *Industrial Review of Japan 1978*, p. 112; *Daily Yomiuri*, 19 June 1977; "Scrapping of Surplus Equipment in Japanese Textile Industry," *JTN*, November 1977, pp. 14–18; and "Japan's Textile Trade Faces Tough Trial Due to High Yen," *JTN*, January 1978, pp. 14–18.

25. "Scrapping of Surplus Equipment," *JTN*, pp. 16–17.

26. On changes in the preference system, see Yamazawa, "Japan's Adjustment," pp. 451–52; and Hirai and Iwasaki, *Seni Gyokai*, pp. 162–63. For detail on MITI policy toward man-made fiber producers, see *Textile Asia*, November 1977, February, March, May 1978; *Daily News Record*, 3 March 1978; and Japan Economic Journal, "Synthetic Fibers," *Industrial Review of Japan 1978*, pp. 112–13. For detail on SDI legislation, see

cerns. During 1978, the volume of imports rose 89.7 percent and exports declined 14.6 percent. Japan's textile trade balance dropped from a surplus of 248.9 billion yen to only 12.9 billion yen. In cotton yarn alone, imports increased by 208 percent and exports decreased by 40 percent.[27] As in 1974, producer associations sought relief through appeals to Japanese textile importers as well as to foreign textile producer associations but with little success. By mid-1978, the Japan Chemical Fibers Association and the Japan Spinners Association were seeking relief through a newly formed ad-hoc import committee within the JTF. Faced with the prospect of a renewed industry consensus and subsequent appeals to the LDP or action by the spinners association under the 1976 Textile Policy Guidelines, MITI officials acted while the JTF committee was still deliberating. In July, MITI officials requested that textile importers exercise self-control in increasing imports of cotton yarn from South Korea and Pakistan.[28]

Again, MITI concessions failed to defuse the textile alliance. In August, the JTF's import committee called on state policy makers to invoke Japan's rights under the Multi-Fiber Arrangement and impose quantitative restrictions on nine specific categories of textile imports. As in 1975, the JTF deliberations had increased the interest convergence of the industrial alliance. All of the major producer associations, with the exception of the woven apparel federation, had representative products in the JTF petition. Organized labor (Zensen) in the textile industry carried the alliance's protests a step further by appealing to the Diet for legislation to restrict textile imports.[29]

Responding to industry protests, members of the LDP Textile Committee called on state policy makers to exclude textiles from the Tokyo

---

*Textile Asia*, May 1978; MITI, *Textile and Apparel Industries*, p. 17; Saxonhouse, "Industrial Restructuring," p. 314; Japan Economic Journal, "Fibers and Textiles," *Industrial Review of Japan 1979*, p. 110; and Gene Gregory, "Scrapping for Survival," *Far Eastern Economic Review*, 11 January 1980, pp. 46–47.

27. Volume and value figures were calculated from Japan Chemical Fibers Association, *Man-Made Fibers of Japan 1983/84*, pp. 88, 38–39, 40–41, 70–71. A major source of the industry's distress was a 25 percent appreciation of the yen versus the U.S. dollar during the first half of 1978 (*Textile Asia*, September 1978).

28. *JTN*, July 1978, p. 14; *Japan Times*, 13 May 1978; *Textile Asia*, July 1978; *Daily Yomiuri*, 13 May 1978; *Mainichi Daily News*, 8 September 1978; and Japan Economic Journal, "Fibers and Textiles," *Industrial Review of Japan 1979*, p. 145.

29. *Daily Yomiuri*, 10 August 1978; and *Textile Asia*, November 1978. For the Japan Spinners Association's activities outside of the JTF import group, see *JTN*, November 1978, p. 18. The committee appeared to time its recommendations to appear the same day the MITI minister convened the Industrial Structure Council and the Textile Industry Council to begin deliberations on extending the 1974 Textile Law.

Round and to rely on bilateral agreements (MFA) to protect the textile industry. Yet subsequent meetings between the textile alliance, the LDP Textile Committee, and MITI officials failed to produce overt protectionist concessions. Ministry officials rejected calls for invoking the MFA on the grounds that Japan's overall trade surplus was already leading to foreign demands that Japan increase imports. Import restrictions, sanctioned or otherwise, would incite foreign trading partners. In an interesting twist of fate, both the LDP Textile Committee and a bill in the U.S. Senate had requested that textiles be excluded from the Tokyo Round. Japanese state policy makers rejected both demands. In response to the United States, moreover, Japanese negotiators threatened to rescind earlier tariff concessions on color film and computers.[30] Appearing before a joint meeting of textile producer and labor associations, the director of MITI's Consumer Goods Industries Bureau stressed the ministry's continued support for self-control by importers of cotton yarn and confirmed that MITI Minister Toshio Komoto had called on South Korea "voluntarily" to restrict cotton yarn exports to Japan.[31] The combination of increasing alliance strength and limited activity in the Diet had finally led a Japanese state policy maker to call for quantitative restrictions on textile imports. Compared to the United States, however, Japanese state policy makers did not appear compelled by domestic pressure to hammer South Korea into accepting such a "voluntary" agreement.

Once again, these revelations did little to ease the concerns of the protectionist alliance. Nor did the textile alliance appear to be placated by the adjustment assistance measures introduced at the close of the year. In November, after only two months of study, the MITI advisory councils recommended a five-year extension of the 1974 Textile Law in hope of improving the structure of the textile industry. Citing limited participation by textile firms in the Textile Law's vertical integration programs, the councils recommended easing the eligibility requirements for state subsidies (loans) to promote such integration.[32] By December, MITI had designated the cotton spinners, wool spinners, and man-made fiber producers as "structurally depressed" and there-

30. *Mainichi Daily News*, 8 September 1978; *JTN*, November 1978, p. 18; and *Textile Asia*, November, December 1978.
31. *Textile Asia*, February 1979; *Mainichi Daily News*, 8 September 1978; and *JTN*, November 1978, p. 18.
32. For detail on the extension of the 1974 Law on Extraordinary Measures for the Structural Improvement of Textile Industries, see *Japan Times*, 9 February 1979; Ike, "Japanese Textile Industry," p. 545; and *Textile Asia*, May 1979, September 1980.

fore eligible for government-guaranteed loans to scrap excess capacity under the 1978 Structurally Depressed Industries Law.[33]

By the end of 1978 JTF and Zensen had broadened their campaigns for import restrictions to include efforts to eliminate preferential tariffs on textile goods.[34] From September through November, reports of meetings among the major synthetic fiber producers raised the prospect that the Japan Chemical Fibers Association would soon be invoking antidumping proceedings against South Korea and Taiwan. Despite claims that evidence of dumping had been obtained, the decreasing volume of imports in key yarn categories led chemical fiber officials to opt for industry-level discussions with South Korean and Taiwanese producers in early December. By 1979, the chemical fibers association joined the JTF in its attack on preferential tariffs allowed under the Generalized System of Preferences.[35]

Although the monthly monitoring system of GSP textile imports had been tightened in April 1979 to prevent abuse, customs officials were unable to cope with the rush of imports that occurred the first few days of fiscal year 1979. Synthetic fiber and yarn imports during a four-day period surged to eleven times the allowable annual quota. From the standpoint of the strength of the industrial alliance, alliance members' convergence of interest on the GSP issue was slightly less than that evident in protests concerning the MFA. The JTF's position on the GSP primarily reflected concern over cotton yarn and fabric imports, and the Japan Chemical Fibers Association was demanding the removal of man-made fiber staple and yarns from the duty-free preferential tariff list. According to one trade publication, as of mid-1979 MITI officials

33. MITI, *Textile and Apparel Industries*, p. 17; and Saxonhouse, "Industrial Restructuring," pp. 314–15. For detail on the often complex and convoluted interaction between MITI and the man-made fiber subsector on the restructuring issue, see Japan Economic Journal, "Fibers and Textiles," *Industrial Review of Japan 1979*, p. 110; Gregory, "Scrapping," pp. 46–47; *Daily News Record*, 19 September 1978; *Textile Asia*, December 1978, November 1979; *Asian Wall Street Journal*, 20 March 1979; Japan Economic Journal, "Fibers and Textiles," *Industrial Review of Japan 1980*, p. 106; and Japan Economic Journal, "Fibers and Textiles," *Industrial Review of Japan 1981*, p. 111.

34. *Textile Asia*, January 1979; and Japan Economic Journal, "Fibers and Textiles," *Industrial Review of Japan 1979*, p. 145.

35. *JTN*, November 1978, pp. 18–19; *Daily News Record*, 21 September 1978; *Daily Yomiuri*, 21 September 1978, 28 June 1979; "Synthetic Fiber Industry Examining Steps against Import Rush," *JTN*, July 1979, p. 14; and *Textile Asia*, December 1978, January, February, April 1979. The outcome of the industry-level discussions is not entirely clear. One report mentions in passing that the mission to Taiwan was successful in persuading officials in that country to "voluntarily" restrain acrylic staple exports. Yet this report contradicts the mid-1979 import rush discussed below. See *Textile Asia*, June 1979.

were responding to the association's requests and the overflow incident by studying the option of a new tariff-quota system and by planning an autumn meeting with representatives from the Ministry of Finance.[36]

As deliberations over the GSP progressed, other members of the textile alliance appealed to state officials through the textile federation. During August 1979, the Japan Spinners Association, the spun-yarn weavers association, and the JTF all requested the implementation of MFA quotas on cotton yarn and fabric imports. Zensen also echoed calls for the implementation of MFA bilateral quotas (in general and specifically on cotton yarn and fabric imports) in meetings with industry officials and in direct appeals to Diet and MITI officials. Finally, in October, the Japan Spinners Association and the Japan Cotton Staple Fibers Weaving Association agreed to put aside their inherent competitive differences to take "joint action" against steep increases in foreign imports.[37]

Faced with an increase in industrial alliance strength (resulting from increased interest convergence among alliance members) but with no accompanying increase in the degree of institutional access on the textile alliance's behalf, MITI officials rejected industry demands that textile products be removed from the GSP. Instead, MITI responded to the textile alliance by turning to a "prior quota approval" system to prevent abuse of the preferential tariff program. The system of allocating quotas to individual importers approved by the cabinet in March 1980 allowed MITI to increase control over small and medium-sized traders, which were found to be responsible for the 1979 import surge in man-made fibers, without compromising the ministry's commitment to continued liberalization. Beyond this response, MITI officials adopted a wait-and-see approach. Despite industry calls for government action against imports of cotton goods, the ministry's strategy was to rely on other JTF members whose export balances were recovering to "persuade . . . [the Japan Spinners Association] . . . to refrain from resorting to protectionist moves."[38] Such intraindustry persuasion had been successful in 1979, when members of the JTF convinced representatives

36. See "Synthetic Fiber Industry," *JTN*, p. 14; and *Daily Yomiuri*, 28 June 1979.

37. *Japan Times*, 25, 29 August 1979; *Daily News Record*, 24 September 1979; and "Japan Textile Federation Investigating MFA Revision," *JTN*, October 1979, pp. 8–20. For detail on the steps leading to the agreement between the spinners and weavers, see *Mainichi Daily News*, 26 October 1979; and *Textile Asia*, September, November 1979.

38. *Japan Economic Journal*, 8 April 1980; and Japan Economic Journal, "Fibers and Textiles," *Industrial Review of Japan 1981*, p. 110.

from the spinners association to agree, albeit reluctantly, to support the renewal of the MFA.[39]

By the end of 1980, MITI's wait-and-see approach appeared to be successful. As desired by MITI officials, the Japan Spinners Association had not moved beyond calls for action under the MFA. Moreover, imports of cotton yarn and fabric appeared to be declining slightly, thereby undercutting the spinners association's ability to press for additional action against imports under the 1976 Textile Policy Guidelines.[40] Yet state policy makers still faced domestic pressure. The improving export conditions for other portions of the textile industry had not diminished the alliance's efforts for Japan to exercise bilateral quotas under the MFA.[41] In addition, although the textile alliance's strength had remained unchanged, MITI officials were unable to prevent an increase in institutional access on the alliance's behalf in December 1980.

Instead of increased pressure from the Diet, MITI officials were subject to the jurisdiction of the Ministry of Finance. The ministry's Tariff Council qualified its recommendation for an extension of the GSP by recommending the suspension of preferential tariffs on portions of the textile industry in which imports had inhibited the ability of domestic producers to "make both ends meet." Aside from silk yarns, these portions consisted of cotton yarn, cotton fabric, and cotton pile fabric. Acting on the Tariff Council's recommendation, the Ministry of Finance suspended the preferential tariff on cotton yarn and fabric effective fiscal year 1981.[42] Thus despite the rejection of such a move months earlier by MITI officials as well as the international scrutiny placed on Japan by the pending renegotiation of the MFA, state policy makers were unable to prevent a policy concession more overt than those granted in the past.

39. Japan Economic Journal, "Fibers and Textiles," *Industrial Review of Japan 1981*, p. 110; and *Women's Wear Daily*, 15 December 1979, 31 January 1980. The first two sources disagree on the date of the spinners association's approval of MFA extension. The first cites late 1980, the second, late 1979. Unless two separate incidents occurred, the second date seems more plausible in light of a unanimous resolution on the MFA passed by the industry in January 1980.

40. Japan Chemical Fibers Association, *Fiber 1983/84*, pp. 70–71.

41. Industry representatives on the Japan Textile Council (Textile Industry Council), for example, called upon Japanese representatives to the GATT Textile Committee to press for modifications in the MFA that would facilitate Japan's use of quantitative restrictions. The Textile Council specifically requested a looser definition of market disruption than that which required consideration of overall bilateral trade surpluses. See *Textile Asia*, June 1981; *Women's Wear Daily*, 31 January 1980; *Japan Times*, 2 August 1980; *Asian Wall Street Journal*, 5 May 1981; and "International Textile Agreement and Japan's Standpoint," *JTN*, September 1981, pp. 28–29.

42. *Daily Yomiuri*, 21 December 1980; and Yamazawa, "Japan's Adjustment."

*Case 3: 1981–1983*

Ronald Dore has argued that the GSP exemptions for the textile industry "seemed largely to have satisfied protectionist instincts" in 1981. Moreover, Dore notes that textile industry pressure for import relief did not reemerge until the Japan Spinners Association became active in late 1983.[43] This image of a two-year hiatus in the textile industry's disputes with state policy makers is extremely misleading. The modification of the GSP merely shifted the industrial alliance's demands back to the Multi-Fiber Arrangement.

Through 1981, the Japan Spinners Association and the MFA sub-committee of the JTF continued to appeal for quantitative restrictions. In the absence of institutional access on the behalf of the textile alliance, MITI's response was to "study" the federation's requests and to ease pressures on the spinners as nonovertly as possible.[44] From May through September, MITI and the FTC acceded to the spinners association's requests for a recession cartel. To facilitate the cartel, MITI officials introduced limited surveillance of thirty-five cotton yarn importers and forty cotton fabric importers. The significance of this package should not be overstated. MITI officials justified the surveillance as a means to monitor real import growth rates and thereby ensure that the rate of production cuts authorized by the cartel would be effective in improving demand.[45] Moreover, as inventories and prices improved during the fourth quarter of 1981, imports of cotton yarn from South Korea and Pakistan surged to record levels. Despite requests for relief by the spinners association and other industry representatives in early 1982, MITI Minister Shintaro Abe rejected the use of quantitative restrictions.[46]

The dispute between the textile alliance and state policy makers shifted to a new access channel in mid-1982. Acting on the recommen-

43. Dore, *Flexible Rigidities*, p. 241.

44. *Japan Economic Journal*, 28 July 1981; *Textile Asia*, June, September 1981; and "International Textile Agreement and Japan's Standpoint," *JTN*, September 1981, pp. 28–29.

45. Dore, *Flexible Rigidities*, pp. 199-202; "Cotton Spinners Extend Anti-depression Cartel until September," *JTN*, September 1981, p. 8; Japan Economic Journal, "Fibers and Textiles," *Industrial Review of Japan 1982*, p. 116; and *Textile Asia*, September 1981.

46. Japan Economic Journal, "Fibers and Textiles," *Industrial Review of Japan 1982*, p. 116; and *Textile Asia*, February, March, April 1982. According to *Textile Asia*, the minister remained committed to the use of administrative guidance to maintain orderly imports. The trade journal also reported that the head of MITI's spinning section had visited South Korea in December but only to discuss import trends in polyester yarn and fabric.

dations of the MITI minister, the Industrial Structure Council and Textile Industry Council established a joint advisory committee to develop guidelines for the Japanese textile industry in the 1980s and beyond. Of the various issues to be addressed by specialized subcommittees, the areas of greatest contention were trade and adjustment assistance measures. In light of recent import trends, the issue of import competition and MITI's reluctance to protect domestic producers were rallying points for the industrial alliance. In the area of adjustment assistance, MITI's desire to reorganize the capacity registration system had also been strongly resisted by small and medium-sized textile producers since MITI proposed such a move in the 1976 Textile Policy Guidelines. The registration system had been introduced under the 1956 Old Textile Act; it empowered MITI officials to "regulate" spinning and weaving capacity through purchases of surplus equipment and the registration of spindles and looms to "discourage further installation." The system set an overall level of allowable spindles and looms and committed the government to purchase surplus equipment.[47]

Discussions in the advisory subcommittees soon revealed that although the core members of the JTF all agreed that MITI officials should invoke the MFA, there was no industrywide consensus on the conditions under which this step should be taken. The Japan Cotton Staple Fibers Weavers Association called for an import ceiling of 10 percent of domestic production to avoid interfering with government-aided restructuring of industry. Zensen representatives called for an import ceiling set at 20 to 25 percent of textile consumption to ensure the long-term survival of the Japanese worker. The Japan Spinners Association and the Japan Chemical Fibers Association demanded concrete steps on import surges but were willing to accept gradual import increases without ceilings. Apparel association representatives, although supportive of the MFA, did not take a strong stand in favor of import restrictions. The combination of disagreements within the textile alliance and the opposition of MITI representatives to any form of restriction resulted in an interim consensus to extend the import regulations introduced in 1976. Since a number of producer associations saw the existing guidelines as being either too limited or merely

---

47. *Mainichi Daily News*, 9 June 1982; and interview held in Tokyo, Japan, April 1984. For detail on the capacity registration system, see MITI, *Textile and Apparel Industries*, p. 13; Ike, "Japanese Textile Industry," p. 539; Hirai and Iwasaki, *Seni Gyokai*, p. 158; and Hornbeck, *Japanese Textile Industry*, p. 20.

"MITI lip service" on the MFA, this consensus was strained.[48] In the absence of increases in the strength of the industrial alliance or in the degree of institutional access, state policy makers had held firm.

The interim recommendations prompted a number of producer associations to make individual demands for import relief outside of the advisory subcommittees.[49] The spinners association also switched tactics by attempting to increase its institutional access to state policy makers. To forestall such a possibility, MITI officials had adopted a limited administrative guidance package in July 1982. Following continued increases in the pace of import contracts for cotton yarn during the first quarter of 1982, as well as estimated increases for April and May, MITI officials had decided to "review and slow" the pace of import contracts.[50] These measures and the interim result of discussions within the import advisory committee, however, failed to ease the Japan Spinners Association's concerns over cotton yarn imports.

On December 11, 1982, the spinners association notified MITI of a plan to petition the Ministry of Finance to institute an antidumping suit against South Korea and a countervailing duty suit against Pakistan. The initial response of MITI officials was to cite the need for "cautious action." On December 21, the ministry announced that it refused to engage in bilateral discussions to restrain imports with either South Korea or Pakistan. The Japan Spinners Association responded by filing suit with the Ministry of Finance in late December. This first actual use of Japan's dumping and countervailing duty laws and the presence of other industries such as steel waiting to file similar actions prompted officials from MITI and the Ministry of Finance to move slowly.[51]

Neither ministry dismissed the Japan Spinners Association's suits at the beginning of the proceedings, which strengthened the spinners association's bargaining position abroad. MITI's consideration of the spinners association's claim created a credible threat of government

48. Interview held in Tokyo, Japan, April 1984; JCSEWA, "Weavers Association Submits Its Opinion Paper to Joint Policy Subcommittee," *Cotton Staple Fiber Information*, 21 September 1982; and *Japan Times*, 23 November 1982. For details on the interim report, see *Textile Asia*, February 1983.

49. For example, the spun-yarn weavers association demanded quotas on imports of Chinese cotton fabric. The Japan Knitting Industry Association called for import surveillance and administrative guidance on sweater imports (*Japan Times*, 23 November 1982; Japan Economic Journal, "Fibers and Textiles," *Industrial Review of Japan 1983*, pp. 114–15; and *Textile Asia*, January 1983).

50. "MITI to Strengthen Guidance on Cotton Yarn Imports," *JTN*, July 1982, p. 17.

51. *Asian Wall Street Journal*, 23 December 1982; *Textile Asia*, January, February 1983; Japan Economic Journal, "Fibers and Textiles," *Industrial Review of Japan 1983*, pp. 114–15; *Mainichi Daily News*, 10 December 1982, 12 January 1983; *Wall Street Journal*, 16 December 1982; and Yamazawa, "Japan's Adjustment."

trade action despite the reluctance of MITI officials to assume such a role. Weighing the costs of an unfavorable Japanese government finding against the costs of voluntary self-restriction, both South Korea and Pakistan opted for that course. In March 1983, Korean textile producers accepted a voluntary export restraint negotiated through meetings with the Japan Spinners Association. MITI's February 1983 decision to pursue a formal investigation against Pakistan also increased the spinners association's leverage in interindustry negotiations. In August, Pakistan eliminated the export rebate program that had prompted the countervailing duty suit. In light of these responses and the slow pace of the ongoing investigations, the spinners association eventually dropped both suits.[52] At first glance MITI officials appear to have avoided overt, formal concessions to the protectionist alliance. Yet by not objecting to the Japan Spinners Association's agreement with South Korea, MITI officials had tacitly approved the first nonunilateral quantitative restriction on textile imports since the emergence of the textile alliance in 1974.

Meanwhile, changes were taking place in the advisory subcommittees that reconvened in early 1983. Industry analysts participating in the deliberations had taken steps to break the MITI-industry deadlock by placing the issue of protection in the context of overall trade balances, Western criticism, and the poor competitiveness of the protected Japanese silk industry.[53] Reaching a consensus in the advisory subcommittees required alliance members to make concessions and at the same time increased the degree of institutional access to state policy makers. Textile alliance members were asked to choose between direct protection and indirect protection (adjustment assistance). MITI officials would have to acknowledge these choices. The Japan Spinners Association and the Japan Chemical Fibers Association opted for concrete steps to check import surges. In the past, both associations had had only limited reliance on adjustment assistance, and they wanted to dismantle

52. The South Korean textile association agreed to hold yarn exports to an annual limit of 270,000 bales for three years, roughly 4.2 percent less than the past five-year average for such exports to Japan. The case against South Korea was dropped in April 1983 and the case against Pakistan in February 1984 (following completion of Pakistani loans to cotton producers in January). Despite Pakistan's compliance on the countervailing duty issue, the Japan Spinners Association still wanted to press Pakistan to follow the Korean example of self-restraint. See *Textile Asia*, May, June, September, November 1983; *Japan Economic Journal*, 26 April 1983; interviews held in Tokyo, Japan, April and May 1984; Japan Economic Journal, "Fibers and Textiles," *Industrial Review of Japan 1984*, p. 122; and Dore, *Flexible Rigidities*, pp. 203–4.
53. This section relies heavily on an interview held in Tokyo, Japan, April 1984.

the capacity registration system to facilitate the expansion of their own weaving operations. In contrast, associations representing small and medium-sized producers reluctantly requested adjustment assistance alone, especially the strengthening of the capacity registration system.[54]

Although the textile alliance was now split over what protectionist policy it favored, the convergence of interest within these two camps was the strongest it had been since MITI's reorganization in 1973. The division was also artificial in that the producer associations that chose adjustment assistance were for the most part not opposed to more overt protectionist policies. Thus, although the Japan Spinners Association and the Japan Chemical Fibers Association accounted for only a small portion of the industry, they were implicitly supported by the rest of the alliance. Thus, though the alliance's strength did not appear to have increased greatly, it was not clear that it had decreased through the advisory committee deliberations.

The guidelines for textile policy revealed in the October 1983 *Vision for the Textile Industry in a New Age* reflected a slightly stronger textile alliance and a slight increase in the degree of institutional access. The guidelines included protectionist concessions on items for which MITI officials opposed protection. They vaguely addressed two import issues that had been of primary concern to the Japan Spinners Association and the Japan Chemical Fibers Association: they called for the use of GATT rules in the case of substantial damage to an industry as a result of "cheap sales" and the use of emergency, temporary MFA quotas in cases of "serious damage" caused by rapid increases in imports. The new guidelines retained the financial assistance measures contained in the capacity registration system and included a vague proposal that the weaving capacity registration programs "should end" sometime in the future. This statement contrasted with the 1976 Textile Policy Guidelines' explicit call for a "phased abolition" of the capacity registration system.[55] In sum, faced with a strong textile alliance and a slight

54. The small and medium-sized firms were primarily represented by the Japan Cotton Staple Fiber Weavers Association, the Japan Silk and Rayon Fibers Weavers Association, and the Japan Knitting Industry Association. By their decision in the advisory council, the spinning and man-made fiber producer associations were not closing the door on adjustment assistance measures. The revised Structurally Depressed Industries Law introduced in May 1983, for example, included explicit coverage for synthetic fiber producers (*Japan Economic Journal*, 31 May 1983).

55. For detail on the guidelines see Japan Economic Journal, "Fibers and Textiles," *Industrial Review of Japan 1984*, p. 122; *Japan Economic Journal*, 8 November 1983; and Textile Industry Council and Industry Structure Council, *Vision for the Textile Industry in a New Age: Towards the Developed Country Industry* (in Japanese), 31 October 1983. Aside from these exceptions, the Textile Vision clearly overlapped with the 1976 guidelines. Pro-

increase in the degree of institutional access, the textile alliance obtained slight protectionist concessions over MITI opposition.

CONCLUSION

From 1974 to 1983, state policy makers and industrial alliances engaged in three major disputes over Japanese textile trade policy. As in the previous chapter, all three cases support the hypothesis that, faced with increasing domestic pressure, state policy makers will act against the dictates of international constraints. Using the indexes developed in the Appendix, Table 6 traces the interaction between domestic pressure and international constraint.

During the time periods of all three Japanese cases, international constraints remained constant (the slight variation in 1978 was the sole exception). Trade as a percentage of GNP hovered between 18.4 and 26 percent, suggesting a vulnerability to retaliation much greater than that of the United States but still at a low to low + level when compared with a broader sampling of postwar industrialized countries. Japan was a marginal supporter surrounded by a multilateral supportership, and its policy makers faced an extremely high threat that trading partners would retaliate in the event of overt protectionist action. Concerns with the threat of retaliation are clearly evident in the responses of MITI to demands from the industrial alliance for overt action against imports.

The combined international economic constraint overshadowed political-military constraints on trade policy choices. Since overt protectionist measures in textile trade policy would come primarily at the expense of East and Southeast Asian exporters, Japan's political-military relations with low-level allies might be disrupted. So long as the United States did not use arguments linking Japanese textile import policy and broader American-Japanese relations, Japanese state policy makers would not face the greater political-military constraint of increased tensions with a strategic ally.

Despite the consistent international constraints, state policy makers

---

grams for gathering and distributing information to importers noted in the new measures were similar to import surveillance. Bilateral opinion sharing with exporters prior to disputes restated the ministry's commitment to unofficial consultations. The new guidelines also pledged to use the Textile Industry Council's Demand and Supply Trade Group, which was created under the 1976 guidelines. See Chapter 5 of the Vision Report, "Securing Smooth Trade Relationship." The strong similarity between the 1976 guidelines and the new textile Vision was also noted by the industry associations (interview held in Tokyo, Japan, April 1984).

*Table 6.* Japanese textile trade policy, case summary

| Case | Domestic pressure | | International constraint | | |
|------|-------------------|------|--------------|--------|-------------------|
| | IAS | DIA | Vulnerability | Threat | Political-military |
| *Case 1* | | | | | |
| 1974 | Mod/Mod − | Low − | Low + | High + | Low |
| 1975 | High | Mod −/Low + | Low + | High + | Low |
| 1976 | High | Low + | Low + | High + | Low |
| Outcome: Administrative restrictions (1975) | | | | | |
| *Case 2* | | | | | |
| 1977 | Low | Low − | Low + | High + | Low |
| 1978 | High | Low + | Low | High + | Low |
| 1979 | High | Low + | Low + | High + | Low |
| 1980 | High | High | Low + | High + | Low |
| 1981 | High | High + | Low + | HIgh + | Low |
| Outcome: Price-based restrictions (1981) | | | | | |
| *Case 3* | | | | | |
| 1981 | High | Low − | Low + | High + | Low |
| 1982 | High/High − | Mod + [a] | Low + | High + | Low |
| 1983 | High/High − | Mod + [a] | Low + | High + | Low |
| Outcome: Nonunilateral quantitative restrictions (1983) | | | | | |

*Note:* The indicator scores are based on the highest level reached in a given year. Abbreviations are used here for industrial alliance strength (IAS) and the degree of institutional access (DIA). The policy outcomes are the most overt types of protectionist policy adopted in the given case study period. For more detail on ranking procedure, see Appendix.

[a] This ranking refers to the initiation of the Japan Spinners Association's antidumping and countervailing duty suits. Since these measures had never been invoked, it is not clear to what extent a successful ruling would be seen as binding on state policy makers' action. I code the advisory council deliberations during 1982 as Mod − (strong potential for hostage) and during 1983 as Mod (state policy maker initiative held hostage).

did not make consistent choices. Administrative restrictions in 1975 gave way to GSP exemptions for cotton textiles in 1981 (reimposing a price-based restriction) and to tacit approval of an interindustry negotiated voluntary export restraint in 1983. Once again, international constraints had not changed; domestic pressures had.

Domestic pressures on state policy makers were sparked by the refusal of textile producer associations to accept rapid surges in textile imports. During 1974, the textile alliance failed to overcome problems with interest convergence and alliance organization. By 1975, however, the Japan Textile Federation's ability to help coordinate a consensus position on the need for concrete action against imports had markedly increased the industrial alliance's strength. Institutional access on behalf of the textile alliance also increased during the period of the first

Japanese case study. Acting on the nonbinding recommendations of the Fair Trade Commission in early 1975, MITI officials introduced a limited import surveillance package as a form of administrative restriction on imports. By April 1975, MITI officials faced pressure from the LDP Textile Committee, the LDP's Diet leadership, and cabinet officials. Yet the degree of institutional access never progressed beyond that point. The ministry's success in separating the silk question from textile industry problems in the minds of Diet officials quieted Diet protests during the Textile Industry Council deliberations. As a result, the 1976 Textile Policy Guidelines were much less overt than the lower advisory council recommendations revealed in late 1975.

In Case 2, the textile alliance quickly regained the levels of industrial alliance strength achieved during the early 1970s. Instead of repeating earlier demands for concrete action such as increases in textile tariffs, however, the JTF played an important role in helping to coordinate industry positions on the MFA and GSP. Having experienced the impact of the last JTF consensus in 1975, MITI officials quickly turned to administrative restrictions while the JTF's ad hoc import committee was still in session. Subsequent reports of MITI calls for self-restraint by South Korea also appeared to stem the spread of institutional access on behalf of the textile alliance. Until 1980, state supporters of the textile industry were primarily limited to the LDP Textile Committee. Yet overlapping jurisdiction with the Ministry of Finance proved to be a source of domestic pressure in early 1981 which MITI officials were unable to circumvent. After successfully holding off the textile alliance's demands in March 1980, MITI officials were forced to accept GSP exemptions for selected textile products in 1981.

State policy makers faced a strong industrial alliance during the entirety of the third Japanese case study. MITI efforts to divide the industrial alliance in advisory council deliberations appear to have had no significant impact on the alliance's strength. In contrast, this case study reveals how the need for consensus within MITI's advisory committees can constrain the action of state policy makers. Despite opposition to the industrial alliance's demands for import protection and state subsidies through the capacity registration system, the need for a government-industry consensus acted as an important source of institutional access to policy makers. The two petitions raised by the Japan Spinners Association, however, acted as a greater source of institutional access. Since these procedures had never been invoked, the spinners association had embarked on a new phase in the industry's relationship with MITI. Despite the long unwillingness of MITI officials to use the threat of government action as a bargaining chip in negotiations with foreign exporters over textile products, the antidumping and countervailing duty suits raised by the spinners association put MITI in the very position it had attempted to avoid. In the end, the Japan Spinners Association partially allowed MITI off the hook by settling for the ministry's tacit acceptance of interindustry negotiated quantitative restrictions.

Finally, these three case studies raise several questions about the predominant theoretical approaches in the political economy literature. Arguments based on international economic structure would suggest that Japan as a spoiler in a multilateral supportership should not have been dissuaded by threats of retaliation from turning to overt types of protectionist policy. This prediction is most accurate for the second Japanese case study. Yet as a marginal supporter, Japan should have avoided the overt types of protectionist policy adopted in the second and third case studies.

International regime approaches also have difficulty in explaining Japan's actions. During the period 1974 to 1983, Japan participated in the renegotiation of two sets of international trade agreements. In addition to negotiations on tariff and nontariff barriers under the Tokyo Round from 1975 to 1979, Japan was active in the negotiations over three successive versions of the MFA. Ironically, the international regime in textiles was becoming more permissive. The MFA's introduction in 1974 allowed the use of nonunilateral quantitative restrictions on cotton, wool, and synthetic textile imports. Subsequent versions of the MFA increased the ability of importing countries to invoke protectionist measures.[56] Yet in all three case studies, Japanese state policy makers refused to exercise their country's rights under the MFA.

According to statist arguments, the "strong" Japanese state should have been able to alter societal structure and at least resist societal pressure. The record here is mixed. Efforts to restructure the textile industry did occur under the 1974 Textile Law, the 1978 Structurally Depressed Industries Law, the 1979 extension of the 1974 law, and the 1983 Vision. In all of these instances state policy makers were most successful when producer associations and MITI officials agreed on the direction of policy. If disagreements occurred, such as in MITI's attempts to alter the capacity registration system, the Japanese state did not match the predictions of the statist approach. Moreover, it is clear that MITI officials are limited in their ability to resist societal pressures. Although avoiding the MFA, state policy makers were unable to avoid the use of administrative restrictions, price-based restrictions, and the

56. Aggarwal, *Liberal Protectionism*, pp. 23–25.

tacit approval of nonunilateral quantitative restrictions. Finally, at a broad level Japanese trade policy choices are predicted by domestic structure arguments. In contrast to the United States, Japanese state policy makers have relied sparingly on overt protectionist measures and have emphasized policies of structural adjustment. An adequate explanation of the specific policies chosen by Japan, however, requires a more nuanced, integrative approach.

# CHAPTER SIX

# West German Textile Trade Policy

For West German state policy makers during the 1960s and early 1970s, promoting open international trade was an integral step for moving beyond the "economic miracle" of the 1950s. Poised between Eastern and Western Europe, West Germany sought integration with both. Markets for exports beckoned in the European Economic Community as long as West Germany could counterbalance protectionist trends in Italy and France. Economic opportunities were also evident in the relatively untapped markets of Eastern Europe. More important, liberal trade policy began to emerge as a means to "rebuild political relations with Eastern Europe and the Soviet Union."[1] Despite the linkage between integration and liberalization, however, West German state policy makers not only backed down on attempts to remove existing textile trade barriers but also granted new quantitative restrictions to a protectionist textile alliance.

What explains the types of protectionist policy chosen during this period? This chapter sets out the international constraints faced by West German state policy makers and analyzes three cases in which industrial alliances demanded action contrary to that dictated by such constraints.

## INTERNATIONAL CONSTRAINTS

West German international economic constraints illustrate a different pattern from those seen in either the United States or Japan. Of the

1. Spero, *The Politics of International Economic Relations*, p. 304.

three countries, West Germany was the most vulnerable to retaliation. The postwar division of Germany had left West Germany with two-thirds of the country's prewar industrial capacity but less than half the domestic market. As a result, postwar industrial recovery and continued growth required access to open foreign markets. West Germany's reliance on export-oriented growth produced an economic miracle during the 1950s but at the price of an entrenched industrial dependence on the export economy. From 1963 to 1969, exports as a percentage of GNP averaged 16.9 percent compared to 3.8 percent for the United States and 11.9 percent for Japan. West German dependence on foreign trade, as measured by trade as a percentage of GNP, averaged 31.6 percent.[2]

Although West German state policy makers had the most to lose in the event of retaliation, they faced a weaker systemic threat that retaliation would occur than did either the United States or Japan. The difference lies in the international economic structure and West Germany's position in that structure during the period of the case studies discussed in this chapter. Hegemony theorists see the 1960s as a transitional period for the international economic structure and the position of the United States in that structure. Lake has argued, for example, that in 1965 the international economic structure shifted from one of hegemonic leadership to a "bilateral supportership" between the United States and West Germany.

By 1963–64, West Germany's economic recovery had pushed the country to the borderline between spoiler and supporter status from the standpoint of international competitiveness. For a supporter in a hegemonic system, the threat of retaliation is mitigated, in part, by the hegemon's concerns with maintaining its leadership of the international economy. At the same time, however, the "size of the sanction" (or side payment) necessary for the hegemon to dissuade the supporter from overt protectionist action is smaller than that needed for dealing with a spoiler since the supporter has a greater stake in free trade. In other words, as the single supporter, and a borderline supporter at that, West Germany would have a difficult time in free-riding on the American hegemony.

For the post-1965 period of the West German case studies, a key question is whether the United States had ceased to be a hegemonic power or had simply become a weaker hegemon. By Lake's criteria that

2. Kreile, "West Germany," p. 192; and Wilhelm Hankel, "West Germany," in Wilfrid L. Kohl, ed., *Economic Foreign Policies of Industrial States* (Lexington, Mass.: Lexington Books, 1977), pp. 107–8. Figures on trade dependence were calculated from International Monetary Fund, *International Financial Statistics*, selected issues.

a hegemon must account for a minimum 15 percent of world trade, the United States falls less than 1 percentage point short of hegemonic status. This ranking alone is not decisive. But the United States by the mid-1960s clearly did not dominate the world economy to the extent that it did during the 1950s or early 1960s. With West Germany a supporter facing a declining hegemon, therefore, its policy makers faced a greater threat of retaliation than in the early 1960s. Whereas a supporter may face less of a threat of retaliation in an international economic structure dominated by a hegemon, in a bilateral supportership each supporter faces the prospect that extensive protectionist action will lead the other supporter to follow suit, a situation relevant to the second half of the decade.[3] Based on these considerations, I set the threat of retaliation faced by West German state policy makers from 1965 to 1969 as roughly equivalent to that faced by a supporter in a bilateral supportership (an increase from low+ to moderate).

*Table 7.* Economic structure of the EEC, 1960s

|  | 1963 | | 1969 | |
|---|---|---|---|---|
|  | PT (percent) | RP | PT (percent) | RP |
| West Germany | 30.9 | 1.04 | 30.8 | 1.01 |
| France | 19.6 | 1.43 | 21.7 | 1.21 |
| Italy | 13.6 | 0.65 | 13.5 | 0.63 |
| Netherlands | 18.1 | 0.91 | 16.8 | 1.12 |
| Belgium/Luxembourg | 17.8 | 0.98 | 17.2 | 1.04 |

*Note:* Percentage of intra-EEC trade (PT) calculated from Statistical Office of the European Communities (Eurostat), *Basic Statistics of the Community, 1970* (Luxembourg: Office for Official Publications of the European Community, 1971), pp. 80–81, 84–85. Rough cutoffs for distinguishing "supporters" from "hegemonic leaders" are 10 percent and 25 percent respectively. The higher cutoff points reflect the smaller number of countries in the regional economic system. Relative productivity data (RP) are based on productivity scores calculated as output divided by employment for manufacturing (including mining and construction). Following Lake, "spoilers" are distinguished by RP scores below the average. RP scores calculated from Eurostat, *Basic Statistics of the Community, 1970*, p. 22; and Peter Flora, Franz Kraus, and Winfred Pfenning, *State, Economy, and Society in Western Europe, 1815–1975*, vol. 2, *The Growth of Industrial Societies and Capitalist Economies* (Chicago: St. James Press, 1987), pp. 405–24, 468–569.

West German state policy makers were not solely concerned with the retaliation from the United States. Such concerns were also at issue on the regional level, a dimension not addressed in any great detail by hegemony scholars. As illustrated in Table 7, the European Economic Community during the 1960s was in a situation of hegemonic leader-

3. Lake, "Beneath the Commerce of Nations," pp. 153–56, 164.

ship. West Germany's share of EEC trade during this period remained significantly greater than that held by other EEC members. Based on intra-EEC trade and average EEC manufacturing productivity, the German hegemony contrasted with the supporter status of France and the spoiler status of Italy. The smaller members of the EEC evolved from spoiler to supporter status during the decade.

As a regional hegemonic power, West Germany faced a clear threat of retaliation in the event of overt protectionist action. To avoid retaliation, West Germany would have either to refrain from such steps or rely on side payments or sanctions to the other members of the EEC. West Germany's vulnerability to retaliation suggests that its policy makers would not favor promoting increased closure through the use of sanctions. Moreover, as only a regional hegemon, West Germany would lack the resources for extensive side payments. Thus, from an economic standpoint, the combination of vulnerability and threat of retaliation (regional as well as international) appeared to rule against the use of overt protectionist policies.

As was true in the United States, international economic considerations were also nested in broader political-military concerns. Whereas American state policy makers saw the broad threat of communist expansion as constraining trade policy choices, West German policy makers were concerned with the impact of trade policy choices on relations with Eastern Europe. By the early 1960s, tension between East and West had produced a decade of Cold War politics, blockades, airlifts, and the Berlin Crisis. West Germany's refusal under the Hallstein Doctrine to maintain formal diplomatic relations with those countries that recognized East Germany had isolated West Germany from Eastern Europe and had become a source of strain within the NATO alliance. Isolation had done little either to reunify Germany or to loosen the Eastern bloc from its support of the Soviet Union in the Cold War.

Faced with this political-military reality, West Germany turned to unofficial trade relations as a means to rebuild contact with Eastern Europe. Michael Kreile has argued that until the mid-1960s, the predominant focus of West Germany's Eastern trade efforts was the reunification of Germany. By 1963, however, state policy makers had begun to expand trade and cooperation agreements to include a number of Eastern European countries. Similar agreements continued through the 1960s and 1970s as part of an active policy of Ostpolitik. Although reluctantly recognizing East Germany as a separate entity in 1972, West German state policy makers continued to emphasize trade policy as a tool to build political ties and reduce tensions.[4] Such political-military considerations ruled against the use of overt protectionist action, especially against the relatively labor-intensive products that characterized Eastern European exports.

Given international constraints against the use of overt types of protectionist policy, to what extent did West German state policy makers favor the use of indirect measures against imports? Once again, West Germany's experience contrasts with that of the United States and Japan. In reaction to the World War II integration of state and society, West Germany's postwar "social market economy" called for limiting state intervention to maintaining economic "order" while leaving "process" to market forces. To ensure order, the state was to focus on maintaining price stability (extended following 1967 to a state focus on investment and wages) and on promoting competition through temporary intervention in the economy. Industry-specific programs were more the exception than the rule. Assistance measures were aimed at promoting the development of regions along the East German border and at encouraging cooperation and rationalization among West German producers. All such measures were open to textile producers. Thus West German state policy makers lacked the aversion to indirect measures characteristic of the United States but at the same time avoided the detailed restructuring legislation adopted by Japan.[5]

CASES

The textile alliance's demands for state policy makers to act on textile trade reflected concerns over actual and threatened increases of "distorted" imports. These distortions included dumping by "low-price" exporters, prices set by nonmarket economies, subsidies on goods produced in

3. Lake, "Beneath the Commerce of Nations," pp. 153–56, 164.
4. Kreile, "West Germany," pp. 204–8; Lehmann, *Chronik der Bundesrepublik Deutschland*, pp. 102–5; and Samuel Pisar, *Coexistence and Commerce: Guidelines for Transactions between East and West* (New York: McGraw-Hill, 1970), p. 60. To facilitate such contacts, the Ostausschuss (Eastern Committee of the German Economy, Ostausschuss der deutschen Wirtschaft) was established in 1952 by the peak industry, trade, and banking associations. The committee's task was to advise the government (and take action) on East-West economic relations in the absence of formal diplomatic recognition of East Germany and Eastern Europe (Kreile, "West Germany," pp. 204–6).
5. Hankel, "West Germany," p. 109; K. H. F. Dyson, "The Politics of Economic Management in West Germany," in Andrei Markovitz, ed., *The Political Economy of West Germany: Modell Deutschland* (New York: Praeger, 1982), pp. 37, 50–54; and Peter J. Katzenstein, *Policy and Politics in West Germany: The Growth of a Semisovereign State* (Philadelphia: Temple University Press, 1987), pp. 83–92.

other EEC countries, and imports diverted to West Germany by the protectionist actions of other countries. Faced with such threats, West German producer associations attempted to paint themselves as supporters of free trade while at the same time demanding protection. Textile associations repeatedly denied that the West German textile industry was protectionist, calling instead on state policy makers to ensure "fair trade" in light of competitive distortions in the international arena. The requisite steps to bring about fairness were not always clear. Textile producers were reluctant to give up the protection they already had, which, in addition to tariffs, consisted of quantitative restrictions carried over from the days of West Germany's balance-of-payments difficulties. With the introduction of the STA and LTA on cotton textiles during the early 1960s, many of the old quotas had been replaced without a confrontation with the domestic textile industry.[6] Because of political difficulties with Eastern Europe, the textile industry began its first major period of competition from imports with quantitative restrictions on Eastern European goods already in place.

In a sense, the West German situation resembles that of the United States before the revelation of the results of the secret tariff negotiations with Japan. The major textile trade policy disputes in West Germany were not fundamentally over increasing protection. Rather, the textile alliance arose to defend that which it already had against the repeated attempts by state policy makers to accelerate the liberalization of textile trade for broader economic and political purposes. The first West German case study details the events leading up to the unilateral West German tariff cuts of 1964. The second case study analyzes state policy maker's attempts to liberalize trade with Eastern Europe. The final case study details the dispute over liberalization measures introduced to forestall revaluation.

### Case 1: 1963–1964

In contrast to the impending death images raised by a relatively healthy textile industry suffering from low government priority during the 1950s, the West German textile industry of the early 1960s stressed its role as an important industry in the throes of structural change.[7] Until 1964, the West German textile alliance consisted primarily of

6. The origins of existing quantitative restrictions are discussed in greater detail in the conclusion to this chapter.

7. The industry's new choice of image reflected the government's focus on technical progress. See Wilfred Wunden, *Die Textilindustrie der Bundesrepublik Deutschland im Strukturwandel* (Tübingen: J. C. B. Mohr [Paul Siebeck], 1969), p. 146.

Gesamttextil, often vocally supported by several of the peak association's subsectoral and regional members. The textile alliance's demands centered on the need for state action against competitive distortions by the other members of the EEC and the need for greater protection against goods being dumped on the West German market. The gradual reduction of tariff rates required for West Germany's integration into the EEC was not disputed by the textile alliance. State policy makers in the BMWi (Bundesministerium für Wirtschaft, Federal Ministry of Economics) voiced support for the industry's concerns. Yet the textile alliance felt that BMWi officials needed to take more concrete and more rapid action.[8] Against this backdrop, state policy makers attempted to accelerate the pace of trade liberalization within the EEC.

By early 1963, Gesamttextil representatives and Länder officials were seriously questioning the federal government's commitment to action against competitive distortions. Despite earlier BMWi promises, viable antidumping measures and steps to compensate German producers for the impact of differential tax burdens among EEC members (compensation through shipments equalization taxes on imports) had yet to appear.[9] In an effort to ease these concerns, BMWi's Minister Ludwig Erhard met with industry and regional officials and pledged to take "drastic steps" in proven dumping cases. Erhard also pledged to assist industry adjustment through modifying financial, credit, and cartel legislation. By April 1963, the Bundesrat had approved a promised alteration in the shipments equalization tax law allowing an increase in shipments taxes on imports of textiles, steel, and paper products. In the Bundestag, however, proposals were emerging that appeared to challenge Erhard's commitment to liberalization. The Bundestag Foreign Trade Committee recommended that internal EEC textile tariffs be reduced by 5 percent instead of the 10 percent mandated for 1963. A number of Bundestag officials also began to consider retroactive antidumping measures.[10]

---

8. Protests came from regional associations primarily in northern Bavaria, Baden-Württemberg, and North Rhine–Westphalia. Protests from subsectoral associations were primarily from cotton weavers and jute textile producers. For examples of regional association and Gesamttextil protests during 1961–62, see *Industrie Kurier*, 6, 14, 21 June 1961, 9 October 1962; *Nachrichten für Aussenhandel*, 1 June, 12 August 1961; *Frankfurter Allgemeine Zeitung*, 2 February 1961, 7, 15 May, 15 June 1962; and *Die Welt*, 2 April 1962.

9. *Nachrichten für Aussenhandel*, 15 June 1962; *Die Welt*, 2 April 1962; *Frankfurter Allgemeine Zeitung*, 6 July 1962; *Handelsblatt*, 5 July 1962; and *Textil-Zeitung*, 4 January, 15 March 1963.

10. *Textil-Zeitung*, 4, 13 March, 10 April 1963, 1 June 1964; *Textil-Mitteilungen*, 8 May 1963. The modified tariff reduction was approved by the Bundestag with no apparent BMWi opposition in June. In contrast, the retroactive dumping proposal was opposed by

Unwilling to wait for either BMWi promises or Bundestag steps to materialize, and facing mounting protests from regional and subsectoral associations, Länder authorities with the largest textile constituencies began to take action.[11] In March, Baden-Württemberg's minister of economics announced the region's intention to introduce a textile and leather industry assistance program. North Rhine–Westphalia's minister president, by contrast, pledged to work for federal assistance programs for the textile industry. In May, the Länder economic ministers from North Rhine–Westphalia, Baden-Württemberg, and Bavaria released a joint statement calling for BMWi action to maintain industry competitiveness. Seeking to keep pressure on the federal government, Baden-Württemberg's economics minister called two months later for harmonizing assistance measures for the textile industry at the regional and national levels.[12]

Faced with rising Länder support for a moderately strong textile alliance, BMWi officials decided to make limited concessions. These concessions, however, reflected a key difference in the orientation of the textile alliance and its Länder supporters. Both groups thought competitive distortions in imported products were disruptive to the West German textile industry. The textile alliance demanded BMWi action against West German trading partners to resolve such distortions, and Länder officials called on BMWi to work against "the ruin and atrophy of the textile industry" through domestic assistance measures because of the failure to solve competitive distortions in the EEC.[13] Following the summer of joint Länder protests, BMWi officials appeared to be responding to both sets of concerns. In August, BMWi officials announced that ministry representatives would soon be taking action against distorted Italian yarn exports and selected cotton textile exports from Hong Kong. Domestically, BMWi officials began discussions on industry rationalization measures with representatives from cotton textile spinning and weaving associations.[14]

---

BMWi officials and "export-oriented" industries and supported by the textile, mining, and chemical industries (*Textil-Zeitung*, 3, 23 April, 23 June, 18 November 1963; and *Frankfurter Allgemeine Zeitung*, 14 November 1963).

11. Regional protests occurred in Baden-Württemberg, Bavaria, North Rhine–Westphalia, Neidersachen, and Bremen (*Textil-Zeitung*, 6 May, 12, 17–19, 21, 23, 28 June, 1 July 1963).

12. *Industrie Kurier*, 28 March 1963; *Die Welt*, 16 September 1963; *Textil-Zeitung*, 4 February, 8 April, 1–3, 8 May 1963. For the specifics of the Baden-Württemberg measures and industry reaction, see *Frankfurter Allgemeine Zeitung*, 15 July 1963; and *Textil-Zeitung*, 25 July 1963.

13. Perhaps the best expression of this distinction lies in the statements of North Rhine–Westphalia's minister-president, reported in *Textil-Zeitung*, 1–3 May 1963.

14. *Textil-Zeitung*, 21 August, 27 October 1963; and *Die Welt*, 16 September 1963.

By the fall of 1963, however, it was becoming clear that BMWi officials would be more responsive to the domestic approach to competitive distortions than to demands for direct action against West Germany's trading partners. In September, BMWi's textile section chief responded to the earlier Länder protests by stressing that the federal government was willing to support industry "self-help" measures and was by no means "writing the industry off." Regarding the textile alliance's concerns with competitive distortions, the section chief noted that the modifications in the shipments equalization tax and a new tax rebate program for West German exporters was a "not insubstantial step" (though rejecting the statements of critics that such steps were mainly a "drop on a hot stone"). The section chief also called on the industry to substantiate its claims of foreign dumping to facilitate government action. By December, the action on the Italian yarn exports pledged four months earlier had failed to materialize. In addition, although Hong Kong's sixty-day grace period for bilateral negotiations on cotton textiles under the LTA had expired in late October, BMWi officials continued to wait instead of taking unilateral action.[15]

Statements in December by the newly appointed BMWi Minister Kurt Schmücker reinforced the implicit distinction between promoting industry rationalization at home and taking direct action against distorted imports. Speaking before Gesamttextil's Executive Committee, Schmücker called for a value-added tax system and antidumping action to meet the problem of competitive distortions. Gesamttextil officials replied by noting that the former would take three to four years to implement and that progress on the latter was unlikely since BMWi officials were opposed to the Bundestag's retroactive antidumping initiative.[16] Industry officials were more receptive to government proposals on domestic measures. Schmücker's efforts at promoting cooperative industry rationalization resulted in the establishment of the Cotton Textile Industry Rationalization Association in mid-January 1964 (Rationalisierungsverband der Deutschen Baumwollindustrie). Two weeks later, BMWi officials revealed that the ministry would aid the Länder governments in providing the necessary financial assistance for the Rationalization Association.[17]

15. *Textil-Zeitung*, 6 September, 27 October, 6 December 1963.
16. *Textil-Zeitung*, 18 December 1963; and *Frankfurter Allgemeine Zeitung*, 18 December 1963.
17. The Rationalization Association's tasks included specialization within the industry, the formation of organizations for purchasing and selling, providing advice and mediation in areas of vertical and horizontal integration, and modernizing industry capacity

Through early 1964, state policy makers faced few protests from the textile alliance. Trade negotiations with Japan and the conclusion of voluntary restraint agreements with Hong Kong on cotton and wool textiles attracted little attention from alliance members. Similarly, joint protests by the "big three" Länder ceased, with only North Rhine–Westphalia's minister-president remaining active.[18] Against this back-drop, on May 13 Schmücker announced a federal government decision to make drastic unilateral tariff cuts on EEC trade effective July 1, 1964. Acting under the leadership of BMWi, the federal cabinet had based its decision on two considerations. First, economic expansion since late 1963 had begun to fuel fears of inflation. Cabinet and Bundesbank officials were expressing concern over the combined im-pact of strong exports and strong government spending on goods and services. The combination of price increases in France and Italy and existing West German tariff levels also threatened to slow the influx of low-cost imports. As such imports declined, inflationary pressures would increase. Second, in preparation for the upcoming Kennedy Round of multilateral tariff negotiations, BMWi officials desired to maximize the benefits of reciprocity. To facilitate tariff concessions by the EEC's trading partners, the EEC would have to show its commitment to trade liberalization. Moreover, West Germany's 1963 trade surplus of $300 million would somehow have to be made to appear less threatening to the country's trading partners. Unilateral tariff reductions would at a minimum offset prices in France and Italy and perhaps ease protection-ist tendencies as these countries retained access to the West German market. Schmücker also hoped that accelerating EEC integration would garner support for external liberalization. The May 13 announcement included a statement of Schmücker's intention to supplement West Germany's unilateral action with a call for a 25 percent reduction in the

---

(*Textil-Zeitung*, 15 January 1964; and *Frankfurter Allgemeine Zeitung*, 20 January 1964). Labor representatives (GTB) protested against the plan's use of public funds for rational-ization, citing the link between increased technological progress and declining employ-ment and wages (*Textil-Zeitung*, 24, 31 January 1964).

18. For detail on the import restrictions, see *Textil-Zeitung*, 8, 13, 27 January, 3, 24 February, 23 March, 10 April 1964. In 1969, with no apparent industry protest, BMWi officials concluded a provisional agreement, requiring EEC approval, with Hong Kong to rectify the fact that the cotton textile restrictions imposed in 1964 had been more restrictive than allowed under the LTA (*Textil-Mitteilungen*, 18 November 1969; and interview held in Bonn, West Germany June 1985). For the minister-president's protests, see *Textil-Zeitung*, 2 March, 17 April 1964. Baden-Württemberg's economics minister continued to release additional components of the rationalization plan (*Textil-Zeitung*, 4 March, 15 April 1964; and *Handelsblatt*, 29 February 1964).

external EEC tariff to take effect before the Kennedy Round negotiations began.[19]

The cabinet proposal for unilaterally reducing intra-EEC tariffs consisted of three steps. First, all tariffs less than 4 percent were to be removed. Second, in anticipation of the planned internal tariff reductions of 10 percent scheduled by the EEC for January 1965 and 1966, all tariffs greater than 4 percent were to be cut in half. Finally, West German goods on which the external tariff was greater than the external EEC standard (roughly three hundred product classifications) were to be reduced to the standard level. Since the unilateral action was not required under the Treaty of Rome, Schmücker announced that the Bundestag would receive the proposed ordinance for review within ten days.[20]

The proposed tariff cuts shocked the textile alliance. Gesamttextil officials demanded that the textile industry be exempted from the tariff plan. Not only would increased imports disrupt the adjustment process for portions of the industry already under pressure from imports, but West Germany was already bearing the brunt of competition from low-price countries because German textile tariffs were lower than their French and Italian counterparts. The federation's protests against the "grave injury" to industry interests were reinforced by action by member associations. In a press conference of southern German textile associations, the knitting association termed the BMWi plan a "massive blow against the German textile industry." The Southwest German Textile Industry Association (representing Baden-Württemberg) called upon the federal government and BMWi to exempt the textile industry from the reduction plan. Association officials also formally notified Baden-Württemberg's Bundestag representatives that pledges of support for the industry's position were expected by the end of May. A few days later, the region's economics minister responded to industry demands by calling for selective tariff reductions with allowances for textile and leather products. A meeting between North Rhine–Westphalia's minister-president and wool weaving association representatives also produced calls for the full exemption of textile, leather, and shoe industries from the planned tariff reduction.[21]

19. *Textil-Zeitung*, 15–17 May 1964; "Bonn to Make Unilateral Tariff Cut," *Times* (London), 14 May 1964; "Germany Chooses Inflation?" *Economist*, 25 April 1964, pp. 401–3; and *Frankfurter Allgemeine Zeitung*, 14, 20 May 1964.

20. *Textil-Zeitung*, 15–17 May 1964; and *Frankfurter Allgemeine Zeitung*, 14, 20, 27 May 1964.

21. *Textil-Zeitung*, 20, 22 May, 1 June 1964; *Frankfurter Allgemeine Zeitung*, 16 May 1964; and *Nachrichten für Aussenhandel*, 29 May 1964. For details on actions by Gesamttextil's

Despite ongoing disputes with textile producers over wages, the primary textile union (Gewerkschaft Textil Bekleidung, GTB) released a statement supporting the producer associations in their rejection of the intended tariff reduction. In a meeting with Schmücker a week after the BMWi announcement, apparel association (BBI) representatives expressed solidarity with the midstream textile producers in demanding that textile products be exempted from the tariff reduction plan. Finally, during the first week of June, the Chemical Fiber Industry Confederation joined the ranks of the textile alliance, arguing in favor of exemption of the textile industry.[22] In sum, state policy makers faced a relatively organized and inclusive textile alliance characterized by extremely high convergence of interest.

Institutional access on behalf of the textile alliance also continued to build. North Rhine–Westphalia's minister-president expressed his opposition to unilateral reductions in textile tariffs in correspondence with Minister Schmücker and in meetings with textile industry officials. Representatives from Bavaria's Ministry of Economics also rejected the unilateral tariff reduction. Finally, in June, responding to the Southwest German Textile Industry Association's call for an accounting on the proposed tariff reduction, the region's Bundestag representatives called the industry's claims legitimate and rejected the BMWi proposal.[23]

The combination of a strong textile alliance, the potential for strong Länder support for the textile industry to spread into the Bundestag, and rising protests by the leather and pulp and paper industries affected the course of the tariff proposal. BMWi officials initially rejected the textile alliance's demands for exemptions and promised to study the economic conditions in industries that might be affected by the reduction. Although BMWi officials continued to adhere to the proposed unilateral tariff reduction plan through the end of May, the threat of Bundestag opposition delayed the introduction of the proposed ordinance to the Bundestag's Foreign Trade Committee by almost two weeks. Cabinet officials found themselves in a difficult position. To meet the July 1 timetable for the onset of tariff reductions, the Bundestag would have to receive and decide on the proposal before the chamber's summer recess. If BMWi officials submitted the tariff proposal in its original form, however, the ministry risked extended debates and a possible rejection. Thus in the federal cabinet's final meeting on the form of the proposed ordinance on June 5, cabinet

regional and subsectoral associations, see *Nachrichten für Aussenhandel*, 29 May 1964; and *Textil-Zeitung*, 22, 23, 25 May, 1, 8, 12 June 1964.

22. *Textil-Zeitung*, 27–29 May 1964; and *Handelsblatt*, 8 January 1964.

23. *Textil-Zeitung*, 12, 26 June 1964.

members modified the initial BMWi proposal to require only a 50 percent tariff reduction on industrial goods with tariffs less than 4 percent.[24]

This concession failed to placate the Bundestag. In the Foreign Trade Committee, Bundestag representatives rejected the BMWi proposal and instead recommended only a 25 percent unilateral tariff reduction effective July 1, 1964. Despite a long debate with Schmücker in which he offered to exempt twenty-five product classifications in the areas of textile, leather, and paper from the proposed tariff reduction, the Bundestag representatives refused to alter their decision. Moreover, the Foreign Trade Committee's call for a 25 percent tariff reduction was made conditional on the receipt of a list of the tariff cuts mandated by the EEC for January 1965 as well as a "fully substantiated and carefully worked out" list of exemptions. On June 25, the day before the Bundestag was to vote on the Foreign Trade Committee's policy recommendation, BMWi officials met again with committee members.[25]

The final compromise plan adopted on June 25 incorporated the federal cabinet's proposal for a 50 percent unilateral decrease in the internal EEC tariff effective July 1, 1964. As a concession to the committee's concerns, however, the tariffs for roughly forty-five product classifications were to be reduced by only 25 percent. Concessions to the textile industry included the primary concerns of Gesamttextil: wool, cotton, and synthetic fabric and wool worsted and cotton yarn.[26] Faced with an increase in the strength of the textile alliance and with the tariff reduction plan held hostage in the Bundestag Foreign Trade Committee, state policy makers were forced to make concessions on tariff liberalization. The receptiveness of members of the Bundestag's Foreign Trade Committee to some form of unilateral reduction, as evident in initial committee proposals, however, limited the degree of institutional access on the textile alliance's behalf.

24. *Textil-Zeitung*, 1, 5, 10, 15 June 1964; and *Frankfurter Allgemeine Zeitung*, 27 May, 6 June 1964.

25. *Textil-Zeitung*, 15, 26 June 1964; and *Frankfurter Allgemeine Zeitung*, 6, 12, 23, 24 June 1964.

26. *Textil-Zeitung*, 26 June 1964; and *Frankfurter Allgemeine Zeitung*, 25, 30 June 1964. In contrast to the Bundestag, the Bundesrat was a strong supporter of the BMWi plan (plus the exemption list as presented by Schmücker). In the end, however, the Bundesrat basically accepted the version of this plan approved by the Bundestag (*Frankfurter Allgemeine Zeitung*, 19, 25, 27 June 1964).

*Case 2: 1964–1967*

The BMWi-Bundestag compromise over unilateral tariff reductions subtly changed relations between the textile alliance and state policy makers. Earlier demands that BMWi officials deal with competitive distortions began to give way to serious questions concerning state policy makers' claims of "understanding" for the textile industry's position.[27] In an effort to mend relations with textile producer associations, BMWi officials adopted a hard-line position in trade negotiations with Japan and Poland during late July 1964. Domestically, state policy makers announced that federal support for the Cotton Textile Industry Rationalization Association would cover one-third of the costs of reducing capacity. Finally, to soften the blow of West Germany's tariff policy, the BMWi state secretary assured Bundestag supporters of the industry that "in cases of market disruption" the EEC treaty would allow state policy makers to revoke the unilateral concessions.[28]

At the same time as BMWi officials were taking steps to ease the textile alliance's concerns over integration with the EEC, however, BMWi officials and representatives from the Foreign Ministry were engaged in opening trade relations with Eastern Europe. As of early 1965, agreements establishing trade missions and/or economic exchange measures had been concluded with Poland, Romania, Hungary, and Bulgaria. By May, reports were surfacing that the West German government had reinterpreted the Hallstein Doctrine to exempt those countries that had acknowledged East Germany "under [Soviet] duress" before 1955.[29]

The prospect of trade liberalization for broader political-military purposes sparked concern in a textile alliance already cautious of its standing in the eyes of state policy makers. Interest convergence among textile alliance members during 1964 had decreased following the passage of the modified unilateral tariff reduction plan. By early 1965, Gesamttextil officials were calling for "similar starting and competitive conditions" and government-industry cooperation to promote industry

27. See, for example, remarks by Gesamttextil's Hans-Werner Staratzke before members of the Northern Bavarian Textile Industry Association (*Textil-Zeitung*, 22 July 1964; and *Handelsblatt*, 20 July 1964).

28. *Textil-Zeitung*, 22, 24, 27 July, 2 August, 21 October 1964; *Nachrichten für Aussenhandel*, 20 October 1964; and *Handelsblatt*, 24 October 1964.

29. "Tackling the Bone in the Throat," *Economist*, 12 September 1964, p. 1009; "When the Shame Has to Stop," *Economist*, 20 March 1965, pp. 1255–56; and "Germany and Romania: Chipping at Hallstein," *Economist*, 29 May 1965, p. 1014.

"self-help" efforts. Other producer associations were more specific in their demands. The Cotton Textile Weavers Association, for example, demanded that the federal government avoid granting liberalization, tariff privileges, or credit assistance to Eastern bloc countries. Beginning in March, BBI and HAKA (men's apparel) representatives used press conferences, letters, and discussions with BMWi officials to protest the dangers of increased outward processing traffic and full textile trade with Eastern Europe. Apparel association representatives specifically cited the threat of Yugoslavian exports of men's apparel and expressed strong opposition to the rumored plans of BMWi officials to expand outward processing traffic with Poland.[30]

Again, BMWi officials sought to ease the textile alliance's concerns. Responding to apparel producers, BMWi officials denied that an agreement had been made with Poland to expand outward processing. Industry observers also saw little likelihood that BMWi officials would turn to additional liberalization in the short term in light of the upcoming September Bundestag elections and the vehement protests of many textile producer associations. These reports appeared to be accurate. In late May, BMWi officials expressed "concern" over the pace of textile imports. By early July, they had rejected demands by retail and wholesale trade associations for the liberalization of imports of Yugoslavian apparel.[31]

In an additional move to ease the concerns of the textile alliance and its supporters, ministry officials met with representatives from Gesamttextil and the Bundestag Foreign Trade Committee. In contrast to Gesamttextil's focus on cooperation within the industry earlier in the year, convergence of interests among members of the industrial alliance improved as Gesamttextil's president shifted his attention to the issue of pressure from imports from low-price, dumping, and developing countries. Yet Gesamttextil representatives still refrained from making explicit demands regarding Eastern European trade. The meeting produced a range of responses. Official press reports cited the participants' agreement on the need for special attention to textile import policy in the future. The industry press hailed the BMWi minister's acknowledgment of the industry's import problems and his broaching the subjects of Eastern European trade and low-price imports. Gesamttextil officials, however, guardedly referred to the meeting as a "step forward" and expressed

30. *Frankfurter Allgemeine Zeitung*, 12 December 1964; *Textil-Zeitung*, 14 December 1964; and *Textil-Mitteilungen/Textil-Zeitung*, 16, 22 February, 13, 24 April 1965.

31. *Textil-Mitteilungen/Textil-Zeitung*, 22 May, 15, 17 June, 8, 13 July 1965. On the CDU's electoral concerns with Erhard at the helm, see "Erhard Fights for His Job," *Economist*, 11 September 1965, p. 974.

special interest in BMWi Minister Schmücker's promise for new procedures to test the prices of goods imported from low-price countries.[32]

For the rest of the summer, both the Bundestag and Gesamttextil
were relatively quiet on issues of textile trade policy. Representatives
from BBI and DOB (women's apparel), however, continued to protest
against liberalizing Eastern European trade, and representatives from
the Foreign Trade Alliance of German Retailers (AVE) protested in
favor of such liberalization.[33] When formal campaigning for the Bundestag
elections opened in early August, BMWi officials "emphatically assured" both industry and trade association representatives that no new
regulations for Eastern European goods would emerge until at least
after the chancellor's inauguration in November.[34] These assurances
appeared to work. Wholesale and retail trade associations shifted from
the Eastern European issue, turning instead to demands for liberalizing
trade with Hong Kong and the European Community. Protests from
producer associations for the remainder of the year consisted primarily
of subsectoral demands lacking any strong sense of interest convergence. By the time of Gesamttextil's annual assembly in December,
association representatives were calling for a range of measures, including government promotion of a common EEC trade policy, interim
antidumping measures, and government consideration of the textile
industry in East-West trade.[35]

The combination of limited convergence of interests and low institutional
access following the Bundestag elections reduced the level of domestic
pressure on state policy makers. In his address to the Gesamttextil
assembly, BMWi's State Secretary Wolfgang Langer rejected increased
protection against imports from Eastern Europe on the grounds that
such protection would lead to the loss of Eastern European markets to
other industrialized countries. More important, increased liberalization
was not ruled out. Langer merely stressed that the further liberalization of Eastern bloc imports was not the government's "current intention." The state secretary noted the ministry's readiness to intervene
against "market distorting" imports and against the unequal division of
imports from Hong Kong among members of the EEC.[36] By April

32. *Textil-Mitteilungen/Textil-Zeitung*, 8, 10, 13 July, 21 August 1965.

33. *Textil-Mitteilungen/Textil-Zeitung*, 27 July, 7 August 1965.

34. *Textil-Mitteilungen/Textil-Zeitung*, 10 August 1965.

35. *Textil-Mitteilungen/Textil-Zeitung*, 4 September, 15 October, 6, 13, 23, 27 November,
16 December 1965; *Die Welt*, 14 December 1965; and *Nachrichten für Aussenhandel*, 15
December 1965.

36. *Industrie Kurier*, 16 December 1965; *Textil-Mitteilungen/Textil-Zeitung*, 29 December
1965; and *Handelsblatt*, 15 December 1965.

1966, state policy makers appeared to be making good on Langer's pledge. BMWi officials revealed that steps would be taken against Hong Kong products routed through third countries and that a market disruption clause would be included in future textile trade agreements with Japan. These promises of future concessions, however, followed negotiations with Japan and Hong Kong in which existing textile import quotas were relaxed (thereby expanding import flows) by roughly 20 percent.[37]

The economic recession of 1966–1967 and restrictive Bundesbank stabilization policies led to little initial change in either the textile alliance's strength or its degree of institutional access. In early 1966 the textile alliance lacked both interest convergence and the participation of apparel producer associations. With few exceptions, Gesamttextil's arguments that BMWi officials should link "structural policy" and import policy contrasted markedly with the demands of regional and subsectoral member associations.[38] As a result, BMWi officials basically rejected the Gesamttextil request. BMWi Minister Schmücker, for example, expressed support for industry concerns on fair international competition, noted efforts at producing a united negotiating front within the EEC against anomalous imports, and promised future meetings with Gesamttextil officials. At the same time, however, BMWi officials downplayed the industry's need for protection and instead emphasized the importance of structural policy (federal "assistance to industry self-help measures"). Aided by modifications in federal tax and cartel regulations, BMWi representatives argued that the textile industry's "model and test case" of structural policy would be the cotton textile rationalization program begun in early 1964.[39]

Gesamttextil officials responded to the BMWi position by rejecting structural policy in favor of direct action against imports. Instead of subsidies and government intervention, top association officials called for limits on imports from East Asia, reduction in imports from nonmarket countries, defense against anomalous imports, dumping legislation, and exemption of textile products from the Kennedy Round.

---

37. Voluntary export restraints on wool products were negotiated with Hong Kong for 1966 and 1967. Far from being overly restrictive, restraint levels for 1966 were set at approximately 850,000 dozen pieces and were allowed to increase 15.2 percent for 1967. Although West German negotiators rejected Japanese demands for extensive liberalization, existing textile quotas on Japanese wool and chemical fiber products were expanded by an average of 26 percent (*Textil-Mitteilungen/Textil-Zeitung*, 1, 26 February, 14 April 1966).

38. *Textil-Mitteilungen/Textil-Zeitung*, 8 February, 1, 10, 31 March, 5, 19 April, 17 May 1966; and *Die Welt*, 28 March 1966.

39. *Textil-Mitteilungen/Textil-Zeitung*, 19 April 1966.

Gesamttextil's rejection of structural policy was reinforced by the results of a poll of cotton textile producers in late April. Despite the BMWi vision of a cotton textile "test case," the poll revealed that only 32 percent of spinners (by capacity) and 10 percent of weavers approved of the government's rationalization measures.[40]

The inability of state policy makers to garner the textile industry's support for structural policy should not overshadow the textile alliance's continued lack of strength and institutional access to alter West German import policy. When BMWi officials introduced import surveillance and price-testing procedures on trade agreements with a number of Eastern bloc countries during May 1966, these measures were not applied to textile trade (despite BMWi Minister Schmücker's promises at the industry-Bundestag meeting the previous year). Similarly, the 1966 Bundestag Finance Committee's assessment of increasing the shipments equalization tax on imported goods had called on the competent ministries to submit product lists for consideration. BMWi officials had argued before Gesamttextil in December 1965, however, that such increases for textile products would be considered only in "exceptional cases." The only clear action on the textile alliance's behalf by mid-1966 was the promised introduction of tighter licensing regulations on Hong Kong wool textile exports routed through third countries.[41]

Through the remainder of the year, the inclusiveness of the textile alliance increased and convergence of interests remained the alliance's weak point. During June, Gesamttextil protests against the unequal distribution of Hong Kong exports across members of the EEC contrasted with HAKA's indictment of West German trade policy as the source of "manipulated, wage-related dumping imports" from Hong Kong and Yugoslavia. By July, the Chemical Fiber Industry Confederation's concerns with the impact of rising imports on industry profits had surfaced in demands that the federal government cease further liberalization concessions, limit quota relaxation, and take action under West Germany's

---

40. *Handelsblatt*, 21 April 1966; and *Textil-Mitteilungen/Textil-Zeitung*, 10 May 1966. Not only had major producers begun their own rationalization efforts, but federal government limits on machinery operation, funding proposals, and West German trade policy were seen as inhibiting the profitability of rationalization along the proposed guidelines (*Textil-Mitteilungen/Textil-Zeitung*, 23 April 1966; and interviews held in Bonn and Frankfurt, West Germany, May and June 1985).

41. For detail on the import-surveillance and price-testing measures, see *Textil-Mitteilungen/Textil-Zeitung*, 12 May 1966; and Kreile, "West Germany," pp. 204–6. For detail on the shipments equalization tax, see *Textil-Mitteilungen/Textil-Zeitung*, 17 May, 27 September 1966; *Industrie Kurier*, 16 December 1965; and *Handelsblatt*, 15 December 1965. For detail on the licensing regulations, see *Textil-Mitteilungen/Textil-Zeitung*, 2 June 1966.

(long-promised and newly introduced) antidumping legislation.[42] In addition to these protests from producer associations, the Cotton Textile Working Group, GTB, and several regional subsectoral associations called for an array of steps against imports.[43]

Institutional access by the textile alliance, however, remained limited. Baden-Württemberg's economics minister, for example, joined Gesamt-textil representatives in protesting against the adverse effects of federal government measures aimed at stabilizing the economic recession. In mid-July, the Bundestag president came out in support of the textile alliance by rejecting "subvention and protection" in favor of "fair or similar competitive conditions." Yet, instead of supporting the alliance's demands for action directly against "unfair" imports, the president called for an initial focus on decreasing the protectionist policies of other EEC countries.[44]

A late September meeting on import policy between representatives from Gesamttextil and BBI and BMWi Minister Schmücker again resulted in a few concessions to the textile alliance. The alliance's peak associations called for an increasingly restrictive import policy, especially in dealing with Hong Kong, and Schmücker expressed the ministry's desire to "consolidate the import burden in textiles." As in the case of the July 1965 meetings between Gesamttextil, the Bundestag Foreign Trade Committee, and Schmücker, the participants spoke of a "turning point" and a "satisfactory first step." Yet in statements to the press and the Bundestag in October and November, Schmücker downplayed the industry's structural adjustment "difficulties" and rejected additional

42. *Die Welt*, 8 June 1966; and *Textil-Mitteilungen/Textil-Zeitung*, 14, 23, 30 June, 7 July 1966; and *Handelsblatt*, 8 July 1966. The new dumping measures modified section 2K of the old tariff law by introducing temporary and provisional antidumping and equaliza-tion tariffs in cases of suspected dumping. If dumping was not found after three months, the importer would be reimbursed.

43. *Textil-Mitteilungen/Textil-Zeitung*, 14, 28 July, 27 August, 20 September 1966; *Industrie Kurier*, 28 July 1966; and *Nachrichten für Aussenhandel*, 13 July 1966. Major individual producers who protested against imports included ERBA AG and J. F. Adolf AG. See *Industrie Kurier*, 4 October 1966; *Handelsblatt*, 5 October 1966; and *Textil-Mitteilungen/Textil-Zeitung*, 21 July 1966. According to one press report, the Cotton Textile Working Group's demands for antidumping action against Turkey reflected the limited impact of a West German VER imposed on Turkey in July. The VER stemmed from negotiations begun in September 1965 (*Textil-Mitteilungen/ Textil-Zeitung*, 30 July 1966). Since this report was the sole mention of trade relations with Turkey that I found during this period, I do not include the VER as a concession to the industrial alliance.

44. *Textil-Mitteilungen/Textil-Zeitung*, 7, 9, 14, 21 July 1966; and *Nachrichten für Aussenhandel*, 13 July 1966. For detail on Erhard's stabilization measures, see "Erhard Vaccinates an Immune Germany from the English Disease," *Economist*, 13 August 1966, pp. 632–33; and "Germany: Two Sensible Moves," *Economist*, 16 July 1966, p. 287.

measures for assisting cotton textile producers. In contrast, Schmücker responded to Gesamttextil and BBI concerns by initiating procedural discussions for trade negotiations with Hong Kong.[45]

By late 1966, political changes in West Germany's ruling coalition had altered the identity of state policy makers facing the textile alliance. Dissatisfaction with Chancellor Erhard and disagreements between the CDU/CSU and FDP in the Bundestag resulted in a new Grand Coalition between the CDU/CSU and the SPD. In subsequent cabinet changes, Chancellor Kurt Kiesinger (CDU) appointed Carl Schiller (SPD) as the new BMWi minister. Appearing before Gesamttextil's annual meeting, Schiller pledged that the new administration would place "special interest" on mining, steel, and textiles. Gesamttextil representatives countered with the long-standing demand for stronger measures against competitive distortions and expressed interest in the negotiations with Hong Kong begun under Schmücker. By mid-December, Hong Kong had agreed to increased import licensing restrictions, limits on relaxing cotton textile quotas, and a protocol on future discussions for wool textile products (which had been restricted since 1964). Gesamttextil officials responded to the three-year agreement by noting that it was both long in coming and by no means a complete solution to the problem of distorted imports.[46] From the standpoint of concessions to the textile alliance, however, the most overt type of protectionist policy in this agreement was simply an administrative restriction (the licensing measures).

Schiller's honeymoon with the textile alliance was short-lived. As West Germany's recession carried over into 1967, employment and production figures in the textile industry continued to worsen. Gesamttextil and GTB representatives again demanded action against competitive distortions and anomalous imports, and Gesamttextil officials appealed to BMWi Minister Schiller to prevent the spread of Eastern bloc trade liberalization to textile products. In a late January Kleine Anfrage, Bundestag supporters of the textile industry called for action against three problem areas in West German textile imports: Eastern Europe, Hong Kong, and Italy's Prato region. BMWi officials responded to the

---

45. *Textil-Mitteilungen/Textil-Zeitung*, 27 September, 15 November, 19 November 1966; and *Handelsblatt*, 14 November 1966.

46. *Industrie Kurier*, 10 December 1966; *Handelsblatt*, 12 December 1966; and *Textil-Mitteilungen/Textil-Zeitung*, 3, 22 December 1966, 24 January 1967. For detail on West German policy in mining and steel, see Katzenstein, *Policy and Politics in West Germany*, pp. 101–3.

PATCHWORK PROTECTIONISM

Bundestag by noting the government's resolve to meet each of these problems.[47]

Examples cited by ministry officials, however, were limited to observing import trends in trade with Eastern Europe and low-price countries, promoting structural adjustment, and working for a common EEC trade policy. Grounds for further industry concern emerged in late January and early February when the federal cabinet agreed to waive the Hallstein Doctrine in an effort to normalize relations with Romania, Hungary, Yugoslavia, and Czechoslovakia. In subsequent Gesamttextil discussions with BMWi officials over import policy, Gesamttextil representatives continued to demand action on the three problem areas noted by the Bundestag. Responding to a CDU/CSU Kleine Anfrage in March, BMWi's state secretary again assured his audience that industry conditions would be taken into consideration (as evidenced by the renewal of restraints on Hong Kong wool textile exports), specifically in upcoming trade negotiations with Japan.[48] Faced with the combination of Gesamttextil and GTB and limited increases in Bundestag pressure on the textile alliance's behalf, state policy makers had again conceded little to the textile alliance.

Against this backdrop, state policy makers turned to the further liberalization of trade with Eastern Europe. In mid-February, the industry press had reported that BMWi's Division IV would soon release a list of goods slated for import increases in Eastern bloc trade. By early April, Gesamttextil, the Cotton Textile Working Group, and BBI, as well as GTB representatives, were demanding action against excessive imports. Yet this convergence of interest was undercut by the midstream associations' focus on competitive distortions and BBI's demand for a greater BMWi role in promoting apparel exports. On 24 April, the textile industry press reported that the cabinet had completed the list of Eastern European products to be liberalized from the

47. *Textil-Mitteilungen/Textil-Zeitung*, 18, 24, 31 January 1967 (additional GTB protests, 23 February, 21 March 1967); and West Germany, Bundestag, *Der Bundesminister für Wirtschaft: Kleine Anfrage*, 5. Wahlperiode, Drucksache V/2503, 23 January 1968, pp. 2–6. In February, North Rhine–Westphalia's economics minister expressed support for the textile industry and pledged action against imports and on Eastern European trade problems (*Textil-Mitteilungen/Textil-Zeitung*, 23 February 1967).

48. *Textil-Mitteilungen/Textil-Zeitung*, 31 January, 23 February 1967; "Germany and Eastern Europe: Push It Out and See If It Floats," *Economist*, 28 January 1967, p. 312; "Something for Mr. Kosygin," *Economist*, 4 February 1967, pp. 395–96; "The Man Who Pulled the Rug Out from under Ulbricht," *Economist*, 11 February 1967, p. 505; *Handelsblatt*, 16, 20 March 1967; and *Nachrichten für Aussenhandel*, 18 March 1967.

offerings of different BMWi sections and was currently debating the proposed increases.[49]

The proposed expansion of quota ceilings for goods on the AlmA product list (Ausschreibung mit laufender Antragsstellung, literally "terms of tender with continuing filing of an application"—goods subject to quantitative restrictions based on earlier applications) raised immediate cries of protest from BBI representatives in April and May. In June, BMWi's state secretary again appeared before the Bundestag defending the federal government's commitment to removing competitive distortions in textile trade such as subsidized imports (from Italy's Prato region) and "manipulated-price" imports (from the Eastern bloc). Gesamttextil officials noted that the government's way of handling competitive distortions was a source of the industry's problems and explicitly rejected the proposed Eastern bloc import plan. Faced with strong opposition from the textile alliance and the strong likelihood of increased opposition in the Bundestag from CDU/CSU and FDP textile supporters, BMWi officials appeared before a Bundestag Fragestunde in late June to assure the industry and its supporters that neither Eastern bloc nor low-price country import liberalization would occur "for the time being."[50]

By mid-June the SPD-led Ministry of Economics had been called before the Bundestag three times to defend its textile trade policy. These demands for explanations from BMWi had primarily come from CDU and FDP textile supporters. In the context of a "fragile" SPD-CDU/CSU ruling alliance, a major dispute over textile trade policy was not in the interests of top SPD officials. By early June, dissatisfaction with the ruling alliance among traditional SPD supporters had cost the party voter support in Ländtag elections in Lower Saxony, Schleswig-Holstein, and Rhineland-Palatinate. In addition, the CDU/CSU remained the dominant political force in the big three textile areas of Bavaria, North Rhine–Westphalia, and Baden-Württemberg.[51] Thus, despite the potential for disrupting relations with Eastern Europe, the indications

49. *Textil-Mitteilungen/Textil-Zeitung*, 10–11 February, 4, 6, 11, 18, 20, 25 April 1967; *Frankfurter Allgemeine Zeitung*, 10 April 1967; and Albert Flaitz, "Wachstums- und Strukturpolitik in der Sicht der deutschen Baumwollindustrie," Vortrag auf die Pressekonferenz an 5. April 1967 in Frankfurt/Main anlasslich der Vorstellung des Unternehmerforums der deutschen Baumwollindustrie, pp. 3, 11–16.

50. *Textil-Mitteilungen/Textil-Zeitung*, 25 April, 9 May, 23–24 June, 30 June–1 July, 4 July 1967; *Nachrichten für Aussenhandel*, 8 June, 1 July 1967.

51. Edinger, *Politics in West Germany*, pp. 305–6; "Socialists Lost in the Crowd," *Economist*, 17 June 1967, p. 232; and Lehmann, *Chronik der Bundesrepublik Deutschland*, pp. 180–97.

of increasing Bundestag support for the strong textile alliance forced state policy makers to back down from liberalization. The absence of greater concessions to the textile alliance reflects the absence of greater institutional access on the alliance's behalf.

## Case 3: 1967–1969

The BMWi pledge to refrain from further import liberalization "for the time being" solved the immediate dispute between West German state policy makers and the textile alliance. Yet the open-ended nature of the pledge left state and societal actors warily exploring the "understanding" that had been reached. By late 1968, textile trade policy became caught up in state policy makers' concerns with a chronic West German trade surplus and pressures for solutions. As in the previous two cases, efforts to rectify broader economic and political concerns at the expense of the textile industry prompted a backlash from the textile alliance.

The turnaround in the textile industry's relations with West German state policy makers in late 1968 is all the more striking in light of earlier BMWi efforts to minimize conflict. The first challenge to the June 1967 understanding came from the demands of Ostpolitik. Before Foreign Minister Willy Brandt's tour of Eastern Europe in August 1967, Gesamttextil and BBI representatives met with BMWi officials to discuss the normalization of relations between West Germany and Romania. BMWi officials had originally intended to relax quotas on Romanian textile and apparel imports as part of a broader liberalization of trade between the two countries. Based on the objections raised by the producer associations, however, BMWi officials and the federal cabinet decided to exempt textile and apparel products from the "de facto liberalization granted to imports from Romania." In meetings with organized labor during November and in a letter to the Bundestag, BMWi Minister Schiller reiterated his ministry's commitment to retaining quotas on imports from Eastern European and low-price countries. On the other hand, Schiller's explicit references to avoiding a "full" liberalization of trade with Rumania and to maintaining "hard-core protection" against Eastern European goods implicitly suggested that partial liberalization was not being ruled out.[52]

State policy makers also noted that producer associations remained

---

52. *Textil-Mitteilungen/Textil-Zeitung*, 27 July, 17 October, 30 November 1967; *Nachrichten für Aussenhandel*, 17 November 1967. On Minister Brandt's tour of Eastern Europe, see "Germany and East Europe I: Sharpish Turn," *Economist*, 12 August 1967, pp. 308–9.

concerned over the issue of competitive distortions in the EEC. The Bundestag Anfrage of early 1967 had called BMWi representatives to task on the relative openness of the West German market to Hong Kong exports when compared with other EEC members as well as on Italy's subsidy policies for textile producers in the Prato region. The June 1967 concessions to the textile alliance, however, had focused on the pressing issue of import liberalization. Moreover, much more complex steps were required to solve the problem of competitive distortions. Equalizing the distribution of Hong Kong exports across members of the EEC would require state policy makers either to compel France and Italy to liberalize their markets or to have West Germany impose more restrictive quotas on Hong Kong goods. The former would be extremely difficult to achieve and the latter would undercut West German efforts to bring about a more liberal EEC. In contrast, to solve the problem of Italy's policy of subsidizing Prato textiles would primarily require action through the European Commission.

In July, protests by Gesamttextil and the Chemical Fiber Industry Confederation illustrated that competitive distortions remained an important concern to several key associations in the textile alliance and had not been silenced by the June understanding.[53] Faced with demands from the textile alliance and the desire to avoid reawakening Bundestag support for the alliance, state policy makers turned to the least unacceptable alternative—resolving the Prato textile issue. Since March 1967, Gesamttextil had lent its weight to wool fabric producers in their attempt to gain import relief from Italian products as allowed under Article 226 of the Treaty of Rome. BMWi officials had responded, however, by noting the failed attempts of other countries to bring such suits before the European Commission. In early June, BMWi officials again rejected the demands of producer associations, this time citing the absence of an industry adjustment program.

In September, by contrast, state policy makers applied to the commission for permission to institute a two-year reduction of Italian imports to facilitate domestic rationalization of the worsted yarn fabric subsector. By November, BMWi Minister Schiller was stressing to textile workers and to the Bundestag that a vital component of his "new course" for the textile industry was his commitment to work against competitive distortions, including a resolution to restrict imports from Prato. Schiller's success in embracing the issue is partially illustrated by industry press reports. Instead of citing the adverse effect of state

53. *Nachrichten für Aussenhandel*, 15 July 1967; and *Frankfurter Allgemeine Zeitung*, 7 July 1967.

policy makers' delays in responding to industry concerns, the press noted that the import penetration rate of 94.8 percent among worsted yarn fabric producers would be helpful in gaining a successful ruling by the commission.[54]

By late November, Prato appeared to be forgotten as producer associations, organized labor, and selected Länder officials had become absorbed in Gesamttextil's demands for alleviating competitive distortions through a more equitable division of third-country imports among EEC members.[55] BMWi officials responded to alliance demands by returning to the stance of understanding that had characterized industry-government relations up to 1964. By December, Gesamttextil representatives found themselves on the same side of the competitive distortions issue as BMWi officials. Both groups were voicing similar demands for a common EEC trade policy that would bring about a more equitable import distribution.[56] Schiller had managed to avoid a repeat of the Bundestag confrontations of June 1967 by selectively and skillfully responding to textile alliance concerns.

In early 1968, however, it became apparent that the convergence of the textile alliance's and state policy makers' positions was more tenuous than the policy makers had believed. In a mid-January SPD Kleine Anfrage, BMWi officials again assured industry supporters in the Bundestag that no "unexpected" concessions in liberalization would occur in textile trade policy "for the time being." In contrast to earlier statements, ministry officials took an additional step by noting that "expected" concessions would include reasonable increases in quota

54. *Handelsblatt*, 16 March, 8 September 1967; *Textil-Mitteilungen/Textil-Zeitung*, 12 September 1967; and *Nachrichten für Aussenhandel*, 8 June 1967. A review of EEC rulings for the late 1960s, however, reveals no mention of West German officials presenting the case before the commission on the Prato issue. The official journals and press releases note only a positive ruling by the commission on an Article 226 petition by the Netherlands. For example, see *Supplément au Journal Officiel des Communautés Européennes: Table Annuelle 1967*, p. 80; and "Décision de la Commission," *Journal Officiel des Communautés Européennes*, no. 180, 3 August 1967, pp. 14–16.

55. Gesamttextil, organized labor, and man-made fiber producers were joined in regional protests by combinations of textile, labor, and Länder authorities in North Rhine–Westphalia, Baden-Württemberg, Bremen, and Bavaria (*Industrie Kurier*, 16 September, 3, 30 November 1967; *Nachrichten für Aussenhandel*, 4 November 1967; *Handelsblatt*, 3, 6 November 1967; and *Textil-Mitteilungen/Textil-Zeitung*, 19 October 1967). On regional protests, see *Blick durch Wirtschaft*, 25 November 1967; *Textil-Mitteilungen/Textil-Zeitung*, 24–25, 28, 30 November 1967; *Die Welt*, 11 December 1967; and *Industrie Kurier*, 30 November 1967.

56. *Industrie Kurier*, 9 December 1967. In early January, Gesamttextil repeated calls for a division of East Asian imports in the EEC (*Textil-Mitteilungen/Textil-Zeitung*, 4, 19–20 January 1968).

ceilings on Romanian goods and liberalization, albeit restricted, of quotas on Eastern European goods in general. Instead of a 1967-style backlash to this reevaluation of ministry policy, the initial protests following the Kleine Anfrage were limited to demands from the BBI for action against Yugoslavian apparel and the North Rhine–Westphalia legislature's calls for overt protection and adjustment assistance measures.[57]

Faced with apparently implicit Gesamttextil support for liberalization in Eastern European trade, BMWi Minister Schiller took an ill-fated step when he noted in February that the government's economic policies were actually improving conditions in the industry. This observation evoked harsh protests from Gesamttextil and the Cotton Textile Working Group. Länder economic ministers meeting in Bonn responded to Schiller's statements by demanding additional protection and financial support for the industry. Schiller responded quickly to head off potential institutional access on behalf of the textile alliance by initiating a meeting with twelve representatives from the three major Bundestag factions. Instead of repeating earlier BMWi statements on the potential for gradual liberalization, Schiller turned the clock back to June 1967. The BMWi minister assured the representatives (who included three past textile producer association officials) that although protection could not be increased, additional liberalization of textile imports would not be likely "for the foreseeable future." In direct response to political support for the textile industry among Länder officials, Schiller also expressed interest in the Länder ministers' demands for action against imports.[58]

Schiller's conciliatory stance and the revelation in the summer of French plans to increase textile protection shifted the textile alliance's attention away from the minister's earlier gaffe to demands for action against France's competitive distortions.[59] By the fall of 1968, BBI was the lone national-level producer association challenging the govern-

57. *Textil-Mitteilungen/Textil-Zeitung*, 16 January 1968; *Frankfurter Allgemeine Zeitung*, 18 January 1968; *Die Welt*, 18 January 1968; and *Textil-Mitteilungen/Textil-Zeitung*, 19–20 January 1968.

58. *Textil-Mitteilungen/Textil-Zeitung*, 5, 6, 22–24 February, 14 March 1968; *Frankfurter Allgemeine Zeitung*, 22 February 1968; *Die Welt*, 2 February, 12 March 1968; and *Bulletin des Presse- und Informationsamtes der Bundesregierung*, 16 March 1968. The minister's statements were made despite appeals by consumer and export associations against textile protection (*Die Welt*, 11 March 1968).

59. For the subsequent fallout from Schiller's statements, see *Textil-Mitteilungen/Textil-Zeitung*, 14, 21–23 March 1968; *Der Volkswort*, 29 March, 11 April 1968. On the protests against France, see *Nachrichten für Aussenhandel*, 6 July 1968; and *Textil-Mitteilungen/Textil-Zeitung*, 23, 25 July, 8, 15, 20 August, 3, 6–7 September, 4–5, 10, 18–19 October 1968.

ment's textile trade policy regarding Eastern Europe.[60] Issues of Eastern European trade as well as the impact of the Soviet invasion of Czechoslovakia on Ostpolitik, however, were eclipsed in late 1968 by concerns over stabilization measures for the deutsch mark (DM).

West Germany's recovery from the 1966–67 recession had been sparked by a restrictive monetary policy, price stability, and a strong export drive. By late 1968, balance-of-payment difficulties in the United States and a chronic trade surplus in West Germany had placed considerable international attention on revaluation of the DM to relieve pressure on the international monetary system. West Germany's experience with revaluation in 1961 as well as strong opposition to revaluation by Schiller and Chancellor Kiesinger, however, prompted a search for alternative means to reduce the West German trade surplus. In late November, cabinet officials announced that instead of revaluation West Germany would impose a 4 percent value-added tax (border tax) on previously tax-exempt West German exports and grant a 4 percent tax rebate on West German imports. The combined measures would decrease West Germany's surplus by a third, from DM 15 billion to DM 10 billion. More important to the textile alliance, imports would be increased by DM 3.7 billion.[61]

The cabinet decision evoked strong protests from Gesamttextil, BBI, and GTB representatives. As in the case of the 1964 tariff acceleration, Gesamttextil officials appealed to the Bundestag and BMWi officials to exempt textile products. Yet the Bundestag Finance Committee's decision (after meeting with Minister Schiller and Chancellor Kiesinger) to reject all demands for exemptions cut off a vital channel of institutional access for the textile alliance. To soften the blow of the import measures, cabinet officials announced that the expected DM 1.3 billion in additional revenues generated by the border tax would be used to assist adversely affected industries. By mid-December, Schiller had revised

---

60. *Textil-Mitteilungen/Textil-Zeitung*, 27–28 September, 3, 15, 22 October, 31 October 1968–1 November 1968; and Bundesverband Bekleidungsindustrie, *Die Deutsche Bekleidungsindustrie Morgen: Kongress der Bekleidungsindustrie 1968*, October 1968, pp. 195–99. Institutional access on the alliance's behalf was also limited to statements by Finance Minister Franz Josef Strauss (CSU-Bavaria) that the burden of Eastern European liberalization be spread across all industries in West Germany (*Textil-Mitteilungen*, 6, 22–23 August 1968).

61. Hankel, "West Germany," p. 117; Kreile, "West Germany," pp. 213–16; Katzenstein, *Policy and Politics in West Germany*, pp. 91–92; "Upping the Deutschmark?" *Economist*, 31 August 1968, pp. 55–56; "How the Pack Tumbled," *Economist*, 23 November 1968, pp. 77–79; "Germany: Forty Million Reasons Why," *Economist*, 17 May 1969, pp. 31–32; "Germany: Will the Gamble Come Off?" *Economist*, 30 November 1968, pp. 65–66; and *Textil-Mitteilungen*, 26 November 1968.

the revenue estimates for assistance programs down to DM 500–700 million. Gesamttextil's Hans-Werner Staratzke responded to the cabinet measures by noting that such steps were "merely a sedative for those industries adversely affected by the government's policy."[62]

By early 1969, the industry press was reporting that the textile, leather, and steel industries had been targeted by the cabinet for assistance measures. Estimates of border tax revenues available for such assistance measures, however, had fallen again to slightly more than DM 195 million. BMWi's concerns that the tax measures would not have sufficient effect on the West German surplus prompted a late February announcement that the ministry was considering liberalizing West Germany's remaining import quotas. Since the bulk of such goods consisted of textile and apparel products, this proposal was greeted by vehement and repeated protests from Gesamttextil and BBI as well as key member associations.[63]

The new liberalization measures announced in mid-March 1969 expanded import quotas on Eastern European and other exporting countries (Japan, India, Pakistan, Yugoslavia, and Taiwan) by 33 percent or roughly DM 430 million. In addition, quotas on goods exported to Eastern Europe for processing and exported back to West Germany (outward processing) were to be increased by DM 50 million. The quota expansion did include limited concessions to the strong textile alliance. Citing the LTA's coverage of the cotton textile trade, cabinet officials exempted cotton textiles from further liberalization. Wool products under Hong Kong voluntary export restraint were also exempted, but cabinet officials noted that the Hong Kong and Japanese restraint agreements would be "examined" for possible liberalization. Finally, in late March BMWi officials exercised the right under the new measures to factor in an industry's "structural and regional problems and difficulties" when determining increases in quota ceilings and announced that textile and apparel quotas would be increased by only 20 percent on a delayed country-by-country basis.[64] The bottom line for the textile

62. *Textil-Mitteilungen*, 26, 29–30 November, 3, 17 December 1968; and *Frankfurter Allgemeine Zeitung*, 14 December 1968.

63. *Textil-Mitteilungen*, 31 January–2 February, 27 February, 4 March 1969. For Gesamttextil and BBI protests, see *Textil-Mitteilungen*, 27 February, 6, 18 March 1969; *Nachrichten für Aussenhandel*, 27 February 1969; and *Die Welt*, 27 February 1969. For protests by member associations, see *Textil-Mitteilungen*, 16 January, 13, 20 February, 14–15 March 1969.

64. *Textil-Mitteilungen*, 20, 28–29 March 1969. Trade with East Germany, by contrast, would not be liberalized according to *Textil-Mitteilungen*, 4 April 1969. The *London Financial Times* (26 January 1969), however, claimed that the textile quota for East Germany was increased by 30 percent. For cabinet deliberations over outward processing quotas, see *Textil-Mitteilungen*, 24–26 April 1969.

alliance was that although the situation could have been worse, in the absence of institutional access textile quotas would still be expanded by a minimum of 20 percent in Eastern European trade.

The first country to benefit from the liberalization package was Yugoslavia. Despite BBI objections, Yugoslavian outward processing quotas were increased in July by 30 percent and normal quotas were increased by 20 percent. One major source of BBI concern was that the import licenses for the expanded quotas were to be divided among West German mail order houses (Quelle, Neckermann, and Otto) instead of apparel producers. In early August, BBI officials were stunned by indications that under pressure from the Foreign Ministry, BMWi officials would be pushing through a full de facto liberalization of Yugoslavian outward processing. BBI representatives protested against such liberalization in appeals to the chancellor, the Ministry of Economics, the Ministry of Finance, and the Foreign Ministry but with little success. Gesamttextil officials were conspicuously silent in the debate over outward processing. BBI justifiably saw outward processing as a threat, but outward processing contracts would require Yugoslavia to import West German yarns and fabric, thereby offering potential benefits to Gesamttextil's membership. Thus BMWi officials believed that Gesamttextil would remain neutral on that issue.[65] In the face of limited vocal opposition and no apparent institutional access on behalf of the textile alliance, BMWi officials submitted a plan to the Ministries of Finance and Foreign Affairs which called for a 67 percent de jure increase in Yugoslavian outward processing quotas. Despite protests by regional textile and apparel associations, the new plan was formally announced in late August.[66]

The import expansion and tax rebate plans of 1968 and 1969 had been an attempt to forestall revaluation of the DM while at the same time maintaining stability in West German prices. By fall 1969, the political alignments on revaluation had shifted and pressures for revaluation were increasing. The renewed debate over revaluation placed Schiller and the SPD in favor of revaluation and Chancellor Kiesinger, Finance Minister Franz Josef Strauss and the CDU/CSU

65. *Industrie Kurier*, 5 August 1969; and *Textil-Mitteilungen*, 17 July, 7–9 August 1969.
66. The new plan also included requests for a 20 percent increase in existing Eastern bloc quotas. I was unable to determine if this 20 percent was just a restatement of measures announced in the spring or a new policy. The latter possibility would stem from cabinet meetings held before the summer vacation. During these meetings, cabinet members had rejected a further increase in border tax measures but had approved additional relaxation in quotas to stimulate imports (*Textil-Mitteilungen*, 24, 31 July, 14 August, 2 September, 16 December 1969; and *Industrie Kurier*, 12, 23 August 1969).

strongly opposed to such a step. As the September Bundestag elections approached, public opinion polls indicated that the SPD and Minister Schiller had public support on the anti-inflation issue and on the appropriateness of using revaluation to forestall price increases. The first step in the resolution of the revaluation debate came before the election as foreign speculation on the potential for DM revaluation prompted Chancellor Kiesinger temporarily to close the currency exchanges (a move for which both Kiesinger and Schiller claimed credit). The second step came at the polls on September 28 when the CDU/CSU lost out to a new SPD-FDP coalition.[67]

On the day of the elections, the Bundesbank also began to allow the DM to float against foreign currencies until a decision could be reached on revaluation. As Bundesbank and BMWi officials carried out discussions on the extent of revaluation, textile producer associations such as Gesamttextil, Gesamtmasche, and BBI protested such a move.[68] The outcome of the Bundestag elections as well as the across-the-board nature of revaluation, however, basically left the textile alliance without institutional access to the policy-making process. In late October, West Germany revalued the DM by 9.3 percent. Speaking before Gesamttextil's annual meeting in December, BMWi's representative (Wilhelm Giel, ministerial director) did not apologize for the revaluation.[69] Instead, Giel stressed the primacy of currency stability in economic policy. Moreover, in response to Gesamttextil's concerns with increases in "anomalous imports" in light of the revaluation, BMWi's representative noted that though sensitive areas in Eastern bloc trade would remain protected, West Germany's trade policy toward Eastern Europe needed to remain flexible. Finally, although the 1968 value-added tax measures and the 1969 quota increases had been intended to forestall DM revaluation, neither was removed once the revaluation had occurred. Instead, beginning in 1970 the new ruling SPD-FDP coalition's goal of

67. Kreile, "West Germany," pp. 215–16; Susan Strange, "The Dollar Crisis, 1971," *International Affairs* 48 (April 1972), p. 194; "Germany: Straussian Economics," *Economist*, 30 August 1969, p. 47; "Hot Money, Cool Handshakes but No Black Eyes Yet," *Economist*, 27 September 1969, pp. 22–24; "When the Dollar Was Devalued," *Economist*, 21 August 1971, p. 55.

68. For examples of protests by these and other producer associations, see *Textil-Mitteilungen*, 21, 30 October 1969; and *Die Welt*, 25 October 1969. For details on DM deliberations, see "German Border Taxes: The Awkward Herr Strauss," *Economist*, 11 October 1969, pp. 73–74; and "In the Trail of the Mark," *Economist*, 1 November 1969, pp. 61–62.

69. *Handelsblatt*, 10 December 1969; *Textil-Mitteilungen*, 11 December 1969; and "Gegen Wettbewerbsverzerrungen in international Handel," *Textile Praxis International*, January 1970, p. C2.

improving relations with Eastern Europe would prompt a new wave of liberalization efforts.

## CONCLUSION

From 1963 to 1969, state policy makers and industrial alliances engaged in three major disputes over West German textile trade policy. As in the cases studied in the two preceding chapters, all three cases support the hypothesis that, faced with increasing domestic pressure, state policy makers will act against the dictates of international constraints. Moreover, the third West German case study illustrates that falling domestic pressure will lead state policy makers to act more in line with international constraints. Using the indexes developed in the Appendix, Table 8 summarizes the interaction between domestic pressure and international constraint.

*Table 8.* West German textile trade policy, case summary

| Case | Domestic Pressure | | International Constraint | | |
|------|------|------|------|------|------|
| | IAS | DIA | Vulnerability | Threat | Political-Military |
| *Case 1* | | | | | |
| 1963 | Mod | Mod − | Low + | Low + (Mod +) | Mod − |
| 1964 | High | Mod | Mod − | Low + (Mod +) | Mod − |
| Outcome: Nonunilateral quotas (1964) | | | | | |
| *Case 2* | | | | | |
| 1964 | Mod | Low + | Mod − | Mod (Mod +) | Mod − |
| 1965 | Mod + | Mod − | Mod − | Mod (Mod +) | Mod − |
| 1966 | Mod + | Low + | Mod − | Mod (Mod +) | Mod − |
| 1967 | High | Mod − | Mod − | Mod (Mod +) | Mod − |
| Outcome: Administrative restrictions (1966)[a] | | | | | |
| *Case 3* | | | | | |
| 1967 | High/High − | Low + | Mod − | Mod (Mod +) | Mod − |
| 1968 | High | Low + | Mod − | Mod (Mod +) | Mod − |
| 1969 | High | Low − | Mod − | Mod (Mod +) | Mod − |
| Outcome: State subsidies (1969) | | | | | |

*Note:* The indicator scores are based on the highest level reached in a given year. Abbreviations are used here for industrial alliance strength (IAS) and the degree of institutional access (DIA). The threat of retaliation scores in parentheses are based on regional economic structure. The policy outcomes are the most overt types of protectionist policy adopted in the given case study period. For more detail on ranking procedure, see Appendix.

[a] The nonunilateral quantitative restrictions on Hong Kong wool textiles introduced in 1964 were renewed in 1965 and 1967. Japanese wool textile quotas were renewed in 1965. For both countries, the renewed quotas were less restrictive than their 1964 versions.

With the exception of slight increases in 1964 and 1965, international economic constraints on state policy makers' action remained constant during the periods covered by all three West German cases. Trade as a percentage of GNP hovered between 29.3 and 35 percent, suggesting a vulnerability to retaliation greater than that faced by the United States and Japan and greater than the postwar average (30.2 percent) for large industrial countries. In contrast, West German state policy makers faced weaker threats of retaliation than their American and Japanese counterparts. West Germany's position as a borderline supporter under American hegemony (1963–64) and as a supporter within a "bilateral supportership" (1964–69) resulted in a low + to moderate − threat. A more pressing threat of retaliation stemmed from West Germany's status as a hegemonic power in the regional economic structure of the EEC.

By the mid-1960s, political-military constraints on West German state policy makers were not as extensive as for the United States. With the gradual reinterpretation of the Hallstein Doctrine, state policy makers began to see overt protectionist action as incurring an economic as well as a political-military cost. In the United States, state policy makers most often rejected industry demands on grounds of broader political-military considerations. Japanese state policy makers, by contrast, were quick to cite the threat of retaliation that awaited overt protectionist action. West German state policy makers, however, primarily cited concerns with economic vulnerability.

As in the case of their American and Japanese counterparts, West German state policy makers failed consistently to follow the dictates of international constraints. Yet the West German cases involved more of a conflict over retaining existing protection than gaining a more overt response from the state. The most overt protectionist measures introduced in each of the case studies were primarily limited to nonunilateral quotas on Hong Kong cotton and wool textiles (1964), administrative restrictions on Hong Kong wool exports (1966), and a state subsidy package based on border tax receipts (1969). In contrast, in 1964 industrial alliances forced state policy makers to back down partially on intra-EEC tariff liberalization. In 1966, industrial alliances forced state policy makers to back down on plans to liberalize trade with Eastern Europe. In 1968, industrial alliances were able to renew state policy makers' pledges to maintain quantitative restrictions on Eastern Europe only to see such pledges disappear in 1969. Once again, international constraints had not changed; domestic pressures had.

In all three cases, domestic pressures were initially sparked by textile producer associations' concerns over "distorted" imports. During 1963 a moderately strong industrial alliance was supported in its efforts by Länder representatives impatient with the pace of state policy makers' action. Industrial alliance strength increased during 1964 as Gesamttextil and BBI turned to joint protests, specifically calling for exemption from BMWi Minister Schmücker's plan to accelerate intra-EEC tariff liberalization. Institutional access on the industry's behalf also shifted from Länder protests to the Bundestag Foreign Trade Committee holding Schmücker's initiative hostage. Yet in contrast to the HR 1 dispute in the United States, the West German textile alliance was unable to gain the support of the Foreign Trade Committee for imposing stricter conditions on the BMWi proposal. As a result, the textile alliance failed to win its demands for total exemption.

In Case 2, the textile alliance had considerable difficulty in regaining the interest convergence necessary to match the level of industrial alliance strength of mid-1964. Following the 1965 Bundestag elections, the industrial alliance also found its institutional access limited to uncoordinated Länder protests, limited statements of support by top Bundestag officials, and nonbinding meetings with BMWi officials. During 1966, this combination of industrial alliance strength and institutional access prompted state policy makers to act on Langer's December 1965 promise to take steps against "market disruption" with the extremely limited licensing measures imposed against Hong Kong. In 1967, by contrast, a second attempt by state policy makers to accelerate trade liberalization sparked the resurgence of the strong textile alliance. The degree of institutional access also began to increase as the SPD's management of West German textile trade policy was increasingly called into question by CDU/CSU and FDP Bundestag members. The threat of renewed support for the textile industry prompted a temporary delay in trade liberalization. A greater degree of institutional access on the alliance's behalf as well as more overt policy concessions, however, failed to emerge.

The third West German case study reveals a strong industrial alliance unable to garner institutional access on the border tax and revaluation issues. Despite demands for exemption, the sole concession to the textile alliance was a proposed state financial assistance plan, which was put into question because of steadily decreasing resources. Schiller's gaffe in stating that government policies were aiding the industry produced a brief return to the days of federal understanding for the industry's concerns. Yet by 1969, the BMWi pledge to forgo liberalization of trade with Eastern Europe had been forgotten and BBI officials found themselves as the lone voice protesting against expanded Yugoslavian trade.

Finally, the three cases raise a number of questions for the predominant theoretical approaches in the political economy literature. International economic structure arguments would suggest that West Germany should have been constrained from the excessive use of overt protectionist action. Drawing from the historical experience of the United States during the 1920s, for example, Lake has argued that the constraints of the bilateral supportership will prompt individual supporters to rely on overt protectionist policies but at more moderate levels. Lake's predictions are partially accurate. West German state policy makers did rely on the limited use of nonunilateral quantitative restrictions during the three cases; however, with few exceptions these restrictions were in place before the industry's first major exposure to import competition and subsequent demands for relief. During the bilateral supportership of the 1920s, the United States also had introduced moderate tariff increases. During the postwar bilateral supportership, by contrast, West German state policy makers relied on a less overt protectionist policies and accelerated tariff reductions. The latter as well as West German trade policy with Eastern Europe are partially accounted for by arguments based on the international economic structure. Specifically, Lake has also argued that the supporter may turn to unilateral action in the attempt to force trading partners towards a more open international economy.[70]

International regime arguments also offer a partial explanation of West German textile trade policy. Following admittance to GATT in 1951, West Germany joined other European countries in relying on import quotas to safeguard balance-of-payments positions as allowed under Article 12. West Germany retained quantitative restrictions on cotton textiles from Japan, India, and Pakistan until the early 1960s. By 1962, West Germany was replacing these measures with bilateral quotas under the STA and LTA.[71] Yet state policy makers did not act entirely in accord with the textile regime. In 1963, West Germany chose not to exercise its option to invoke unilateral action under the LTA even

70. Lake, "Beneath the Commerce of Nations," p. 161.

71. GATT, *Textile and Clothing in the World Economy*, 4 May 1984, p. 64; Gerard Curzon and Victoria Curzon, "The Management of Trade Relations in the GATT," in Andrew Schonfield, ed., *International Economic Relations of the Western World, 1959–1971: Politics and Trade*, vol. 2 (London: Oxford University Press, 1976), pp. 255, 260–61; Gesamttextil, *Textilindustrie in Spannungsfeld deutscher und europaischer Wirtschaftspolitik: Festgabe für Hans-Werner Staratzke* (Frankfurt: St. Otto Verlag, 1979), pp. 13–18, 28–29; Aggarwal, *Liberal Protectionism*, p. 74; and Jürgen Wiemann, *Selective Protectionism and Structural Adjustment: European Response to the Growing Competition from Developing Countries, The Case of the European Community's Textile Policy* (Berlin: German Development Institute, 1983), p. 67.

though Hong Kong's grace period under the regime had long since expired. In 1964, West Germany restricted imports of Hong Kong cotton textiles and renegotiated the Japanese quota as allowed under the LTA. West Germany's successful push for a voluntary restraint agreement covering Hong Kong wool textile exports, however, was not covered by the LTA.

Regime approaches have greater difficulty explaining trade policy choices in the second and third West German cases. From 1964 to 1969, West German state policy makers continued to rely on quantitative restrictions on Japan and Hong Kong under the LTA. As a result, the LTA was not a source of dispute between the textile alliance and state policy makers. State policy makers' efforts to remove quotas on Eastern European trade, however, are not explained by regime arguments. With the exception of Coordinating Committee restrictions on Western exports to communist countries, there were no regime constraints on West German trade with Eastern Europe. During the 1960s these countries were members neither of GATT nor of the textile regime. The sole provision for nonmembers of the LTA was that they should not be treated more leniently than the regime's participants if their exports were "causing or threatening to cause market disruption."[72] Following this criterion, West German state policy makers should not have liberalized quantitative restrictions on Eastern European textile imports.

According to statist approaches, the fragmented West German state should at least have been able to resist societal pressure. Again, this argument is only partially accurate. State policy makers were able to resist societal pressure on the border tax measures and on liberalization of Eastern European trade during the late 1960s. In the dispute over unilateral tariff cuts and the efforts to accelerate Eastern European trade during the mid-1960s, however, state policy makers were forced to make concessions and, in the case of the latter, to back down. As expected by statist arguments, West German state policy makers had little success in directly altering industry structure. The failure of the 1964 Cotton Textile Rationalization Association, for example, placed a damper on subsequent cooperative efforts aimed at structural change. Liberalization efforts in the face of limited domestic pressure, however, allowed West German state policy makers indirectly to promote industry rationalization.

Finally, policy predictions based on domestic structure are basically

72. Pisar, *Coexistence and Commerce*, pp. 49, 60, 102–7; and reprint of the LTA (Article 6, Section C) in Aggarwal, *Liberal Protectionism*, p. 220.

accurate. Katzenstein has argued that in part because of the combination of a decentralized state and centralized society, West German policy choices have fallen between the U.S. model of "limited, ad hoc protectionist policies" and the Japanese model of "structural transformation" and short- to medium-term protectionist policies. West German state policy makers have turned to a combination of the selective use of overt types of protectionist policy and limited industry assistance measures. The absence of major sectoral adjustment programs for the textile industry following the experience of the Cotton Textile Rationalization Association also appears to bear out Katzenstein's argument that West German state policy makers have forgone the task of managing structural change to societal actors.[73] Accounting for more specific policy choices, however, requires a more detailed focus on the interaction between state and societal actors than that offered by a domestic structure framework.

73. Katzenstein, *Small States*, p. 23; and Katzenstein, *Policy and Politics in West Germany*, pp. 15–35, 93.

# CHAPTER SEVEN

# Choosing between Protectionist Policies: The Sources and Fate of the Patchwork

Postwar protectionism is distinguished by markedly different choices made by state policy makers among types and coverage of protectionist policy in response to what initially appears to be a similar threat: domestic industry calls for increasingly overt forms of import relief in the face of international constraints against the use of such measures. The preceding chapters illustrate that a more nuanced, integrative approach to trade policy choices than that offered by the literature on international political economy is necessary to account for the resulting protectionist patchwork.

In accordance with the international economic structure, state policy makers in the United States should have responded to textile industry demands with protectionist policies less overt than those actually adopted, and textile trade policy in Japan and West Germany should have been more overtly protectionist than it actually was. Regime arguments predict a similar pattern of policy responses for the United States and Japan and provide only a partial understanding of West German trade policy choices. Statist arguments appear unable to account for the tendency of the weak American and West German states and the strong Japanese state to behave in similar manners; state policy makers in all three countries at times resisted and at times were forced to concede to the protectionist demands of strong societal groups. Domestic structure arguments come the closest to accounting for textile trade policy choices by predicting the relative emphasis state policy makers in the different countries placed on broad strategies of protection and adjustment.

Patchwork protectionism, however, lies beneath the surface of these cross-national differences in protection and adjustment and holds the potential to spark increased tension in the international political economy. Accounting for this patchwork requires a nuanced and integrative approach to the sources of trade policy choices.[1] This chapter discusses the findings and implications of the integrative approach introduced and tested in the preceding chapters.

## TEXTILE TRADE POLICY CHOICES AND THE DEGREE OF INSTITUTIONAL ACCESS

The case studies support the general hypothesis posed by this book: when faced with rising domestic pressure—reflecting the combination of industrial alliance strength and the degree of institutional access— state policy makers turned to increasingly overt types of protectionist policy despite international constraints against such choices. Domestic pressure forced American state policy makers to put quantitative restrictions on textile imports despite the political-military costs such steps could entail. Domestic pressure forced Japanese state policy makers to move beyond cartel and subsidy policies to more overt protectionist policies despite the threat of retaliation stemming from Japan's structural position in the international economy. Domestic pressure also forced West German state policy makers to retain overt protectionist policies despite international economic pressures for accelerated liberalization. Given this pattern of policy responses, I would expect that cross-national and intranational differences in trade policy choices among protectionist policies will reflect differences in domestic pressure and international constraints. The case studies reveal a much more specific finding: the greatest source of variation in textile trade policy choices appears to lie in the degree of institutional access achieved by state officials on behalf of industrial alliances.

Table 9 summarizes the textile trade policy choices of the United States, Japan, and West Germany. As argued in the Appendix, the ordinal scales used to rank the components of domestic pressure and international constraint sacrifice a degree of precision for the sake of integrating quantitative and qualitative data. Moreover, the small num-

---

1. The integrative approach overlaps the recent "institutionalist" arguments calling for a focus on the impact of the state and state institutions on American foreign policy making. The two approaches differ in the integrative approach's cross-national perspective and narrower focus on the degree of institutional access. For detail on the institutional approach, see G. John Ikenberry, David A. Lake, and Michael Mastanduno, eds., *The State and American Foreign Economic Policy*, special issue of *International Organization* 42 (Winter 1988).

*Table 9.* Summary of textile trade policy choices

| Case | Domestic pressure | | International constraint | | |
|---|---|---|---|---|---|
| | IAS | DIA | Vulnerability | Threat | Political-Military |
| United States, 1954–57 | High– | High–/ Mod+ | Low– | High–/Mod+ | High–/Mod+ |
| Outcome: Nonunilateral quantitative restriction | | | | | |
| United States, 1957–60 | Mod | Mod+ | Low– | High– | High–/Mod+ |
| Outcome: Nonunilateral quantitative restriction (attempted) | | | | | |
| United States, 1960–62 | High/ High– | Mod+ | Low– | High– | High–/Mod+[a] |
| Outcome: Unilateral quantitative restrictions | | | | | |
| Japan, 1974–76 | High | Mod–/ Low+ | Low+ | High+ | Low |
| Outcome: Administrative restrictions | | | | | |
| Japan, 1977–81 | High | High+ | Low+ | High+ | Low |
| Outcome: Price-based restrictions | | | | | |
| Japan, 1981–83 | High/ High– | Mod+ | Low+ | High+ | Low |
| Outcome: Nonunilateral quantitative restrictions | | | | | |
| Germany, 1963–64 | High | Mod | Mod– | Low+ (Mod+)[b] | Mod– |
| Outcome: Nonunilateral quotas | | | | | |
| Germany, 1964–67 | High | Mod– | Mod– | Mod (Mod+)[b] | Mod– |
| Outcome: Administrative restrictions (quotas renewed but relaxed) | | | | | |
| Germany, 1967–69 | High | Low– | Mod– | Mod (Mod+)[b] | Mod– |
| Outcome: State subsidies | | | | | |

*Note:* The indicator scores are based on the highest level reached in a given case study. The policy outcomes are the most overt protectionist policy adopted in a given case study period. This table is based on the summary tables for the United States, Japan, and West Germany.

[a] Level for those actions not sanctioned by the STA and LTA.

[b] Threat of retaliation score in parentheses based on regional economic structure.

ber of cases precludes more detailed statistical measures of correlation that would be helpful in assessing the accuracy of the ordinal scales. With these caveats in mind, Table 9 offers a rough starting point for assessing the sources of divergent trade policy choices that characterize patchwork protectionism.

The integrative approach introduced in this book reveals that the international and domestic pressures facing state policy makers in the United States, Japan, and West Germany were similar but not exactly the same. State policy makers in the United States and Japan faced high levels of international constraint against the use of overt types of protectionist policy, albeit from different sources. Political-military considerations were primary for American state policy makers whereas economic considerations were of greater importance for their Japanese counterparts. West German state policy makers, by contrast, faced a more balanced and slightly more moderate level of international constraints. Yet despite having greater latitude to choose overt types of protectionist policy than American and Japanese state policy makers, West German state policy makers faced weaker levels of domestic pressure for such a response.

Industrial alliances in all three countries called for action against imports, and in all three countries these demands were initially resisted by state policy makers. Except for the second American case study, these demands were backed by the emergence of strong industrial alliances. As seen in Table 9, however, the degree of institutional access achieved by these alliances varied across the individual cases. In those instances when the degree of institutional access failed to surpass the moderate − level (distinguished by the strong potential for an electoral or hostage threat), industrial alliances were unable to press state policy makers into accepting overt measures beyond the use of administrative restrictions.

In contrast, state policy makers turned to quantitative restrictions in cases when the degree of institutional access reached the moderate + level (distinguished by the strong potential for state officials to initiate a specific, binding recommendation on state policy makers' action). The one exception to this finding is the first West German case study in which quantitative restrictions were not the primary focus of the debate. Finally, the most overt responses to the demands of industrial alliances appear to have occurred when these alliances achieved high degrees of institutional access. Such access through the Ministry of Finance, for example, contributed to the Japanese textile alliance's success in achieving exemption from preferential tariffs in 1981. The third U.S. case study, as argued in Chapter 4, offers less definitive support for the link between degree of institutional access and overt policy responses in that Kennedy's turn to unilateral quotas in 1962 appeared to follow more from fears of potential institutional access undercutting the 1962 Trade Expansion Act than from the actual level of institutional access that existed at the time.

The conclusion that differences in trade policy choices appear to reflect different degrees of institutional access raises an additional question: what accounts for differences in the degree of institutional access? Several arguments can be raised here. For example, the answer offered by the statist and domestic structure approaches—cross-national differences in historically determined state structures—is partially undercut by the presence of intranational as well as cross-national differences in the degree of institutional access achieved by industrial alliances in the nine cases. A more extensive sample of cases of intrasectoral trade policy disputes drawing from a number of manufacturing sectors would be necessary to determine whether cross-national differences were indeed more prevalent than intranational differences in institutional access.

A second argument that opposing societal coalitions captured the support of state actors, thereby closing off access channels to the industrial alliance, is undercut by the relative absence of such countercoalitions in the debate over textile trade policy. In the United States, associations representing importers of Japanese textiles attracted little support in Congress. Associations of importers in Japan appeared to have little impact on the LDP Textile Committee or on the Ministry of Finance's decision to exempt portions of the industry from preferential tariff measures. MITI and the importers associations clearly held a similar interest in promoting textile trade, but this overlap did not prevent concessions to the textile alliance.

In contrast to the United States and Japan, the West German textile alliance faced an active countercoalition of retail and wholesale trade associations. The textile alliance's demand for action on Eastern European imports also challenged the export programs of West Germany's capital goods industries. Despite this opposition, the textile alliance still appears to have gained greater access to the policy-making process than the trade associations. Capital goods industries, by contrast, have been a dominant force in peak business associations and as such are likely to carry greater weight in formal and informal discussions with state policy makers. Yet the failure of both the textile alliance and export-oriented industries to modify the DM revaluation during the late 1960s suggests that neither societal actor has succeeded in "capturing" the state.[2]

A tentative response to the question of institutional access lies in answering two other interrelated questions: first, what determines the access channel selected by an industrial alliance, and second, what determines the access channel's receptivity to the demands of an industrial alliance? Intuitively, industrial alliances should choose access channels based on past successes and the nature of relief offered

2. Kreile, "West Germany," pp. 201, 203, 213–16; and Katzenstein, "Conclusion: Domestic Structures," pp. 316–17.

through the channel. The American textile alliance's past success in obtaining import relief had come through appeals to Congress for tariff relief before 1934 and through wielding the threat of unilateral congressional action against Japan during interindustry negotiations in 1937. The 1934 Reciprocal Trade Act shifted authority over tariff policy decisions to the executive. Twenty years later, the textile alliance appealed to the tariff policy access channel for import relief as embodied in the Committee for Reciprocity Information. By 1955, the textile alliance had again turned to Congress. To keep pressure on state policy makers, the textile alliance also appeared to follow a "shotgun approach," scattering its efforts across a wide number of access channels including the secretary of agriculture, the Tariff Commission, and the Office of Defense and Civilian Mobilization. With the exception of congressional action, however, these access channels did not offer binding input on the policy-making process.

What determined Congress's limited receptivity to the textile alliance's demands? Specifically, why did the degree of institutional access through Congress fail to move beyond the high– to moderate+ level? Support for the textile industry in Congress primarily reflected the geographical concentration of the industry in the South and the Northeast. Faced with a strong industrial alliance, congressmen and senators responded to their constituencies. But the congressional committee system and the experience and interests of those individuals staffing key positions acted as a check on the industry's supporters. The leaders of the House Ways and Means Committee and the Senate Finance Committee as well as the Speaker of the House opposed concessions to the industry and played a substantial role in restraining protectionist legislation during the 1950s and early 1960s.[3]

Presidential action also appears to have played a role in constraining protectionist forces in Congress. Eisenhower's concessions on the 1958 extension of the RTA avoided a showdown such as occurred in 1955 and removed an opportunity for the textile alliance to hold state policy makers hostage. Eisenhower's initiation of VER negotiations with Hong Kong, his willingness to authorize a Tariff Commission review of the

3. Destler, *American Trade Politics*, pp. 26–27; and Bauer et al., *American Business*, pp. 59–79. Given the role of other state officials in shaping policy choices, an interesting direction for future research would be a systematic, cross-national analysis of how state officials (as distinct from state policy makers) balance international and domestic factors. Although this issue has been addressed to some extent in the literature on bureaucratic politics, this literature has been dominated by a focus on American politics. For example, see Graham T. Allison, *Essence of Decision* (Boston: Little, Brown, 1971); and Morton Halperin, *Bureaucratic Politics and Foreign Policy* (Washington, D.C.: Brookings Institution, 1974).

textile alliance's Section 22 petition, and the administration's posturing on a possible import duty on foreign goods also allowed state policy makers to appear active in response to the 1958 Pastore Subcommittee protests. These steps basically placed the alliance's congressional supporters "on hold" until the collapse of the negotiations with Hong Kong in early 1960. Finally, Kennedy's strategy of holding the textile alliance hostage by trading off the STA and LTA for industry support of the 1962 Trade Expansion Act also appears to have played a role in limiting congressional action on the industry's behalf.

How did the Japanese textile alliance select its access channels? In contrast to its American counterpart, the Japanese textile industry's most recent success in gaining relief before the onset of major postwar import competition had concerned the issue of textile exports. Years of trade disputes with the United States had increased the industry's reliance on MITI as a source of restructuring assistance through the Diet and as the industry's negotiator. The 1971 conclusion of the bitter "textile wrangle" with the United States altered this relationship when industry demands to the Diet and to MITI officials failed to dissuade the latter from finally accepting American demands over the industry's opposition. In the post-1974 debate over import policy, the Japanese textile alliance limited its appeals primarily to MITI and the Diet even though, as noted in Chapter 2, neither channel offered the best opportunity for successfully gaining access with influence. Additional access channels attempted by the industrial alliance included the prime minister and the Ministry of Finance, but these were given only secondary attention by alliance members.

What determined the wide variation in the degree of institutional access achieved by Japan's textile alliance? All three Japanese case studies illustrate the industry's use of different access channels. From 1974 to 1976, the industrial alliance relied primarily on direct appeals to MITI and appeals to the Diet for action on the industry's behalf. As argued in Chapter 2, MITI's internal restructuring had placed consideration of the textile industry in the broader context of consumer goods industries. Thus, in the absence of advisory council deliberations, the industry's influence through direct access channels to the policy-making process was limited. Similarly, appeals to the Diet never surpassed the moderate− to low+ level of institutional access. One explanation based on state structure would be the Diet's relatively limited power and authority in the policy-making process. Yet LDP forces in the Diet were highly responsive to demands from the silk industry and appeared to place considerable pressure on MITI. Moreover, although the silk industry's experience is not well suited for drawing broader inferences, the perception of the Diet as a "rubber stamp" of MITI policy is increasingly seen as less accurate among analysts of Japanese politics. A more plausible explanation lies in the composition of the LDP Textile Committee. Although responsive to the textile alliance's demands, the committee was staffed primarily with silk delegates of the LDP textile faction. Thus, during the early 1970s, the Textile Committee's primary focus was on the silk industry's concerns.[4]

The higher degrees of institutional access at the times of the second and third Japanese case studies reflect the shift of the textile alliance to secondary access channels. Appeals in the late 1970s to modify Japan's preferential tariff policy fell within MITI's jurisdiction as well as within the purview of the Ministry of Finance's Tariff Council. The council's 1980 decision to respond to the textile alliance's demands for exemption appeared to be based on the adverse economic impact of low-tariff imports on portions of the Japanese textile industry. In contrast to the nonbinding nature of the Tariff Commission's recommendations to American state policy makers, the Ministry of Finance's recommendations on tariff policy were binding on MITI. The 1983 moderate+ degree of institutional access also reflects a shift from the industry's traditional access channels. In brief, the Japan Spinners Association stepped outside of MITI advisory council deliberations to invoke Japan's antidumping and countervailing duty legislation. Once again, both MITI and the Ministry of Finance were involved in the decision-making process. In contrast to 1980, however, the guidelines for reaching a decision under this legislation and thus the potential for binding input on the policy-making process were unclear. The spinners association's decision to drop the suit against South Korea in favor of a voluntary export restraint appeared to leave state policy makers relieved and the nature of the access channel untested.

What determined the West German textile alliance's relatively low levels of institutional access to the policy-making process? Compared to the United States and Japan, the West German textile alliance relied primarily on direct appeals to state policy makers to mitigate the pace of liberalization despite the limited binding input such channels would actually offer and the limited receptiveness of ministry officials to the alliance's demands. Not only were industry sections set within broader divisions of BMWi, but the ad hoc meetings between ministry officials and textile alliance representatives did not incur the burden of consensus decision making evident in Japan. The textile alliance's preference for direct appeals appears to reflect the nature of the relief BMWi

4. Interview held in Tokyo, Japan, April 1984.

officials could offer. Since BMWi was the primary state source behind the liberal direction of West German trade policy, the ministry would be the source of relief for the industry either through direct action or action on the alliance's behalf at the level of the EEC.

This strategy of "going to the source" in selecting access channels was supplemented during times of crisis by appeals to key committees in the Bundestag. Appeals to the Bundestag Foreign Trade Committee (1964) and the Bundestag Finance Committee (1968), however, were undercut by committee members' support for liberalization and revaluation. Finally, the textile alliance found its most receptive access channels at the regional level. Because of the textile industry's concentration in key Länder such as Bavaria, North Rhine–Westphalia, and Baden-Württemberg, coordinated Länder protests on the industry's behalf were difficult for state policy makers to ignore. By accepting regional adjustment programs for the textile industry and by meeting with Länder officials, state policy makers were often able to prevent Länder opposition to West German trade policy from sparking greater degrees of institutional access by Bundestag officials and other state actors. The industrial alliance's most receptive audience thus had only a limited impact on the policy-making process.

## THE FATE OF THE PATCHWORK

From a policy standpoint, the integrative approach suggests an increase in the use of more overt types of protectionist policy in the future. The United States will be less likely to act as a check on overt protectionist policy choices in the international economy. American state policy makers no longer face the political-military constraints against overt protectionist action that characterized the 1950s. By the mid-1970s, the scenario of strategic allies abandoned to the economic wave of communism had become less compelling with Soviet-American détente and the economic recovery of Western Europe and Japan. By the mid-1980s, the Soviet Union, the potential source of such a communist economic wave, was questioning the appropriateness of the "Soviet model" as part of a broader strategy of restructuring (*perestroika*). Political-military considerations are likely to increase for Japan and West Germany, however, as the United States places greater emphasis on the linkage between foreign trade and sharing the defense burden by NATO and Japan.

International economic constraints on American state policy makers have also changed since the early 1960s but not enough to compensate for the decline of political-military constraints. The shift in status from hegemon in world trade to supporter in what Lake has termed a "multilateral supportership" has slightly decreased the threat of retaliation faced by the United States in the event of overt protectionist action. In contrast, America's vulnerability to retaliation as measured by trade as a percentage of GNP has increased but only from 6.7 percent (1954–62) to 16.6 percent (1980–85). Japanese and West German vulnerability scores for the 1980s remain higher, standing at 24.5 percent and 50.4 percent respectively.[5] As international constraints fall, American state policy makers will have less cause than their Japanese and West German counterparts to resist domestic pressure for overt protectionist policies.

Domestic pressure is unlikely to wane in either the United States, Japan, or West Germany. Destler has argued that the capacity of trade policy-making institutions in the United States to resist protectionist pressures is eroding. In Congress, the decline of the committee system and its ability to insulate congressional officials from their constituencies are likely to increase the receptiveness of this access channel to the entreaties of industrial alliances.[6] In Japan, efforts by opposition and LDP Diet members to increase their expertise in certain areas and to play a more active role in the policy-making process are likely to increase the potential for greater institutional access. Moreover, the nature of the access embodied in Japan's antidumping and countervailing duty laws remains untested.[7] Finally, West German state policy makers are likely to face the potential for greater institutional access from the European Community level as member states engage in the push toward a single market by 1992.[8]

The remaining question, therefore, is whether strong industrial alliances will emerge to take advantage of such access channels. Because of the dynamic nature of interest convergence among producer associations, predictions here can rapidly become outdated. It is plausible to assert, however, that import-competing industries in the United States, Japan, and West Germany will continue to face pressure from

5. International Monetary Fund, *International Financial Statistics*, selected issues.

6. Destler, *American Trade Politics*, pp. xii, 59–60.

7. For detail on the interaction between MITI and the Diet since the early 1980s, see T. J. Pempel, "The Unbundling of 'Japan, Inc.': The Changing Dynamics of Japanese Policy Formation," *Journal of Japanese Studies* 13 (Summer 1987), pp. 271–306.

8. For detail on the current push toward integration, see "1992: A Survey of Europe's Internal Market," *Economist*, 16 July 1988.

current as well as future waves of newly industrializing countries.[9] Convergence of interests among and within producer associations is also likely to hinge on factors such as producers' export orientation, reliance on intrafirm trade across national boundaries, and joint ventures with foreign producers. Aside from such relatively recent exceptions as the American automobile industry, these characteristics are more common among Japanese and West German producers.

For those industrial alliances seeking more overt protection, success will begin at home through strategies of increasing organization, inclusiveness, and interest convergence. The continued formidable presence of the American textile alliance, for example, reflects its shift from the days of ACMI to the American Fiber, Textile, Apparel Coalition. For those state policy makers seeking to curtail domestic pressure, the integrative approach suggests two routes: alter the potential degree of institutional access and alter the strength of industrial alliances. The attractiveness of modifying state institutions to increase the flexibility of trade policy makers is mitigated by the difficulty of such a task and issues of the public accountability of policy-making officials. Thus, despite the protectionist fervor in the United States during the 1980s, neither the 1984 nor 1988 trade acts shifted final decision-making authority over "unfair trade" issues from the president to nonelected officials.[10]

Targeting the strength of industrial alliances appears as a more viable option. To buy breathing space in the short run, state policy makers should ideally target concessions at the core producer associations of the industrial alliance. Kennedy's strategy with ACMI, MITI's focus on the Japan Spinners Association, and BMWi's focus on Gesamttextil entailed costs but minimized the use of overt protectionist action. As a longer run strategy, state policy makers should attempt to tie concessions on overt protectionist measures to policies encouraging exports and international investment and linking protection to mandatory progress on industry adjustment. Such strategies can fragment the convergence of interests of the industrial alliance while also creating pockets of competitiveness in the industry's domestic market.

In summary, the future of the international economy will hinge on

9. For background on NICs, see Thornton F. Bradshaw et al., eds., *America's New Competitors: The Challenge of the Newly Industrializing Countries* (Cambridge, Mass.: Ballinger, 1988).
10. Lande and VanGrasstek, *The Trade and Tariff Act*, pp. 12–23; and "New Trade Law: Wide Spectrum," *New York Times*, 24 August 1988.

the trade policy choices of its dominant members. Insights into the direction these choices will take lie in focusing on the intersection of domestic pressures and international constraints on state policy makers' action.

APPENDIX

# *Operationalization*

As noted in Chapter 1, a major hindrance to the analysis of postwar protectionism has been the absence of a framework to integrate qualitative and quantitative data. I will here introduce a tentative effort to fill this gap through detailed operationalization and the use of ordinal indexes. In this book I rely on the indexes merely to trace changes in the independent and dependent variables. The small number of cases precludes more detailed statistical measures of correlation that would be helpful in assessing the accuracy of the ordinal scales. I leave this task for future research.

## INTERNATIONAL CONSTRAINTS

International constraints against the use of overt types of protectionist policy stem from economic and political-military factors. The level of international economic constraint faced by state policy makers is based on the country's vulnerability to retaliation and the threat of retaliation (Table A1). Vulnerability is distinguished by relatively high levels of trade dependence, measured here by trade (exports plus imports) as a percentage of gross national product.[1] I derive an ordinal vulnerability scale from an unweighted average of vulnerability scores for fourteen industrialized countries. Averages for individual countries are calculated based on five-year intervals over the period 1955 to 1985. The fourteen countries are the small and large industrial democ-

1. For the strengths and weaknesses of this indicator, see Richard N. Rosecrance and Arthur Stein, "Interdependence: Myth or Reality," *World Politics* 26 (October 1973), pp. 1–27.

racies emphasized by the political economy literature: United States, United Kingdom, West Germany, France, Japan, Italy, Canada, Austria, Belgium, Denmark, the Netherlands, Norway, Sweden, and Switzerland. For detail on the determination of cutoff points for moderate and high levels of vulnerability, see Table A1, note a.

*Table A1.* Index for international economic constraint

| Rank | Vulnerability to Retaliation (percent)[a] (Trade/GNP) | Threat of Retaliation[b] Actor | IES |
|---|---|---|---|
| 1. High + | 80–100 | SP | SUPs + SPs |
| 2. High | 70– 79 | SUP | SPs |
| 3. High – | 60– 69 | HEG | SPs |
| 4. Moderate + | 50– 59 | HEG | SUPs + SPs |
| 5. Moderate | 40– 49 | SUP | SUP + SPs |
| 6. Moderate – | 30– 39 | SUP | SUPs + SPs |
| 7. Low + | 20– 29 | SUP | HEG + SPs |
| 8. Low | 10– 19 | SUP | HEG + SUP(s) + SPs |
| 9. Low – | 0– 9 | SP | HEG ( + SUPs) |

[a] Vulnerability scale derived from unweighted average of vulnerability scores for fourteen industrialized democracies from 1955 to 1985 (calculated at five-year intervals). The cutoff points for moderate and high levels of vulnerability reflect the average for large industrial countries (30.2 percent) and the average for small industrial countries (62.8 percent) respectively. Average vulnerability for large and small industrial countries combined for the period 1955–85 equals 46.5 percent. *Source:* Calculated from International Monetary Fund, *International Financial Statistics,* selected issues.

[b] Table A1 proposes rough combinations of major economic actors—spoilers (SP), supporters (SUP), and hegemons (HEG)—and ranks possible combinations by the systemic threat of retaliation faced by the actor within a given international economic system (IES). The rankings are tentative. Moreover, the differences within the high, moderate, and low categories are less than those between categories. *Source:* Derived, in part, from Lake, "Beneath the Commerce of Nations," pp. 151–59, 162–67.

The second component of international economic constraints, the threat of retaliation, draws from David Lake's arguments on international economic structure.[2] Lake conceptualizes the international economic structure as consisting of different combinations of three dominant actors: spoilers, supporters, and hegemons. Lake attempts to refine Charles Kindleberger's qualitative distinction between medium-sized and large countries by setting out quantitative demarcations of size and by dividing medium-sized countries according to relative productivity. For example, spoilers are those countries that account for

2. Lake, "International Economic Structures"; and Lake, "Beneath the Commerce of Nations."

between 5 and 15 percent of world trade but are characterized by levels of productivity (manufacturing, agricultural, and service) below the world average. Supporters account for the same percentage of world trade as spoilers but are distinguished by above-average productivity. Finally, hegemonic countries exhibit above-average productivity and account for 15 percent or more of world trade.

Lake has acknowledged that distinguishing hegemonic countries from nonhegemonic countries according to a quantitative cutoff point is a tentative as well as arbitrary exercise. Such classifications must also be grounded in the historical interpretations of the relative position of countries in the international economy. Quantitative identifications as well as qualitative identifications should be cross-checked against alternative conceptualizations to increase methodological rigor. Thus, as seen in the case studies, I rely on Lake's criteria only as a starting point for identifying supporters, spoilers, and hegemons in the issue area of trade policy.

A key point is that the threat of retaliation faced by a given country is based not only on whether it is a spoiler, supporter, or hegemon but on the composition of the international economic system within which the country interacts with its trading partners as well. Table A1 proposes rough combinations of these major economic actors and different international economic systems. These combinations are derived, in part, from historical analysis of international economic structures. I rank these combinations according to the systemic threat of retaliation faced by the actor in question.

These rankings are tentative. Moreover, the differences within the high, moderate, and low categories are less than those between categories. Yet these rankings of systemic threats of retaliation are informed by several considerations. First, since Lake measures relative productivity against the average productivity scores of members of the international economic system, there must always be countries below the average (either spoilers or large numbers of smaller countries that essentially act as protectionist free-riders). The systems presented in Table A1, therefore, reflect combinations of spoilers and supporters or hegemons. Second, Lake notes that hegemonic countries will weigh the consideration of protectionist action against the negative impact such action will have on the hegemon's leadership. This can facilitate the ability of spoilers to free-ride on the hegemon (act with less fear of retaliation). Third, Lake argues that there are finite limits on the ability of hegemons (and more pressing limits on supporters in the absence of a hegemon) to use positive inducements instead of retaliation in seeking to prevent countries from adopting protectionist measures. Thus the greater the number of spoilers in an international economic system, the more extended are the resources of the hegemon. Finally, in the absence of a hegemon, the greater the number of supporters, the less the threat of retaliation faced by the single supporter that chooses to adopt overt types of protectionist policy.

Political-military considerations serve as the second source of international constraint. Vinod Aggarwal has accurately argued that trade issues are often "nested" in broader strategic concerns. Building on this idea, I measure political-military constraints according to a set of potentially adverse political-military consequences that could occur in the event that state policy makers adopted overt types of protectionist policy. I derive these consequences from three primary concerns of state policy makers: war, spheres of influence, and alliance politics.

Aggarwal's observation on nesting is borne out by a wide array of examples. For West Germany, international trade serves as a means to retain ties with the German Democratic Republic. For the United States, trade policy has often been seen as the "carrot" to draw countries away from Soviet influence and as the "shield" to ensure the viability of American allies. For Great Britain and France, trade policy serves to maintain political ties with old colonial territories. In all these instances, trade policy choices that disrupt import flows or provoke retaliation by trading partners can incur political-military costs. The

*Table A2.* Index for political-military constraint

| Rank | Political-military constraint[a]<br>(adverse political-military consequences) |
|---|---|
| 1. High + | War against allies of primary strategic importance |
| 2. High | War against primary opponent |
| 3. High − | Loss of support from strategic allies |
| 4. Moderate + | Increased tension with strategic allies |
| 5. Moderate | Disrupted relations with intermediate-level allies |
| 6. Moderate − | Disrupted relations with opponent's allies (primary/intermediate) |
| 7. Low + | Disrupted relations with strategic neutrals |
| 8. Low | Disrupted relations with low-level allies |
| 9. Low − | Disrupted relations with nonstrategic neutrals |

*Sources:* The literature here is extensive. See, for example, R. J. Barry Jones, *Conflict and Control in the World Economy: Contemporary Economic Realism and Neo-Mercantilism* (Atlantic Highlands, N.J.: Humanities Press, International, 1986), p. 115; John Spanier, *Games Nations Play*, 6th ed. (Washington, D.C.: Congressional Quarterly, 1987), pp. 155–59; Vinod Aggarwal, *Liberal Protectionism: The International Politics of Organized Textile Trade* (Berkeley and Los Angeles: University of California Press, 1985), pp. 27–28; and Joan Edelman Spero, *The Politics of International Economic Relations*, 2d ed. (New York: St. Martin's Press, 1981), pp. 27–28, 185–89, 348–51, 357–59.
[a] This rough ranking reflects state policy makers' concerns with war, spheres of influence, and alliance politics.

higher the cost, the less important low levels of international economic constraints against overt protectionist action are likely to be for state policy makers. Broader concerns with political-military costs would override economic considerations. To measure these costs, I rely on the rough ranking of adverse consequences presented in Table A2.

## DOMESTIC PRESSURE

State policy makers also face domestic pressures for the adoption of overt types of protectionist policy. Domestic pressure hinges on the strength of industrial alliances and the degree of institutional access. Industrial alliances are coalitions of producer associations, each association representing a subsector within a single major manufacturing industry. I calculate industrial alliance strength by combining indicators of the alliance's organization, inclusiveness, and convergence of interests. The ordinal indexes for these indicators appear in Table A3. By averaging the relevant rankings on the indicators, I derive a rough measure of industrial alliance strength (see note to Table A3).

My conception of industrial alliance strength seeks to bridge aspects of societal structure with a more dynamic conception of coalition politics. The indicator for organization measures the organizational structure of the members of the industrial alliance. Alliances of producer associations consist of different combinations of separate associations, federations, and merged associations.[3] The weakest alliance organization occurs in alliances of separate associations, associations that encompass a single production process such as spinning or weaving. These associations represent the narrow interests of their members, thereby encouraging resistance to cooperation with other associations. In a federation, separate (and merged) associations are brought together under a peak or umbrella association but retain their separate identities. Although federations establish an organizational framework for cooperation, they still face the problem that their member associations are responsible to their own membership first and to the federation second. As a result, organizational conflicts between producer associations do not disappear in an industrial alliance dominated by a federation. In contrast, merged

---

3. David B. Truman distinguishes only between unitary and federated organization. The latter is an "organization of organizations"; the former is a "single organization." The key to this distinction, according to Truman, is the implications for group cohesion. Yet not all single organizations have the same breadth of organized interests. For this reason, I divide Truman's unitary association into separate and merged associations. See Truman, *Governmental Process*, pp. 115–16.

*Table A3.* Index for industrial alliance strength

| Rank | Organization | Inclusiveness (percent) | Interest convergence |
|---|---|---|---|
| 1. High+ | Single merged | 88-100 | On a specific measure |
| 2. High | Federation of merged and/or federations | 77-87 | On more than one specific measure |
| 3. High− | Federation of merged and separate | 66-76 | On a specific measure and on another type |
| 4. Moderate+ | Federation of separate | 55-65 | On a specific measure and on dissimilar types |
| 5. Moderate | Federation plus merged outside of federation | 44-54 | On one type |
| 6. Moderate− | Federation plus separate outside of federation | 33-43 | On more than one type |
| 7. Low+ | Separate plus merged | 22-32 | On similar types (high, mod, or low, see Table A5) |
| 8. Low | Separate plus separate | 11-21 | On similar and dissimilar types |
| 9. Low− | Single separate | 0-10 | No agreement |

*Note:* I calculate industrial alliance strength by averaging the numerical scores for organization, inclusiveness, and interest convergence. The lower the average score, the stronger the industrial alliance. When outside societal support for the alliance exists (labor, other peak associations, etc.), I subtract one numerical rank per supporter from the sum of the three indicators before calculating the average.

associations directly represent several production processes. In the absence of loyalties to individual associations, the merged association brings a greater degree of organization to the industrial alliance than separate associations.

As an indicator of industrial alliance strength, however, organization is of little relevance without also considering the proportion of the industry that the alliance represents (inclusiveness). To measure inclusiveness, I average each producer association's employment and production figures as a percentage of the industry's total employment and production. Combining the results for those producer associations that constitute the industrial alliance provides a rough measure of inclusiveness. Yet producer associations rarely release information on the extent of their representation in terms of the industry as a whole. Instead, these subsectoral associations tend to claim representation as a proportion of a given subsector, such as 45 percent of cotton spinning or 90 percent of man-made fiber production. Thus, determination of the inclusiveness of an industrial alliance often requires two preliminary steps. First, I calculate the proportion of total industry production and employment accounted for by a given subsector. Second, I multiply this figure by the percentage of subsectoral representation claimed by the producer association. These steps are required to provide a more rigorous conception of the actual inclusiveness of an industrial alliance. A common alternative method used by scholars has been to look at total industry employment, acknowledge the existence of industry spokesgroups, and assume that these groups represent the entire industry. As illustrated in Chapter 3, such an approach can overestimate the strength of societal actors.

The third and final component of industrial alliance strength is convergence of interests. I base this measure on a comparison of the demands of industrial alliance members by type of protectionist policy. Through interviews and a rough content analysis of primary sources, I determine whether producer associations are in agreement on the general type of protectionist policy demanded from state policy makers (tariffs, unilateral quotas, nonunilateral quotas, administrative restrictions, state subsidies, production cartels).[4] Each of the six types of protectionist policy discussed here serves as a category for more specific "measures." For example, unilateral quotas can be applied across the board, by country, and by specific product. The more precise the agreement among industrial alliance members on the steps demanded from state policy makers, the greater the convergence of interest.

The strength of the industrial alliance alone, however, is no guarantee that the alliance will achieve its demands. Industrial alliances also require high degrees of institutional access to generate domestic pressure. Industrial alliances attempt to gain access to state policy makers either through direct appeals or through the efforts of state officials on the alliance's behalf. Yet the issue of access is often clouded by the failure to distinguish between points of access (number of access channels) and nature of access (influence provided through a given access channel). Focusing on the former establishes the variety of access channels available to societal actors. In the latter lies a more dynamic conception of how different access channels affect the ability of societal actors to influence the policy-making process. I measure this nature of

4. This book does not systematically deal with the question of the sources of producer associations' demands. For detail on the sources of industry preferences, see Stephen D. Krasner, "The Tokyo Round: Particularistic Interests and the Prospects for Stability in the Global Trading System," *International Studies Quarterly* 23 (December 1979), pp. 491–531; Gerald Helleiner, *Intra-Firm Trade and the Developing Countries* (New York: St. Martin's Press, 1981); Gourevitch, "Breaking with Orthodoxy"; and Milner, "Resisting the Protectionist Temptation."

*Table A4.* Index for degree of institutional access

| Rank | Type of input by industrial alliance or state supporter |
|------|----------------------------------------------------------|
| 1. High + | Binding recommendation |
| 2. High | Binding recommendation (final decision pending) |
| 3. High − | Binding recommendation (decision procedure initiated) |
| 4. Moderate + | Binding recommendation (strong potential for initiation) |
| 5. Moderate | State policy-maker initiative held hostage<br>Strong electoral threat<br>Set broad parameters empowering (but not requiring) state policy maker action |
| 6. Moderate − | Electoral threat (strong potential)<br>Hostage threat (strong potential) |
| 7. Low + | Limited indications of support for the industrial alliance (electoral, legislative, or other) |
| 8. Low | Nonbinding recommendations or advice |
| 9. Low − | None |

access—degree of institutional access—according to an ordinal scale of different types of input on the policy-making process (Table A4). These types range from the absence of input to binding recommendation on state policy makers' action. Moderate degrees of institutional access are distinguished by strong electoral threats, holding state policy makers' initiatives hostage, or setting broad parameters that empower (but do not require) action by state policy makers. The nature of the access channel selected by the industrial alliance is an integral part of domestic pressure.

## Type of Protectionist Policy

Roughly six types of protectionist policies are available to state policy makers. Drawing on the literature on trade policy, I rank these according to their ability to disrupt imports and to provoke retaliation by trading partners.[5] Price-based restrictions (tariffs) and unilateral quan-

5. The rankings in Table A5 and the analysis presented in this section are based on Giersch, "The New Protectionism"; Balassa, "World Trade"; Trade and Development Board, *Growing Protectionism*; Aggarwal, *Liberal Protectionism*, p. 34; Lipson, "Transformation of Trade"; Franko, "Current Trends in Protectionism"; Carl J. Green, "Legal Protectionism in the United States and Its Impact on U.S. Economic Relations," in Japan-U.S. Economic Relations Group, *Appendix to the Report of the Japan-U.S. Economic Relations Group*, (Washington, D.C.: The Group, 1981), pp. 14–15; Yamazawa et al., "Trade and Industrial Adjustment," pp. 35–36.

titative restrictions are the most overt types of protection and the most likely to provoke retaliation and disrupt imports. Nonunilateral quantitative restrictions (voluntary export restraints, voluntary restraint agreements, and orderly marketing agreements) and administrative restrictions (gray area measures such as import guidance and surveillance) are more moderate protectionist policies and, as such, are less likely to provoke retaliation and to disrupt imports. The two types of protectionist policy least likely to provoke retaliation and disrupt imports are state subsidies and production cartels. The ordinal rankings for types of protectionist policy appear in Table A5.

*Table A5.* Index for type of protectionist policy

| Rank | Policy |
| --- | --- |
| 1. High + | Price-based restrictions |
| 2. High | Price-based restrictions and unilateral quantitative restrictions |
| 3. High − | Unilateral quantitative restrictions |
| 4. Moderate + | Nonunilateral quantitative restrictions |
| 5. Moderate | Nonunilateral quantitative restrictions and administrative restrictions |
| 6. Moderate − | Administrative restrictions |
| 7. Low + | State subsidies |
| 8. Low | State subsidies and production cartels |
| 9. Low − | Production cartels |

Price-based restrictions refer to those policy instruments that allow imports but influence prices of imports. Tariff barriers can offset the price advantage of foreign competitors by placing a duty on imports. Import prices can also be increased through dumping and countervailing duty actions. In cases of dumping, domestic actors seek to levy duties on foreign exporters who sell goods at a price below some conception of "fair value." In cases of countervailing duties, domestic actors also seek to levy duties on foreign exporters, but duties are linked to the subsidies received by the exporter for production or sale. Although dumping and countervailing duty suits raise tensions among trading partners, tariffs dominate the category of price-based restrictions and evoke the greatest ire in international trade. Memories of the predominant role of tariffs during the 1930s have made price-based restrictions the policy most likely to provoke retaliation from trading partners. For these reasons, multilateral trade negotiations under GATT have primarily focused on reducing tariffs.

Quantitative restrictions regulate the amount of imports allowed into a country in a given period. Tariff quotas combine the two types of restrictions by placing a special tariff rate on a specific quantity of goods. Once the quota is filled, goods are imported at the normal tariff rate. Aside from tariff quotas, quantitative restrictions can be imposed unilaterally or under the rubric of nonunilateral (bilateral or multilateral) agreements. Because there is no consultation with trading partners, unilateral quotas follow price-based restrictions as the protectionist policy most likely to provoke retaliation. Unilateral quantitative restrictions disrupt imports by severely limiting their quantity. This disruption is limited, however, because small quantities of imports can still have a dramatic effect on the importing market by undercutting domestic prices.

Nonunilateral quotas are least likely to provoke retaliation and disrupt imports. These quotas take many different forms. Under voluntary export restraints or voluntary restraint agreements, the government or relevant producer associations of the exporting country "volunteers" to restrict exports of specific goods to ease trade tensions. Orderly marketing agreements are more formal agreements between exporting and importing countries to restrict exports to specific levels. The ranking for nonunilateral quotas in Table A5 reflects the fact that these quotas are a product of negotiations and are often subject to the enforcement ability (and willingness) of the exporting country.

Administrative restrictions refer to the "gray area" of remaining, often vague measures that directly affect imports. Measures such as import surveillance, government recommendations for restraint by importers, and import inspection procedures are often a source of tension in trade relations. Yet these measures are less likely to provoke retaliation and disrupt imports than their more overt counterparts. Import surveillance occurs when state officials monitor import flows and feed the information back to major importers to avoid "excessive and speculative" imports. State policy makers' recommendations for import restraint move beyond simple monitoring by suggesting actual modifications in the pace of import contracts. Finally, inspection and product-testing procedures slow the pace of imports in the name of general political objectives such as public safety.

Finally, the two types of protectionist policy least likely to provoke retaliation and disrupt imports are forms of monetary and nonmonetary adjustment assistance. Both measures seek to increase the ability of domestic producers to compete with foreign products by altering the costs of production. State subsidies for producers include outright grants, low-interest loans, and tax credits for investment or export.

Measures for employees include employment subsidies and relocation and retraining assistance. Nonmonetary adjustment assistance measures, by contrast, refer to exemptions from domestic legal constraints. Antitrust, pollution, and safety regulations can be modified to increase the international competitiveness of domestic producers. These measures are often difficult to discern, thereby reducing their ability to provoke retaliation by trading partners. This analysis focuses on production cartels allowed as exemptions to antitrust regulations.

# Index

Abe, Shintaro, 132
ACMI. *See* American Cotton Manufacturers Institute
Administrative guidance, 4; MITI and, 44–45, 124, 127
Administrative restrictions: automobiles and, 9; definition of and index for, 199–200; steel and, 6; textile and apparel and, 3-6. *See also* Type of protectionist policy; *entries for individual countries*
Aggarwal, Vinod, 14, 20, 26, 30, 101, 194
Agricultural Adjustment Act: 1956 and, 39; Section 22 of 1933 and, 38–39n, 97, 102, 184
All Japan Apparel Federation: alliance participation of, 133; characteristics of, 74, 77; Federation of Clothing Manufacturers and, 77n.
Amalgamated Clothing Workers of America, 71, 103-4
American Apparel Manufacturers Association, 66, 70
American Cotton Manufacturers Institute: alliance participation of, 94–109, 111, 188; characteristics of, 66–68, 75–76, 83, 188
American Fiber, Textile, Apparel Coalition, 70, 188
American Importers of Japanese Textiles, Inc., 71
Apparel Associations Inter-Association Committee, 66, 69. *See also* Committee for the Apparel Industries

Apparel Industry Committee on Imports, 66, 69, 104
Apparel Industry Federation. *See* BBI
Atkinson, Michael, and William Coleman, 24n
ATMI. *See* American Cotton Manufacturers Institute
Automobiles: patchwork protection in, 8–10
AVE. *See* Federation of German Textile Retailers
AWG. *See* BMWi; Foreign Trade Act

Basis Price System, 7
BBI: alliance participation of, 153, 156–57, 160–64, 167–71, 174; characteristics of, 81–82, 84–85
BDI. *See* Federation of German Industry
BMWi: advisory councils and, 51; AlmA product list and, 163; Bundesrat and, 52, 148, 154n; Bundestag and, 52, 148–50, 152–54, 157, 159, 161–68, 171, 174, 186; Bundestag Foreign Trade Committee and, 148, 153–54, 160, 174, 186; Cartel Law and, 58–59; European Community and, 54–60, 165; Federal Cartel Office and, 60; Foreign Office and, 53, 170; Foreign Trade Act and, 55; Fragestunde and, 163; Kleine Anfrage and, 52, 161–62, 165–67, 174; Länder authority and, 61–62; Länder officials and, 148–53, 160, 163, 166–67, 174; Ministry of Finance and, 60, 170; political penetration of, 48; structure of,

erIndex

Voluntary Export Restraint (*cont.*)
Hong Kong and, 101–2; United States versus Japan and, 97–99, 107. *See also* Quantitative restrictions; *entries for individual countries*

West Germany. *See* Germany, West
Women's Outerwear Industry Association. *See* DOB
Workers councils, 85

Yarn Industry Association: characteristics of, 81, 83. *See also* Cotton Textile Working Group
Young, Oran, 15

Zenminrokyo, 78
Zensen: characteristics of, 78–79, 85; textile alliance and, 127, 129–30, 133

Library of Congress Cataloging-in-Publication Data

Friman, H. Richard.
   Patchwork protectionism: textile trade policy in the United
States, Japan, and West Germany / H. Richard Friman.
      p.  cm.—(Cornell studies in political economy)
   Includes bibliographical references.
   ISBN 0-8014-2423-2 (alk. paper)
    1. Textile industry—Government policy—United States.  2. Textile
industry—Government policy—Japan.  3. Textile industry—Government
policy—Germany (West)  4. Free trade.  5. Protection.  I. Title.
II. Series.
HD9856.F75 1990
382'.45677—dc20                                      89-27400

# Cornell Studies in Political Economy

EDITED BY PETER J. KATZENSTEIN